Environmental Law in spain

Environmental Law in Spain

Second Edition

Mar Campins Eritja
Lucía Casado Casado
Juan Emilio Nieto Moreno
Antoni Pigrau Solé
Isabel Pont Castejón

This book was originally published as a monograph in the International Encyclopaedia of Laws/Environmental Law

General Editor: Roger Blanpain
Associate General Editor: Michele Colucci
Volume Editor: Kurt Deketelaere

Wolters Kluwer
Law & Business

Published by:
Kluwer Law International
PO Box 316
2400 AH Alphen aan den Rijn
The Netherlands
Website: www.kluwerlaw.com

Sold and distributed in North, Central and South America by:
Aspen Publishers, Inc.
7201 McKinney Circle
Frederick, MD 21704
United States of America
Email: customer.service@aspenpublishers.com

Sold and distributed in all other countries by:
Turpin Distribution Services Ltd.
Stratton Business Park
Pegasus Drive, Biggleswade
Bedfordshire SG18 8TQ
United Kingdom
Email: kluwerlaw@turpin-distribution.com

Printed on acid-free paper.

ISBN 978-90-411-5318-0

This title is available on www.kluwerlawonline.com

FSC
MIX
FSC® C103993

The Authors

Mar Campins Eritja obtained a Ph.D. in Law at the Universitat de Barcelona. She is a Tenured Professor in Public International Law (European Community Law) in the Department of International Law and Economics at the School of Law of the Universitat de Barcelona. For several years, she also served as a Vice-Dean and as a Vice-Rector for International Policy at the University of Barcelona. Her major areas of study, teaching and research are Environmental Law, European Community Law, and Public International Law. Dr Campins Eritja has leaded and participated in several research projects concerning International Law, European Law, and Environmental Law issues, and she is the author of some books and articles for specialized law journals in these fields, and in particular on international and European environmental law. Dr Campins Eritja is a member of the Spanish Association of Professors of International Law and International Relations. She is also member of a High Quality Consolidated Research Working Group of the University of Barcelona, as well as a member of the Water Institute of the Universitat de Barcelona and of the Tarragona Centre for Environmental Law Studies (CEDAT). She is also a member of the Board of Editors of the *Revista Catalana de Dret Ambiental* (*Catalan Journal of Environmental Law*).

Lucía Casado Casado graduated as a Ph.D. in Law at the Universitat Autònoma de Barcelona. She is a Tenured Professor in Administrative Law in the Department of Public Law at the Universitat Rovira i Virgili (Tarragona). Her major areas of study, teaching and research are Administrative Law and Environmental Law. She has participated in various research projects in the ambits of administrative law, environmental law, media law and immigration, and is the author of various books and articles on these subjects. She is research coordinator and head of projects at the Tarragona Centre for Environmental Law Studies (CEDAT), as well as being a member of the High Quality Consolidated Research Group on *Territory, Citizenship and Sustainability*, at the Universitat Rovira i Virgili. She is a member of the Board of Editors of the *Revista Catalana*

de Dret Ambiental (*Catalan Journal of Environmental Law*) and the journal *Actualidad Jurídica Ambiental* <www.actualidadjuridicaambiental.com>. She is the Spanish correspondent for the *IUCN Academy E-Law Journal*, for whom she writes reports on regulations and environmental jurisprudence. She is also a member of the Spanish Association of Professors of Administrative Law and the Association of Spanish Environmental Law.

Juan Emilio Nieto Moreno obtained a Ph.D. in Law at the Universitat Autònoma de Barcelona. He is Associate Professor of Administrative Law at the Universitat Autònoma of Barcelona and researcher at the Institute of Law and Technology. Dr Nieto has been linked professionally to environmental law since 1997. In particular, he is an expert in the environmental assessment of plans, programmes and projects. He has authored several publications and conferences, and participates as a professor in several courses on environmental subjects. He is involved in various projects, both at a European and national level. In addition, he usually acts as a consultant to the Generalitat of Catalonia and several Catalan local administrations in environmental matters. He is a partner in the Group of Investigation on Integrated Management of Coastal Zones, amongst others.

Antoni Pigrau Solé obtained a Ph.D. in Law from the Universitat de Barcelona. He is a Full Professor in Public International Law in the Public Law Department of the Universitat Rovira i Virgili (Tarragona). For several years, he has served as Vice-rector and as a General Secretary. His major areas of study, teaching and research are Public International Law and European Community Law, in particular, Environmental Law, Human Rights, International Humanitarian Law and Criminal International Law. Dr Pigrau Solé is the author of several monographs and articles on International Law and he has also participated in various collective works. Dr Pigrau Solé is the Director of the Tarragona Centre for Environmental Law Studies (CEDAT) and the Leader of the High Quality Consolidated Research Group on *Territory, Citizenship and Sustainability* at the Universitat Rovira i Virgili. He is Editor-in-Chief of the *Revista Catalana de Dret Ambiental* (*Catalan Journal of Environmental Law*) and Spanish Correspondent of the *Yearbook of International Humanitarian Law*. He is member of the Spanish Association of Professors of International Law and International Relations.

The Authors

Isabel Pont Castejón obtained a Ph.D. in Law at the Universitat Autònoma de Barcelona. She is a Tenured Professor of Administrative Law at the Autonomous University of Barcelona. She has been professionally linked with Environmental Law since 1985. She has done research and published articles and books, coordinated conferences, and organized environmental courses on the diverse subtopics and tools of Environmental Law, especially focusing on the role of the different levels of Public Administrations in their elaboration and implementation. She has also acted as a Magistrate for the Judicial Administrative Review Court of Catalonia for two judicial years. Since 1998, she has combined her part-time job as a university professor, with providing legal advice on environmental matters to different public bodies at the regional and state level, and amongst them, the Port Authority of Barcelona. She has been appointed Counsellor of the Regional Advisory Committee on Sustainable Development of Catalonia and Counsellor of the Juridical Advisory Commission for the Regional Government. Nowadays, she is the General Secretary of the Autonomous University of Barcelona.

The Authors

Table of Contents

List of Abbreviations

AENOR	Spanish Association for Standardization and Certification
AGAC	Chemical Analysis Water Network
AGHD	Hydrometer Water Network
AGPZ	Piezometry Water Network
BAPMN	Background Air Pollution Monitoring Network
CAMP	Comprehensive Atmospheric Monitoring Programme
CAP	Common Agricultural Policy
CLP	Classification, Labelling and Packaging of Substances and mixtures
COAS	Drinking Water Control
COCA	Water Quality Official Control
D	Decree
EC	European Communities
EDAR	Inventory of Waste-water Depuration Facilities
EMAS	Environmental Management and Audit Scheme
EMEP	European Monitoring Evaluation Programme
ENAC	National Certification Entity
EWC	European Waste Catalogue
EU	European Union
GDP	Gross Domestic Product
HWEL	Hazardous Waste European List
ICA	Water Quality Information System
ICONA	Institute of Nature Preservation
IPPC	Integrated Pollution and Prevention Control
IRYDA	Institute of Agricultural Development and Reform
ITGE	Technological and Geomining Institute of Spain
LD	Legislative Decree
PAEE	National Plan of Scientific Research and Technological Development on the Savings and Energetic Efficiency Plan
PAPIF	Action Plans Against Forest Fires

List of Abbreviations

PORN	Natural Resources Plan
PNIR	Integrated National Waste Plan
PRUG	Management and Use Rector Plans
RD	Royal Decree
REACH	Registration, Evaluation, Authorisation and Restriction of Chemical Substances
RLD	Royal Legislative Decree
SAICA	Water Quality Information Automatic System
SAIH	Hydrological Information Automatic System
UH	Hydro-geological Units
ZAC	Air Polluted Areas
ZSE	Emergency Areas

Preface

Regarding environmental matters, the Spanish Constitution establishes a system of shared powers between the State and the Autonomous Communities. Thus, the Autonomous Communities (17) have assumed powers over environmental matters. This description of Spanish environmental legislation and policy mainly deals with State legislation, although some remarks have been made related to Autonomous Communities' legislation. For the correct understanding of the structure of the legislation in Spain, special attention should be given to the State's basic legislation as well as the issue of shared and exclusive powers.

All translations of legal texts are unofficial.
Barcelona-Tarragona, December 2010

Dr Mar Campins Eritja
Dr Lucía Casado Casado
Dr Juan Emilio Nieto Moreno
Dr Antoni Pigrau Solé
Dr Isabel Pont Castejón

General Introduction

Chapter 1. General Information

§1. Geography and Population

1. The Kingdom of Spain has a total area of 505,938.13 km2, spreading over the continental territory, the Balearic and Canary Islands, and the territories of Ceuta and Melilla, in northern Africa. This is about 15% of the total area of the European Union (EU). In 2006, the Spanish Sustainability Observatory published a report called ‘Changes in land use in Spain: implications for sustainability’, which was based on information from the European Environment Agency’s CORINE project (Coordination of Information on the Environment) Land Cover. According to this report, land use in Spain is as follows: almost 50% is used for agriculture, 47.1% is forested with natural vegetation and open spaces; 0.9% is wetland and water surfaces, and 2.1% is artificial surfaces. The area covered by artificial surfaces increased by 29.5% during the 1987/2000 period, which is almost equal to a third of all the land that was covered by artificial surfaces in previous centuries. This figure reached almost 50% on the coast, of which Spain has some 8,000 km on the Mediterranean Sea, the Cantabrian Sea and the Atlantic Ocean.

2. On 1 January 2010, Spain had a population of 46,951,532. Of this total, 41,242,592 were of Spanish nationality. The remainder were foreigners and made up 12.2% of the total population. Of these, 2.3 million were EU citizens. The average population density is 92.39 per km2, although the population is distributed very unequally with high concentrations in urban areas on the Mediterranean and Cantabrian coasts and in some inland areas such as Madrid, Saragossa and Seville. About 6.84% of the Spanish population lives in non-peninsular territories. The annual rate of population growth decreased from 0.8 in the 1975–1985 decade to 0.3 in the 1985–1995 decade, and reached zero in 1997. However, the figure was 1.18% between 2002 and 2003 and grew to 2.38% between 2008 and 2009, for the most part because of immigration. The birth rate in 2007 was 492,527 and the death rate was 385,361; the number of adoptions was 3,592 and the number of abortions was 112,138. Average life expectancy is 78.01 years for men and 84.37 years for women. The average number of children per woman was 1.25% in 2002 and grew to 1.40% in 2009 (1.33% for Spanish women and 1.69% for foreign women. 16.65% of the total population is over the age of 64). As a result of these factors, the typical pyramid-shape graph showing the age of the population has changed and become more similar to the situation in other countries of the EU. The higher life expectancy together with the decrease of the birth and mortality rates has led to an ageing of the population. Also, the population is distributed very unevenly throughout the country, with large parts of the interior that are sparsely populated and semi abandoned, in contrast with a high concentration of the population on the coast.

3. An uneven and varied land surface relief (including the Central Plateau and several mountain chains crossing the territory in all directions) characterizes Spain from a geographical point of view. The Central Mountain Chain and the Pyrenees can be mentioned among these mountains. The highest point in the peninsular territory is the Mulhacén (in Sierra Nevada, Granada, 3,478 m), while the Teide (3,718 m) and the Puig Major (1,445 m) are the highest points in the Canary and Balearic Islands respectively. The longest rivers are the Tajo (1,007 km) and the Ebro (910 km). The high number of mountain chains, together with the large climatic differences, explains the important contrasts in rainfall and temperature, between the Spanish regions. Rains – abundant in the North and quite scarce in the South-east – are spatially and temporally distributed in a very irregular way. As a result of these factors, very humid areas in the North and Northwest of the Iberian Peninsula together with semi-arid areas – mainly in the South of Spain – can be found. This situation has led to the creation of varied ecosystems of high biodiversity.

4. All of the Iberian Peninsula lies in the temperate zone, with summer maximum temperatures in July and August and winter minimum temperatures in January and February, but the uneven land surface relief and the influence of the seas cause large differences between the regions and annual oscillations. Three different areas can be distinguished: the Central Plateau and the Ebro Valley (very cold winters and very hot summers), the Atlantic coast (mild winters and cool summers), and the Mediterranean coast (warm winters and very hot summers).

5. Spain has few natural resources. The amount of non-energy mineral resources (abundant some time ago) have been significantly reduced because of over-exploitation in the beginning of the industrialization process. However, Spain has always had to import energy mineral resources excepting coal to a certain extent.

The available energy resources are mainly related to hydroelectric energy, as well as to the increasing exploitation of renewable energy sources such as solar, wind or geothermal energies (the latter two are used to a lesser extent).

6. The Spanish coast is quite long with 7,876 km along the Mediterranean and Atlantic littoral zones. The presence of many beaches and sunny weather in much of the country during the greater part of the year constitute important factors for attracting tourism, which has played a major role in the Spanish economic development. Moreover, an outstanding diversity of natural spaces and ecosystems with high levels of quality can be found in Spain. Water constitutes the most important renewable resource to be taken into consideration. The Spanish pluvial index is one of the lowest in the EU countries (about 725 mm). High temperatures intensify evaporation, and this means that only one-third of the rainfall becomes a potentially available water resource. In addition, water resources are quite unevenly distributed over the national territory (rainfall varies from 1% to 20% between extreme zones, and there are quite important variations from year to year).

In the north of Spain, annual rainfall usually exceeds 800 mm. Often, in the north-east (Galicia, Asturias, Cantabria, the Basque Country) it exceeds 1,500 mm. These levels are also reached in certain isolated mountain zones in the rest of the territory. In areas close to the Pyrenean Mountains as well as the western area of the Central Plateau, the annual rainfall varies from 600 to 800 mm. In most of the national territory (the Central Plateau, Ebro Valley, the Mediterranean littoral excepting its south-eastern part, a part of the Guadalquivir Valley and most of the archipelagos), annual rainfall varies between 400 and 600 mm. The driest areas (under 400 mm) are to be found in the interior of the country and especially in the South-east (Almeria, Murcia, Alicante) and the Canary Islands, where rainfall is between 100 and 300 mm.

On the other hand, the existence of mountain chains very close to the coast brings about a peculiar fluvial typology characterized by short rivers running over steep slopes. These rivers do not have abundant flows. The main rivers flowing into the Atlantic Ocean are the Miño, Duero, Tajo, Guadiana and Guadalquivir. The Ebro, Júcar and Segura flow into the Mediterranean Sea. A significant part of their courses runs through regions with limited or irregular rainfall. This has a negative impact on the quantity and stability of their flows.

7. All these factors lead to a situation in which naturally obtained water resources can only satisfy one-third of the demand for water. That is why constructing reservoirs for capturing excess rainfall during the rainiest years was of paramount importance in Spain. A reservoir capacity of 54.4 million m3 was reached in 2009. During the same year, water reserves reached 23.9 million m3.

The Júcar, Segura and South water basins are the most critical points in terms of the deficit between water resources and existing demand. This problem has been addressed by combining measures to better control the use of the available water resources, and transfers of water resources from other basins.

§2. Legal and Political Structure

8. The military forces that arose against the Second Republic of Spain obtained victory in the Spanish Civil War (1936–1939). Until the death of General Franco in 1975, Spain had no Constitution and was subjected to a dictatorial regime, which prevented the citizens from exercising their fundamental rights. Isolationism characterized Spanish foreign policy during this period. After General Franco's death, a transition from dictatorship to democracy took place and Spain progressively reincorporated into the international and European contexts.

9. The Constitution of 1978 restored the Spanish constitutional tradition, the history of which dates back to 1812. Article 1 of the Constitution states that Spain constitutes itself into a social and democratic State observing the rule of law that proclaims liberty, justice, equality and political pluralism as the superior values of its legal system.

The political form of Spain is a parliamentary Monarchy. The King is the head of the State and assumes the highest representation of Spain in international relations. The King exercises the functions expressly attributed to him by the Constitution and the law. The Acts of the King are countersigned by the President of the Government and, when appropriate, by the competent ministers.

10. The legislative power rests with the Parliament (*Cortes Generales*) composed of two Chambers: the Congress and the Senate. Members of the Congress are elected by universal, free, equal, direct, and secret ballot. The electoral district is the province. Act 5/1985 (which has been amended several times) regulates the general electoral regime.

The Senate is the chamber of territorial representation, but, as a matter of fact, the provisions regarding its composition clearly give prevalence to the provinces (which elect a number of members by universal suffrage) rather than to the Autonomous Communities (which can certainly appoint a limited number of Senators).

In accordance with Title III of the Spanish Constitution, the legislative process as well as the conclusion of international treaties involves both Chambers. Besides general Acts and Statutes, the Spanish Constitution foresees that very important matters (e.g., fundamental rights and public liberties) shall be regulated by a special sort of Act (Organic Act), whose approval is subject to more stringent requirements.

11. The President of the Government, the Vice-Presidents and the Ministers form the executive power. Pursuant to Article 97 of the Spanish Constitution, the Government directs domestic and foreign policy, civil and military administration, and the defence of the State. It exercises its executive functions and regulatory powers in accordance with the Constitution and the laws. Following the electoral results and after having consulted the political parties present in the Congress, the King proposes a candidate for President of the Government. Once the candidate has received a favourable vote in the Congress, the King appoints the President of the Government. The other members of the Council of Ministers are appointed and removed by the King on the proposal of the President of the Government.

12. Judicial power is an independent power, exclusively subject to law. The Organic Act on the Judicial Power (Organic Act 6/1985 of 1 July) regulates the establishment, functioning and government of courts and tribunals, as well as the legal status of judges, magistrates and personnel in the judicial administration's service. Together with the civil jurisdiction, a military jurisdiction also exists (strictly limited to hearing cases within the military framework and certain exceptional cases of suspension of civil rights and liberties according to the Constitution). The General Council of the Judicial Power is the competent body for deciding on appointments, re-posting, inspection and discipline of judges and magistrates (Article 122 of the Constitution, and Organic Act 1/1998 of 10 January).

The Constitution also deals with the Constitutional Court. This is composed of twelve members – magistrates – in accordance with Article 159 of the Constitution and the Organic Act 2/1979 of 3 October on the Constitutional Court. The Constitutional Court hears appeals on the grounds of unconstitutionality against Acts and regulations, appeals against violation of the rights and liberties referred to in Article

53(2), and conflicts of competence between the State and the Autonomous Communities or between the Autonomous Communities themselves.

13. One of the most noteworthy peculiarities of the Spanish political structure is the territorial organization of the State (including municipalities and provinces – at the local level – and Autonomous Communities).

Article 2 of the Constitution recognizes and guarantees the right to autonomy of the nationalities and regions. Title VIII of the Constitution and the different Statutes of Autonomy develop the content of this principle. Spain currently counts seventeen Autonomous Communities (Basque Country, Catalonia, Galicia, Andalusia, Asturias, Cantabria, La Rioja, Murcia, Valencia, Aragon, Castile-La Mancha, Canary Islands, Navarre, Extremadura, Balearic Islands, Madrid, and CastileLeón), besides Ceuta and Melilla, which have a special regime.

14. The concept of 'power' determines the meaning of autonomy. It is related both to notions of 'matter', as well as 'function', and can be defined as the capacity of a particular territorial administration to assume specific functions (legislative, implementing or enforcement functions) regarding a specific matter. Articles 148 and 149 of the Constitution list the criteria regarding the distribution of the powers between the State and the Autonomous Communities. The respective Statutes of Autonomy deal with this matter in a more precise way. Article 148 of the Constitution includes those matters regarding which the Autonomous Communities can hold powers. Article 149(1) of the Constitution lists the matters regarding which the State has assumed exclusive powers. So, both Article 149(1) of the Constitution and the specific Statute of Autonomy determine who holds the concrete power in a specific matter. Article 149(3) states that the matters not attributed expressly to the State by the Constitution belong to the Autonomous Communities if expressly included in their respective statutes. Powers over matters not assumed by the Statutes of Autonomy shall belong to the State. Furthermore, Article 150 of the Constitution establishes that the State may transfer or delegate to the Autonomous Communities by an Organic Act those faculties on matters within the competence of the State, which because of their own nature are susceptible to transfer or de-legation. In general terms, the distinction between 'exclusive' and 'shared' powers is quite common in Spanish constitutional law. 'Exclusive power' means that either the State or the Autonomous Communities have the full decision-making power over the specific matter or function. In cases of 'shared powers', both the State and the Autonomous Communities hold powers regarding a specific matter or function (for instance, in environmental matters).

15. Each Autonomous Community has a Parliament (with legislative powers), a President and a Council of Government, which directs the policy and the administration of the Autonomous Community. These functions are obviously carried out within the framework of the powers assumed by the specific Autonomous Community.

16. Regarding local administration, Spain is sub-divided into provinces, which in turn consist of municipalities. The governments of the municipalities and provinces respectively are the City Council and the Provincial Council. The government bodies for the archipelagos are the Island Councils. Act 7/1985 of 2 April on the Local Regime regulates the basics of the autonomy of the local entities. Local entities have no legislative power, but only regulatory power to develop and implement the State and Autonomous Communities legislation in the management of their specific interests, especially in the framework of certain public services within their respective territories).

§3. Economic Characteristics

17. Spain is a full member of the EU since 1 January 1986, and entered into the Euro area on 1 January 1999. The process of integration into the EU has had a large impact on Spain, since it accelerated economic development and brought the Spanish economy close to the levels of the rest of the European countries. The agricultural sector has lost importance and the Spanish economy opened to foreign markets. The economic capacity of the public sector has been also enlarged. The Gross Domestic Product (GDP) was USD 152,100 million in 1975, and USD 626,300 million in 1997 and up to EUR 1,117,624 million in 2009. The economy has been growing annually in a continuous way (with a medium growth rate of 1.9% for 1977–1987 and 2.6% for 1987–1997, reaching 3.8% in 1998). Between 2001 and 2002, economic growth was at approximately 2%. However, between 2008 and 2009, there was roughly a 3.6% decrease as a result of the global economic and financial crisis. The GDP per capita passed from USD 4,280 in 1975, to USD 7,920 in 1985, and USD 33,100 by the end of 2008.

The inflation rate passed from 16.1% in 1975 to 9.6% in 1985, 3.4% in 2002 and 0.8% in 2009. At the end of 2009 there were 17,449,700 people in work in Spain, of which 15,114,600 earned a salary. The unemployment rate remains the highest in the EU. It was 4.3% of the labour force in 1975, 21.1% in 1985, 20.8% in 1997 and 20.09% of the active population in 2009, which is equivalent to 4 million people out of work. The public deficit represented 1.8% of the GDP in 1981, 4.5% in 1985 and 0.2% in 2001. In 2009, the figure was 12.5% compared with the EU average of 6.1%. The public debt was 12.8% of GDP in 1975, 43.7% in 1985 and 67.5% in 1997. It later decreased to 53.8% in 2002, compared with the EU average of 62.3%. The General National Budget for 2010 estimates that the public debt will increase to 62.5% of the GDP. The current account balance experienced a deficit in 2001 equivalent to 3.1% of GDP. In 2008, the total sum of all exports was EUR 189,227,9 million and that of imports was EUR 283,387,8 million.

The total public budget was ESP 23,226.877 million in 1999; EUR 216,832,83 million in 2004, and EUR 329,896 million in 2009.

Public expenditure in investments was 21.1% of GDP in the period 1977–1986 and 21.8% in the period 1987–1996. Public expenditure in research and development was 0.4% of GDP in 1981, 0.6% in 1985, 0.86% in 1997 and 1.27% in 2007, a figure which is much lower than the EU average of 1.91%. Public expenditure on education has risen from 1.8% of GDP in 1975 to 3.3% in 1985 and 4.3% in 2007, compared with the 6.4% average in the Organization for Economic Co-operation and Development (OECD) countries.

Public expenditure in defence was 2.1% of GDP in 1975, 2.4% in 1985 and 1.2% in 2002. Although these are lower figures than in previous years, in 2009, military spending still represented 13.04% of the total state expenditure, 1.64% of the GDP and 5.11% of the National Budget.

Total expenditure on social welfare was about EUR 135,620 million in 2002, or 20.1% of GDP. In 2006, Spain spent 20.9% of its GDP on social welfare, a long way off the European average of 26.9%.

Spain has received major funding from the EU for environmental protection programmes: between 1994 and 2003, it got about EUR 3,500 million from structural funds; and between 2000 and 2006 it received an additional provision of around EUR 12,000 million financed by the Cohesion Fund, as well as other contributions from the LIFE programme. During the period between 2007 and 2013, Spain will receive something in the region of EUR 35,217 million from the Cohesion Fund.

18. There were 3.29 million active companies at the end of 2009. 53.9% of these had no salaried employees. Only 2.27% employed twenty workers or more. The highest percentage of small businesses are to be found in the service sector, excluding trade(83.7% have two or less employees), and in the trade sector (81.3%). By contrast, most of the large companies are found in the industrial sector, with 8.2% of these companies employing twenty or more salaried employees. The property of the enterprises is concentrated as follows: stocks of small enterprises are usually controlled by families, and stocks of bigger enterprises are usually concentrated in a few hands. Of Spain's autonomous regions, Catalonia has the largest percentage of active companies with 18.5% of the total as of 1 January 2010, followed by Madrid (with 15.3%) and Andalusia (with 15.1%).

Foreign buying of Spanish company shares and *vice versa* is currently limited to big enterprises, but has significantly increased in the last years (mainly since the integration of Spain into the EU). Most cross-border investments are in the financial sector, insurance, manufacturing (concrete, food, shoes, paper and graphic arts), and energy and water management.

19. The economic structure has changed. The economic centre of Spain has shifted away from agriculture (and industry to a lesser extent) to services. The labour force increased from 13.02 million people in 1975 to 13.59 million in 1985, 16.12 million in 1997, 18.8 million in 2003 and 30.4 million in 2007 of which 49.4% were women. Its distribution per sector was as follows: in 1975 agriculture accounted for 22.1%, industry for 38.4% and services for 39.6%; in 1985 agriculture accounted for 18.3%, industry for 31.7% and services for 49.9%; in 1997 agriculture accounted for 8.1%, industry for 20.2%, construction for 9.8%, and services for 61.9%; in 2002 agriculture accounted for only 6%, industry for 19.2%, construction for 11.9%, and services for 62.9%); in 2007 agriculture accounted for only 4.6%, industry for 16.0%, construction 13.2%, and services for 66.2%. Agrarian activities mainly include agriculture (64.6% in 2007) and stockbreeding (35.4%). The most important agricultural products of Spain are meat, fruit and vegetables, olive oil, cereals and wine. The number of livestock in 2007 was estimated at 164.4

million poultry, 18.8 million sheep and goats, 23.4 million pigs and 5.7 million cattle. The average farm size in 2007 was 23.85 ha, with farms of less than 20 ha constituting 78.9% of the total number of farms but representing only 15.9% of the total surface dedicated to agricultural activities. By contrast, 4.9% of farms covering more than 100 ha covered 56.1% of the exploited land.

The fishing sector must also be included in the primary sector. Spain was during decades one of the most important fishing powers in the world, both because of the size of its fleet and the catch volume. But that privileged position was substantially altered by the changes brought by the Law of the Sea and the joining of the EU. Nevertheless, in 2007 Spain still had a fleet of more than 11,000 vessels with almost 800,000 tonnes of gross register tonnage and a value of EUR 1.6 billion.

Industrial activities include manufacturing, mining, the petroleum industry and the production of electricity, gas and water (83%, 8% and 9% respectively of the total turnover for 2007). Companies with 250 or more workers (i.e., about 1,000 of the 150,000 companies with salaried employees, that make-up the Spanish industry), contribute 52% of the total industry's turnover. The sectors that contribute the most to turnover are car manufacturing (7.1%); electricity production and distribution (7%); petroleum, natural gas and nuclear fuel (6.9%); and basic chemical products (3.1%).

The energy sector must be placed, with some specific characteristics of its own, inside the industrial field. The gross internal consumption of primary energy in 2008 was 142,070,000 equivalent oil tonnes. Spain has traditionally been dependent on oil and gas, completing its energetic needs with coal, hydroelectric energy and other renewable energies. The last twenty years have witnessed a significant reduction of oil dependency (47.8% in 2008) in favour of coal (9.8%) and nuclear energy (10.8%), a significant increase in the use of natural gas (24.5%) and a slight reduction of hydroelectric energy (1.4%). Other renewable energies reached 6.1% in 2008. The public sector has had an important influence on the energy field until recent years, due to the prevailing EU policies, the liberalization of the sector, and a wave of privatizations of public enterprises. Nonetheless, economic control remains in a few hands in each of these sub-sectors. The degree of self-sufficiency in primary energy (i.e., the relation between internal production and total energy consumption) was 21.6% in 2008, which means that Spain imported 78.4% of its primary energy requirements.

Regarding the tertiary sector, also called the services sector, we must differentiate non-market services, offered by the public sector for free or at subsidized prizes, and market services (commerce, hotel business, transport, telecommunications, credit and insurance, business services, etc.). The first kind of service has significantly increased its part of Spanish production due to rising prices and the expansion caused by the decentralization of the Spanish administration and its increasingly important role in the education, health and welfare fields.

In 2008, market services accounted for 1,368,497 companies in the sectors of transport and storage, the hotel trade, information and communications, real estate, professional, scientific and technical activities, administration and auxiliary services, artistic, recreational and entertainment activities and other services. Market services employ almost 6 million workers and turned over EUR 454 billion in 2008.

Particularly important is the tourist sector, which represents around 6.5% of turnover and 16% of employment in the sector. With more than 50 million tourists per year (52,231,098 in 2009), Spain is one of the most important tourism-receiving countries in the world.

20. It has been calculated that in 2003 the environmental market in Spain represented 1.6% of GDP. This figure includes the water sector minus irrigation, the waste sector, atmosphere and renewable energies. It excludes forestry, ecological agriculture, 'green' tourism and street cleaning. Taken together, these sectors provide a total of approximately 256,000 jobs. In 2007, there were 16,643 companies and 20.592 establishments linked to the environmental sector (recycling, production and distribution of electricity, gas, steam and hot water, water collection, purification and distribution, and environmental remediation), with around 25% growth compared with 2006.

21. According to data from the Survey on Business Expenditure on Environmental Protection for 2008, expenditure on environmental protection by industrial establishments increased to 3,129.4 million in 2008, with an increase of 3.9% compared with the previous year. The most important investments were made in reducing atmospheric emissions (down 0.7% on the previous year), waste water management (up 4.5% on the previous year) and waste management (up 5.6% on the previous year).

§4. Social and Cultural Characteristics

22. According to the Human Development Indicator elaborated annually by the United Nations Programme for Development, Spain occupied twenty-first position in 1997 and twentieth in 2004, but rose to fifteenth in 2009, on the basis of the following reference data: life expectancy from birth of 80.7 years, 97.9% adult literacy with 96.5% enjoying schooling, together with a per capita GDP of USD 31,560.

23. In the educational field, in particular, during the academic year of 2007–2008, an estimated total of 8,093,660 students were enrolled in all levels of the education system, of which about 73.5% were in the public school system and 27.5% were in the private system. These were distributed as follows: 1,643,016 students in Infant Education (1,049,762 public schools and 593,254 in private schools); 2,607,384 in Primary Education (1,751,267 public schools and 856,117 in private schools); 1,829,874 in Compulsory Secondary Education (1,210,357 in public schools and 619,517 in private schools); 584,693 in Upper Secondary Education (423,391 in public schools and 161,302 in private schools); 37,440 in Distance Upper Secondary Education (all at public schools except for 1,707). At university level, 1,391,253 students were enrolled in the first and second cycles of the 2008–2009 academic year; approximately 90% of them in public universities and 10% in private universities.

24. Different languages co-exist in Spain. The official languages are Spanish for the whole country and Catalan, Basque and Galician in their respective Autonomous Communities. According to a European Commission survey from 2005, that allowed respondents to name two mother languages, 89% of the population has Spanish as their mother tongue, 9% Catalan, 5% Galician and 1% Basque. There is also the Aranese language (a variety of Occitan spoken in the Aran Valley in the north-east of the province of Lleida). Aranese is official in this valley and, since the new 2006 Statute of Autonomy, throughout Catalonia. Aranese is the mother tongue of around 2,800 people.

25. The predominant religion, with more than 70%, is Catholicism which is favoured with a special backing from the State, due to the Concordat signed with the Vatican State. However, in recent years, a significant implantation of other religions has taken place, especially Protestant confessions. According to survey data from the Spanish Government's Centre for Sociological Research for July 2010, 74% of the population states that it is Catholic, 15.2% were non-believers; 7.2% were atheist and 2.1% were followers of other religions. More than half of those who stated they were believers also stated that they almost never attended religious services.

26. The percentage of civil marriages has increased, slowly but steadily, constituting 46.3% in 2007 out of a total of around 204,772. 1.56% of the total corresponds to same-sex marriages. Equally, the number of divorces and separations has slowly increased, reaching a total of 141,304 that same year.

27. The foreign population residing in Spain at the end of 2008 numbered 4,473,499 people, of which 1,794,229 were EU citizens. Furthermore, the number of foreigners with a residence permit to carry out studies was 41,881, of whom 52 were EU citizens. During 2008, 84,170 people were given Spanish nationality, of which 1,424 were EU citizens. In 2008, 2,052,406 foreign workers were in employment in Spain. The number of foreigners who applied for asylum in 2008 was 4,517, of whom 2,455 were successful in their application. 498,977 immigrants entered Spain in 2009, of whom 29,635 were Spaniards and 469,342 were foreigners (144,867 of these being EU citizens). 323,641 people emigrated. Of these, 107,120 were EU citizens, including 35,372 Spaniards.

28. In 2008, there were 16,741,400 main residences in Spain. The housing market in Spain is characterized by a striking tendency towards home ownership. In the year 2008, 80.4% of residences were owned.

29. Editorial output in 2009 reached 74,521 titles and booklets with a total of 183,87,000 copies. Of these 77.4% were published in Spanish; 11.2% were in Catalan, 2.5% in Galician and 1.4% in Basque. In the same year, in Spain, there were 100 paid daily newspapers with an average distribution per publication of 40,663,20 copies. In 2008, 28 million units of recorded music were sold (CDs and others).

Additionally, in 2007, 1,776 films were shown at 2,140 cinemas to audiences totalling 116.9 million. In 2008, approximately 51% of Spanish homes had an internet connection.

30. The total number of automobiles in 2006 was 28,531,183. Of these, 4,835,670 were trucks and vans; 58,286 were buses and minibuses; 20,636,738 were private cars; 2,042,298 were motorbikes; 196,866 were tractors; and 761,325 were other vehicles (not including those registered as special vehicles, trailers or mopeds. In 2007, a total of 2,350,098 new vehicles were registered

31. In 2008, 196,143 people were convicted through penal procedures, of whom 179,080 were men and 53,364 were foreigners. This represented an increase of more than 21.9% over the year before. In 2008, there were 73,558 people incarcerated in Spain, of which 67,608 were men and 26,201 were foreigners.

§5. Main Environmental Problems

32. Among the main environmental problems affecting Spain, three different groups can be distinguished: (a) common problems affecting all countries of the EU (universal problems such as the depletion of the ozone layer or climate change); (b) problems commonly affecting Mediterranean countries (marine pollution, soil erosion and desertification); and (c) environmental problems specific to Spain, frequently linked to deficiencies in infrastructures (such as water depuration and waste management).

33. The specific environmental problems in Spain are related to the socio-economic structure, the distribution of the land and physical characteristics. The movement of the population, from areas more affected by erosion and desertification to bigger cities and the littoral zone, appears to have an especially relevant environmental impact. Agriculture has been progressively confined to certain areas (not necessarily the most appropriate areas for agriculture in terms of soil quality and water resources). The industrial sector has historically developed in a context of state protectionism. This has led to lower efficiency and scarce preparation for international competition. Environmental concerns have rarely been taken into consideration by the Spanish industry. Finally, the development of the tourist sector has not observed environmental criteria either at early or at subsequent stages of the process. That is why damages that are impossible to restore have been caused in different areas of the country.

34. The main social-ecological challenges in the opinion of the Spanish Ministry of the Environment are:

- the concentration of population and economic activities on the coasts, where more than 40% of the population resides, and in Madrid, where 12% of the population resides;

- the increase in greenhouse gas emissions which rose 32.1% between 1990 and 2001 – a figure far above the limits established in the Kyoto agreement, whose objective is 15% above the 1990 levels by 2010;
- the tendency towards the use of less sustainable modes of transport (road and air) instead of more sustainable ones (sea and rail), with the corresponding increase in nitrogen oxide and ammonia emissions;
- growing material consumption (18% growth in the period between 1996 and 2000) and the corresponding growth in wastes;
- threats to land and sea ecosystems (the urbanized area grew by 40% between 1990 and 2000); the fragmentation of land due to land transport infrastructure, which increases stress to ecosystems; and
- over-exploitation of fishing zones in waters adjacent to Spain, despite the reduction in the Spanish fishing fleet.

The Ministry considers the construction, tourism and transport sectors the most critical in terms of pressure on the land and environment in Spain.

35. The defective implementation and enforcement of environmental law constitutes a relevant environmental problem in Spain. The insufficiency of both technical and human resources for the public administration undertaking such actions is the main cause of this problem.

This situation has been progressively changing since the middle 1980s. Priority actions of the Department of the Environment and Rural and Marine Affairs are currently focused on: adequate use of water resources, restoration of water quality, control of deforestation from forest fires or natural causes (nearly 15,400 forest fires in 2009, with more than 110,000 ha affected), control of erosion (which affects almost half of the national territory), control of desertification (18% of the country is considered to be at high or very high risk of desertification), restoring of the littoral environment, reduction and adequate management of wastes, and nature conservation.

36. Among the activities that are progressing positively, the Ministry of the Environment emphasizes the following: the purification of urban waste waters; the reduction in contamination from nitrates in subterranean waters; an increase in protected natural areas; less pollution in rivers; higher quality of water on coastal beaches; growing participation by businesses in environmental management, and the development of renewable energy sources.

37. For example, Spain enjoys a network of national parks that consist of the following areas:

- Teide (Canary Islands, 18.990 ha).
- Timanfaya (Canary Islands, 5,107 ha).
- Picos de Europa (Asturias, Cantabria and Castile-Leon, 64,660 ha).
- Ordesa and Monte Perdido (Aragon, 15,608 ha).
- Garajonay (Canary Islands, 3,986 ha).
- Doñana (Andalusia, 54,251 ha).

- Caldera de Taburiente (Canary Islands, 4,699 ha).
- Aigüestortes and Estany de Sant Maurici (Catalonia, 14,119 ha).
- Sierra Nevada (Andalusia, 86,208 ha).
- Tablas de Daimiel (Castile-La Mancha, 1,928 ha).
- Archipelago de Cabrera (Balearic Islands, 10,020 ha).
- Cabañeros (Castile-La Mancha, 40,856 ha).
- Atlantic Islands (Galicia, 8,480 ha).
- Monfragüe (Extremadura, 18,118 ha).

1,440 locations representing almost 14.5 million ha formed part of the National List of the Natura 2000 Network in 2007 (made up of Special Areas of Conservation (SACs) and Special Protection Areas (SPAs) for birds). 26.81% of the Spanish national territory (14,375,930 ha) is covered by EU Natura 2000 Network and other protected natural spaces. In Spain there are twenty-two biosphere reserves and forty-four wetland reserves under the Ramsar Agreement.

38. The structure of public expenditure both in environmental protection and in the use and management of natural resources constitutes the most reliable indicator of the aforementioned priorities. Total public budget of the Ministry of the Environment, Rural and Marine Environments in these concepts rose to EUR 4,034,7 million in 2010. This was distributed as follows:

Programme	*(Thousand Euros)*
Program for Sustainable Rural Development	244,550,00
Protection of fishing resources and sustainable development	47,676,48
Environmental Management and General Services	225,431,67
Water Management and Infrastructures	1,811,214,25
Regulations and Territorial Organization of Water Resources	290,518,71
Water Quality	471,834,57
Protection and Improvement of the Environment	55,770,61
Protection and Improvement of the Natural Environment	371,903,39
Action on the coast	280,829,10
Action to Prevent Pollution and Climate Change	121,188,55
Research and Development of the Information Society	4,232,13
Meteorology	109,517,69
Total	4,034,668,05

Source: State Budget 2010

This table clearly shows the priorities of the Spanish Department of the Environment and Rural and Marine Affairs. Most of the total expenditure, which constitutes nearly half of the budget, is devoted to hydrological resource management and infrastructure, followed by programmes related to water quality and the protection and improvement of the natural environment.

39. In 2009, apart from the above policies in the field of waste management and the implementation of Water Framework Directive (WFD), the most significant environmental policies of the Government were: the adoption of the Spanish Strategy for Sustainable Mobility; the creation of the Desertification Observatory and the National Inventory of Soil Erosion; the adoption of the Reforestation Plan for 2009–2012 (45 million trees); the creation of the State Council for Natural Heritage and Biodiversity; and the adoption of the Act on sustainable development of the rural environment and the Act on Sustainable Economics.

Chapter 2. Basic Principles of Environmental Law

§1. Definitions and Notions

40. One of the most important problems in environmental law is the lack of general consensus on the definition and the scope of the concept itself. This problem is not specific to Spanish law. The concept of environment can be used in multiple senses from different points of view: spatial (world, local, regional), substantive (biosphere, social environment, cultural environment) or on the basis of its foundations (anthropological, cosmological). This brings about a wide range of legal problems related to the delimitation of the specific subject covered by environmental law, the identification of the interests and goods to be protected, and the setting up of a system of rights and obligations. Apart from certain regulations on particular matters, the concept of environmental law crystallized after World War II (especially from the 1960s). This could explain the insufficient consolidation of a general theory on environmental law.

41. On the other hand, environmental law does not aim to regulate the matter from a sectorial point of view, but to influence the overall legal system. The challenge thus consists of integrating environmental law in the traditional juridical areas (criminal, civil, etc.), as well as to include environmental concerns in the different policies (agriculture, energy, transport, etc.). 33. In the absence of any legal provision on the delimitation of environmental law, it is commonly understood that it should deal with soil, air, water, natural resources and nature protection. Waste is also included within this concept, since its final destination will affect any of the elements mentioned (as is also the case for dangerous substances and radiation). Doctrinal efforts to include energy, transport, agriculture, zoning, land use and historical patrimony in the domain of environmental law have been made. This, however, appears to be too wide a concept of environmental law. This monograph will therefore refer to these latter subject-matters only as far as any environmental aspect or impact is concerned.

42. In any case, the concept of environment has some specific characteristics that cannot be ignored by the legal instruments aiming to protect it. The first of them consists of the dynamism of the subject covered by environmental law, its capability of changing due to natural or human causes. The configuration of the environment as a whole system constitutes the second characteristic to be taken into account. This means that the concept of environment does not only involve a group of elements (air, water, soil, flora, and fauna) seen statically, but also their continuous interaction. Finally, the environment constitutes a global concept, since interactions among the different components do not only take place at local or regional levels, but also at world level (irrespective of the existing administrative and political frontiers). This last characteristic explains the development of international environmental law during the last decades.

On the other hand, legal intervention in the environmental field is permanently influenced by economic factors, which means that consideration must be given to the social and economic development model, as well as the social and economic costs in the enforcement of environmental law. Finally, environmental law is also influenced by the progressive enlargement of scientific knowledge regarding the types and intensity of human activities that the environment can bear. The research on technical applications that facilitate the development of activities in such a way as to cause a lesser negative environmental impact, can also be mentioned.

§2. Constitutional Provisions

43. Article 45 of the Constitution is the reference point for the legal system of environmental protection in Spain. The text of Article 45 is as follows:

> (1) Everyone has the right to enjoy an environment suitable for the development of the person, as well as the duty to preserve it.
> (2) The public authorities shall look to the rational use of all natural resources with a view to protecting and improving the quality of life and preserving and restoring the environment, basing themselves on an indispensable collective solidarity.

44. For those who violate the provisions of the foregoing paragraph, penal or administrative sanctions, as applicable, shall be established and they shall be obliged to repair the damage caused. ('unofficial authors' translation) 36. Article 45 is included in Chapter III ('Guiding Principles of Economic and Social Policy') of Title I ('On Fundamental Rights and Liberties') of the Constitution. That is why any violation of this right cannot constitute the object of any specific proceeding in front of the Constitutional Court foreseen in Article 53(2) of the Constitution (limited to the rights and liberties included in Chapter II of Title I). For the same reason, it is not included in the matters that should be regulated by Organic Act (Articles 53(1) and 81 of the Constitution). On the contrary, pursuant to Article 53(3) of the Constitution, the recognition, respect and protection of the principles recognized in Chapter III, such as the environment, shall guide legislation, judicial practice and the actions of public authorities. They may also be evoked before ordinary jurisdiction through proceedings established in the laws. The legislation thus fixes the scope and limits of this right in a more precise way.

45. Environmental protection in the Spanish Constitution thus has different faces: as a right of the citizens (linked to their personal development), as an environmental protection duty, and as a commitment of the public authorities. Its being a social right implies that its effective exercise depends on positive actions by the public authorities. This necessarily involves the establishment of public policies to achieve a suitable environment for the development of individuals. Following Article 45, it particularly implies the promotion of the rational use of natural resources, as well as actions addressed to protect, improve and restore the environment (including the establishment of penal or administrative sanctions for those who damage the environment, and the setting up of appropriate mechanisms to ensure the effectiveness of the obligation to repair the damage caused). The duty of preserving the environment imposed on the citizens is the reverse of the right to enjoy it. This duty is linked to the necessary collective solidarity, which materializes in specific limitations for those activities that could cause adverse effects to the environment. In the context of the distribution of powers as explained above, public authorities are expected to undertake actions at three different levels: prevention, restoration and punishment.

46. The prevention principle, expressed in the reference to the rational use of natural resources, implies awareness of the fact that restoration is not always possible, or could be costlier than the establishment of measures which impede or reduce the risk of damage. Environmental Impact Assessment (EIA) and a permanent control of activities that are likely to cause environmental pollution are among the large number of measures to be taken at this level.

47. The restoration principle involves the obligation of the public authorities to act once the damage has been caused. For this purpose, public authorities should be fitted with the necessary powers and instruments (including legal instruments) to ensure that the party, whether a natural or a legal person or a public administration, who causes the damage bears the costs of restoration.

48. The sanction principle is the normal consequence of any breach of the legislation regarding environment protection. The difference between criminal and administrative sanctions gives rise to problems regarding the delimitation of the different liabilities, and the setting up of adequate mechanisms aiming to observe the *non bis in idem* principle.

Chapter 3. Historical Background

49. Remote precedents dealing with environmental subjects can be found in the Spanish legislation. More recently, Article 1 of the Decree 2414/1961 of 30 November, on Unpleasant, Unhealthy, Noxious and Hazardous Activities, refers to the concept of environment. However, the first piece of legislation that can be relevant to the concept and policy of the environment in Spain is Act 38/1972 of 22 December, on the Protection of the Atmosphere. The foreword of this Act justifies the refusal to elaborate a general Act on the Environment and the preferred option of a sectorial approach. This Act also states the commitment of the State to protecting the environment.

Since then, legal provisions on protection of the environment were included either in specifically environmental legislation (Act on Protected Habitats of 1975, Solid Urban Waste Act of 1975, Act on Marine Pollution from Ships and Aeroplanes of 1977) or in general legislation (Act on Agrarian Reform and Development of 1973, Mining Act of 1973, Act on Research and Exploitation of Hydrocarbons of 1974). Other contemporary legislation (such as the Roads Act of 1974) does not contain any reference to environmental matters.

50. Administrative structures specifically linked to the environment in Spain appeared in 1971, in the framework of the preparatory works of the Stockholm Conference. The National Institute for Nature Conservation (linked to the Ministry of Agriculture) and the Inter-Ministerial Committee for the Improvement of the Environment were created in the same year. In 1972, the Government Delegated Commission on Environment as well as the Inter-Ministerial Commission on Environment were created for the purpose of coordinating the environmental actions of the different ministries. This objective was not, however, achieved. The creation of the new Ministry of Public Works and Urbanism in 1977 had a relevant impact. It assumed competence on coasts, harbours, hydrological infrastructures, urbanism and housing. The Under-Secretariat of Territorial Planning and Environment, which included the General Directorate of Environment, was created within this ministry. Even though the General Directorate was expected to play a relevant role in inter-ministerial coordination, it faced many difficulties in imposing its own criteria on other ministries and even on bodies within its own ministry, mainly due to the low administrative level of this body. On the other hand, this General Directorate did not directly manage any natural resources (sea water, continental water, natural areas, forests, fauna or air) which were in the hands of other general directorates or ministries.

51. Some years later, as a result of the increasing need of incorporating the European environmental legislation into the Spanish legal system, the General Directorate of Environment assumed competence as the national authority with regard to certain legislation. This led to the creation of higher-level administrative bodies: the General Secretariat of Environment (1990), the Secretariat of State on Water Policies and Environment (1991), and the Ministry of Public Works, Transport and Environment (1993). Finally, the Ministry of Environment was created in 1996

(Royal Decree 758/1996 of 5 May 1996). This ministry holds the competencies formerly dispersed among the Ministries of Public Works, Transport and Environment, the Ministry of Agriculture, Fishery and Food, and the Ministry of Industry and Energy. Nevertheless, some jurisdictions that affect the environment are still under the authority of other ministries today. Among them, are those related to marine environment natural resources, those related to the monitoring of mine use and those associated with the monitoring and saving of energy. The administrative structure of the Ministry of the Environment has been modified on several occasions, the last one being by means of Royal Decree 1823/2011, of 21 December, Royal Decree 1887/2011, of 30 December and Royal Decree 401/2012 of 17 December. The name of the Ministry was changed to the Ministry for the Agriculture, Food and Environment, and it takes over most of the responsibilities of the now defunct Ministry for the Environment and Rural and Marine Affairs. Its role is to propose and execute the Government's policies regarding the fight against climate change and the protection of natural heritage, biodiversity and the sea, and regarding water, rural development, agriculture, fisheries and food. The aim is to bring together under one department all the responsibilities of the State linked to the natural environment and the protection of the land and biodiversity and the promotion and defence of agriculture, livestock, forests, fisheries and food production.

The general structure of the Ministry can be summarized as follows: (1) the State Department for the Environment, which is responsible for the (a) the Spanish Office for Climate Change, which has General Directorate status; (b) the General Directorate of Environmental Quality, Environmental Assessment and Natural Heritage; (c) General Directorate for the sustainability of the Coast and the Sea; and (d) the General Directorate for water resources (2) the Under-Secretariat for Agriculture, Food and Environment (3) the Secretariat for Agriculture and Food. Among the consultation agencies that the Ministry uses, the two most important are National Water Council, created in 1988 (RD 927/1988 and abolished by RD 1383/2009), Environmental Advisory Council, created in 1994 (RD 224/1994, 14 February 1994), the National Council on the Climate, created in 1998 (RD 177/1998, 16 February 1998), and the State Council for Natural Heritage and Biodiversity, created in 2009 (RD 948/2009), the Inter-Ministerial Commission for the Climate Change (RD 1886/2011, of 30 December), and the Commission for the Coordination of the Policies regarding the Climate change(RD 1823/2011, of 21 December).

52. Finally, the concept of environmental crime was introduced for the first time in the Criminal Code by the Organic Act 8/1983 of 25 June. Title XVI of the Spanish Criminal Code (Organic Act 10/1995 of 23 November) deals with crimes related to territorial organization and development, protection of the historical patrimony and environment. It includes a Chapter (Articles 325–331) devoted to crimes against natural resources and the environment, as well as another Chapter (Articles 332–337) on crimes related to the protection of flora and fauna and finishes with the common provisions (Articles 338–340). Article 325 defines the basic environmental crime as any breach of the Acts or general legislation protecting the environment that directly or indirectly involves emissions, discharges, radiation, extractions, excavations, dumping, noise, vibrations, injections or landfills, in the atmosphere, soil, subsoil, sea, or inland or underground waters (even if affecting trans-boundary areas). Underground water abstraction that could seriously damage the natural balance is also deemed to be an environmental crime. The latest modifications to the articles relating to environmental crime is found in Organic Act 15/2003 of 25 November of the Penal Code (BOE 26.11.2003) and Organic Act 5/2010, of 22 June (BOE 23.6.2010).

53. Recently, Act 10/2006, of 28 April, which modifies Act 43/2003 on Mountains, modified Act 50/1981, of 30 December, on the Regulation of the Organic Statute of the Public Prosecutor's Office in order to create Environmental sections in each Public Prosecutor's Office of the Supreme and Provincial Courts that specialize in crimes relating to territorial organization, the protection of historical heritage, natural resources and the environment, the protection of flora, fauna and domestic animals, and forest fires. Furthermore, it states that the Public Prosecutor should name a prosecutor to deal with crimes relating to territorial organization, the protection of historical heritage, the environment and forest fires, and that he or she should have the status of Chief Prosecutor and will, among other things, supervise and coordinate the special environmental sections and unify the criteria that they` apply.

Chapter 4. The Role of Government Institutions in the Shaping and Administration of Environmental Law and Policy

§1. The Governmental Institutions and Their Competencies

54. In environmental matters, the Spanish Constitution establishes a system of shared powers between the State and the Autonomous Communities, which have some legislative powers. In accordance with Article 149(1.23) of the Constitution, the State holds exclusive powers on 'basic legislation on environmental protection without prejudice to the faculties of the Autonomous Communities to establish additional standards of protection' and 'basic legislation on woodlands, forestry projects, and livestock trails'. Its exclusive powers thus are within the realm of basic legislation, rather than to the whole environmental sector.

55. The legal discussion has primarily focused on the scope of the notion of 'basic legislation'. The Constitutional Court defined basic legislation as uniform legislation valid all over the country which ensures the existence of common legislative grounds in matters of a general interest superior to the particular interest of any Autonomous Community. The Autonomous Communities, respecting this basic legislation, can establish more specific rules (Constitutional Court Decision 1/1982 of 28 January). In accordance with the most recent jurisprudence of the Constitutional Court, which has progressively been varying its position, the essence of the basic legislation consists in establishing sufficient and homogeneous minimum provisions for all of the country, which can be developed by the Autonomous Communities that have assumed powers with regard to the specific matter at hand (Constitutional Court Decision 102/1995 of 26 June).

56. Another dispute focuses on the hierarchical level that norms containing basic legislation should have. Although the term 'legislation' in Spanish law suggests that a formal Act or Statute may be required, the Constitutional Court adopted a substantive approach (with certain vacillations). It is not necessary that basic legislation should have the form of an Act. It can be contained in administrative regulations or even in administrative enforcement acts (Constitutional Court Decisions 163/1995 of 8 November and 329/1993 of 12 November). Furthermore, the Constitutional Court has accepted that if the State did not establish basic legislation regarding any matter, the Autonomous Communities may exercise their legislative powers. In this case, the Autonomous Communities should respect the legal basics (meaning substantive notions that rationally result from the current legislation, whether express or implied). This does not impede the State from establishing basic legislation in the future (Constitutional Court Decision 64/1982 of 8 February).

57. Besides its analysed paragraph 23, Article 149(1) of the Constitution also lists other matters affecting the environment regarding which the State holds exclusive powers, among others:

– criminal legislation – Article 149(1.6);
– civil legislation – Article 149(1.8);

- legislation, regulation, and concession of water resources and projects when the waters run through more than one Autonomous Community – Article 149(1.22);
- public works of general interest or whose realization affects more than one Autonomous Community – Article 149(1.24); and
- the basics of the mining and energy system – Article 149(1.25).

58. Pursuant to Article 148(1.9) of the Constitution, the Autonomous Communities can hold powers regarding environmental protection. This includes the development, implementation and enforcement of the State's basic legislation, as well as additional legislation addressed to achieve higher levels of environmental protection. All the Autonomous Communities have assumed generic powers on environmental matters as well as specific powers on matters linked to the environment. For instance:

- regulation of the territory, urbanism, and housing – Article 148(1.3);
- agriculture and livestock – Article 148(1.7);
- woodlands and forestry – Article 148(1.8);
- fishing in inland waters, hunting, and river fishing – Article 148(1.11); and
- promotion and regulation of tourism within their territorial areas – Article 148(1.18).

To summarize (even though some peculiarities exist), it is up to the State to enact basic legislation. The Autonomous Communities hold development and implementation powers and may also enact additional legislation aiming to achieve higher levels of environmental protection. Enforcement usually falls upon the Autonomous Communities. The administrative organization of the Autonomous Communities has also evolved to include the majority of environmental jurisdiction in one department, or regional ministry which is specific to the autonomous government.

Coordination and cooperation between the central administration and the autonomous administrations of the state are channelled through the Environmental Sectorial Conference at which all are present and which is presided over by the Ministry of the Environment.

59. The Act 7/1985 of 2 April regulating the Basics of the Local Regime, defines the scope of the powers of the local authorities regarding the environment. It should be noted again that these authorities have no legislative power, but only regulatory power materializing in municipal ordinances. Municipalities have competence for environmental protection to the extent their interest is concerned (Article 137 of the Constitution). Sectorial legislation (waters, coast, etc.) specifies certain local competencies regarding these specific matters. Pursuant to the Act regulating the Basics of the Local Regime, municipalities are compulsorily responsible for the public services of waste collection and treatment, sewers and waste water treatment. Other public services may be required, depending on the population of the municipality.

Municipalities basically undertake actions at two levels: (a) elaboration of municipal ordinances, since they have regulatory powers; and (b) environmental management, since they have executive powers. The municipalities should furnish public services alone or in association. To the extent small municipalities, with a limited budget, cannot afford to supply the aforementioned public services, the Provincial Councils and Island Councils assist them.

§2. THE ACTUAL ROLE OF THE GOVERNMENTAL INSTITUTIONS

60. Spanish governmental institutions basically face certain important problems in the practice of environmental protection.

As mentioned above, the first problem is the absence of a general Act on Environment. The option for a model of sectorial regulation reduces the coherence and congruence of the adopted measures and leads to a fragmented administrative action.

The second problem concerns the delimitation of the powers between the different public administrations. Keeping in mind the wide understanding of the 'basic legislation' concept as defined by the Constitutional Court in its 102/1995 Decision, the basic legislation established by the State has sometimes had a high level of concreteness. This has limited the extent of the legislative powers of the Autonomous Communities. In such cases, the Autonomous Communities have been limited to adopting measures to enforce the State's basic legislation and to establishing additional measures aiming to achieve higher levels of environmental protection.

In addition, the incorporation of Spain into the EU has further complicated the discussion on competencies, given that European Directives – which tend to be quite specific – have de facto substituted the basic legislation. The State and the Autonomous Communities have continuously tried to keep a certain margin of legislative decision-making power even in these circumstances. It must be noted that pursuant to the Community principle of institutional and procedural autonomy, the appointment of the competent national body to implement and execute the obligations deriving from European law must be decided on the basis of the constitutional provisions applying in each country (Constitutional Court Decision 80/1993 of 8 March).

The third problem is related to the large number of competent authorities in environmental matters, as a result of the existing fragmentary legislation and distribution of powers. The dispersion of competencies of the authorities dealing with economic activities that are likely to cause adverse environmental effects, together with the insufficient level of administrative coordination, has a negative impact on the effectiveness of public environmental policies. It should also be taken into account that, in addition to the Central Government and the Autonomous Communities, local councils also have significant competencies regarding the environment, such as waste management and waste water management. In this sense, the implementation of Directive 96/61/EC on Integrated Pollution Prevention and Control (IPPC) constituted an outstanding challenge for the Spanish authorities.

Recently an additional problem has arisen as a result of the Spanish Government's reorganization of its ministries. The amalgamation of the Department of the Environment and the Department of Agriculture, Fisheries and Food into the new

Department of the Environment and Rural and Marine Affairs, and the appointment of a Minister in charge of the new department may have improved the integration of environmental policies in the areas of agriculture and fishing, but it has also lead to the break up of some units and technical groups that had hitherto played a very important role in the development of environmental policies and to the general weakening of these policies.

Chapter 5. Sources of Environmental Law

61. This section deals only with the legislation of the State. Previous remarks on basic legislation, shared and exclusive powers, and legislation of the Autonomous Communities should be taken into account for a correct understanding of the structure of environmental legislation in Spain. The following Spanish Acts are the main national sources of law relating to pollution control and nature conservation.

I. General and Administrative Legislation

- Spanish Constitution of 27 December 1978 (BOE 29.12.1978), Articles 45, 53, 93, 94, 95, 96, 148, 149.
- Civil Code of 24 July 1889, Articles 1.902–1.908.
- Act 7/1985 of 2 April, on the Basics of the Local Regime (BOE 3.4.1985), as partially amended by Act 11/1999 of 21 April (BOE 22.4.1999).
- Organic Act 10/1995 of 23 November, Criminal Code (BOE 24.11.1995 and 2.3.1996), Articles 325–340.
- Act 6/1996 of 15 January, on Social Voluntary Activities (BOE 17.1.1996), Article 4.
- Act 7/1997 of 14 April, Establishing Measures addressed to the Liberalization of Both Regimes of the Land and Professional Associations (BOE 15.4.1997).
- Act 55/1999 of 29 December, on Fiscal, Administrative and Social Measures (BOE 30.12.1999).
- Act 26/2007, of 23 October, on Environmental Liability (BOE 24.10.2007).
- Act 17/2009, of 23 November, on free access to professional activities and their exercise.(BOE 24.11.2009).
- Act 25/2009, of 22 December, on modification of several regulations in order to update them to the Act on free access to professional activities and their exercise (BOE 23.12.2009).
- Act 2/2011, of 4 March, of Sustainable Economy (BOE 5.3.2011).
- RD 2/2008, of 20 June, which approved the rewritten text of the land law (BOE 26.6.2008).
- RD 1188/2001, of 2 November, which regulates the composition and the functions of the National Climate Council (BOE 3.11.2001).
- RD 2355/2004, of 23 December, which regulates the structure and the functions of the Environment Advisory Board (BOE 14.1.2005).
- RD 12/2008, of 11 January, which regulates the composition and the activities of the Council for the National Parks Network (BOE 12.1.2008).
- RD 865/2008, of 23 May, which regulates the composition, functions and activities of the Inter-Ministerial Commission for the Rural Environment, the Council for the Rural Environment and the Committee of Rural Development Associations (BOE 24.5.2008).
- RD 1424/2008, of 14 August, which specifies the State Commission for Natural Heritage and Biodiversity in terms of its composition, functions, governing regulations and its specialized committees (BOE, 12.9.2008).

- RD 2090/2008, of 22 December, which approves the Regulations extracted in part from Act 26/2007, 23 October, on Environmental Responsibility (BOE 23.12.2008).
- RD 948/2009, of 5 June, which specifies the composition, functions and regulations governing the State Council for Natural Heritage and Biodiversity (BOE 20.6.2009).
- RD 1383/2009 of 28 August, which specifies the composition, organic structure and the functioning of the National Water Council (BOE 29.8.2009).
- RD 495/2010, of 30 April, which approves the basic organic structure of the ministerial departments (BOE 6.5.2010).
- RD 367/2010 of 26 March, to amend various regulations in the area of environment to adapt to the Act 17/2009 of 23 November, on free access to professional activities and their exercise and Act 25/2009, of 22 December on modification of several regulations in order to update them to the Act on free access to professional activities and their exercise (BOE 27.3.2010).

II. Water Protection

- Act 21/1977 of 1 April, Prevention of Marine Pollution Caused by Discharges from Vessels and Aeroplanes (BOE 4.4.1977).
- Act 22/1988 of 28 July, Coast Act (BOE 29.7.1988), as modified (mainly) by the Act 2/2013 of 29 May, on the protection and sustainable use of the coastal zone (BOE 30.5.2013).
- Act 27/1992 of 24 November, on State and Merchant Marine ports (BOE 25.11.1992 and 12.12.1992).
- Act 11/1999 of 21 April, amending Act 7/1985 of 2 April, Basics of the Local Regime and Other Measures for the Development of the Local Government on Traffic and Waters (BOE 22.4.1999). It modifies Articles 17 and 25 of Act 29/1985 of 2 August (BOE 189, 8.8.85).
- Act 46/1999 of 13 December, Modification of Act 29/1985, on Water (BOE 14.12.1999). Only the first transitional clause remains valid.
- RLD 1/2001 of 20 July, which approves the rewritten text of the Water Act (BOE 24.7.2001) (Correction of Errors BOE 30.11.2001). Partially modified by Act 24/2001 of 27 December, on Fiscal and Administrative Actions and Social Order (BOE 31.12.2001), Act 16/2002 of 1 July, on Integrated Prevention and Pollution Control (BOE 2.7.2002), Act 53/2002 of 30 December, on Fiscal and Administrative Actions and Social Order (BOE 31.12.2002) and by Act 62/2003, of 30 December, on Fiscal and Administrative Actions and Social Order (BOE 31.12.2003).
- Act 10/2001 of 5 July, on the National Hydrological Plan (BOE 6.7.2001). Correction of Errors of Act 10/2001 of 5 July (BOE 2.8.2001). Modified by RLD 2/2004 of 18 June) BOE 19.6.2004).
- RLD 4/2007, of 13 April, which modifies the rewritten text of the Water Law, approved by RD 1/2001, of 20 July (BOE 14.4.2007).

- Act 41/2010, of 29 December on Protection of Marine Environment (BOE 30.12.2010).
- Act 2/2013, of 29 May, on the protection and sustainable use of the coastal zone (BOE 30.5.2013).
- RD 849/1986 of 11 April, Regulation on the Hydrological Public Domain. Develops the content of Titles I, IV, V, VI and VII of the Act 29/1985 of 2 August (BOE 30.4.1986 and 2.7.1986). Partially amended by RD 1315/1992 of 30 October (BOE 1.12.1992), RD 995/2000 of 2 June (BOE 20.6.2000), and RD 606/2003 of 23 May (BOE 6.6.2003).
- RD 927/1988 of 29 July, Regulation on the Water Public Administration and Hydrologic Planning. It develops Titles II and III of the Act 29/1985 of 2 August (BOE 31.8.1988 and 29.9.1988). Modified by RD 117/1992 of 14 February, RD 439/1994 of 11 March, 1541/1994 of 8 July, and 2068/1996 of 13 September.
- RD 1471/1989 of 1 December, Administrative Regulation for the Implementation and Enforcement of the Act 22/1988 of 28 July (BOE 12.12.1989), amended by RD 1112/1992 of 18 September (BOE 6.10.1992).
- RD 11/1995 of 28 December, Treatment of Urban Waste Water (BOE 3.2.1996). Developed by RD 509/1996 of 15 March (BOE 29.3.1996), and amended by RD 2116/1998 of 2 October (BOE 20.10.1998) RD 1664/1998 of 24 July, Water Basins Hydrological Plans (BOE 11.8.1998).
- RD 261/1996 of 16 February, about the protection of waters against contamination from nitrates originating from agrarian sources.
- RD 140/2003 of 7 February, which establishes the sanitary criteria for water quality for human consumption.
- RD 907/2007, of 6 July, which approved the Regulations governing Hydrological Planning (BOE 7.7.2007).
- RD 903/2010, 9 July, on the evaluation and management of flood risks (BOE 15.7.2010).
- RD 60/2011, of 21 January, on environmental quality standards concerning water policy.

III. Air Pollution

- Act 21/1992 of 16 July, Industry (BOE 23.7.1992).
- RLD 339/1990 of 2 March, Statutory Instrument of the Act on Motor Vehicles Traffic and Road Safety (BOE 14.3.1990).
- Act 16/2002, of 1 July, on the prevention and integrated control of pollution (BOE 2.7.2002).
- Act 1/2005, of 9 March, on trading of greenhouse gases emission allowances (BOE 10.3.2005), amended by Act 13/2010 of 5 July, amending the Law 1 / 2005 of 9 March, on trading of greenhouse gases emission allowances, to improve and extend the general system of emissions trading to include aviation (BOE 6.7.2010).

- Act 34/2007, 15 November, on air quality and the protection of the atmosphere (BOE 16.11.2007).
- Act 40/2010, of 29 December, on the geological storage of carbon dioxide.(BOE 30.12.2010).
- D 833/1975 of 6 February 1975. Develops Act 38/1972 of 22 December (BOE 12.9.1985). Amended by RD 547/1979 of 20 February (BOE 23.3.1979), RD 1613/1985 of 1 August (BOE 12.9.1985), RD 1154/1986 (BOE 19.6.1986), RD 717/1987 of 27 May (BOE 6.6.1987), and partially amended by RD 1321/1992 of 30 October (BOE 3.2.1993).
- RD 1513/1988 of 9 December, which regulates the maximum lead content in petrol (BOE 19.12.1988).
- RD 653/2003 of 30 May, about waste incineration (BOE 14.6.2003 and 18.9.2003).
- Real Decreto 1428/2003, de 21 de noviembre. General Regulation on Traffic for the Implementation and Enforcement of the RDL 339/1990 on Motor Vehicles Traffic and Road Safety (BOE 23.12.2003).
- RD 430/2004 of 12 March, which establishes new norms on the restriction of emissions of certain contaminating agents originating from large combustion facilities into the atmosphere and which fixes certain conditions for the monitoring of emissions into the atmosphere from petroleum refineries (BOE 20.3.2004).
- RLD 5/2004 of 27 August, which regulates the emission rights trading system of greenhouse gasses (BOE 28.8.2004).
- RD 1866/2004 of 6 September, which approves the National Emission Rights Assignation Plan 2005–2007 (BOE 7.9.2004).
- RD 1264/2005, of 21 October, which regulates the organization and functioning of the National Emissions Rights Registry. (BOE 22.10.2005).
- RD 1315/2005, 4 November, which establishes the systems for monitoring and verifying greenhouse gas emissions in those installations governed by Act 1/2005, 9 March, which regulates emissions trading. (BOE 9.11.2005).
- RD 227/2006, of 24 February, which complements the legal system that governs the limiting of volatile organic compound emissions in specific paints and varnishes and in car body paint (BOE 25.2.2006).
- RD 777/2006, of 23 June, which modifies RD 1866/2004, of 6 September, which approves the National Plan for Assigning Emissions Trading Rights, 2005–2007. (BOE 24.6.2006).
- RD 1370/2006, of 24 November, which approves the National Plan for Assigning Emissions Trading Rights, 2008–2012. (BOE 25.1.2006), amended by RD 1402/2007, of 29 October. (BOE 30.10.2007).
- RD 508/2007, 20 de abril, regulates the supply of information regarding emissions in accordance with the E-PRTR Regulations and the integrated environmental authorizations. (BOE 21.4.2007).
- RD 509/2007, of 20 April, which approves the Regulations for the development and execution of Act 16/2002, of 1 July, on the integrated control and prevention of pollution. (BOE 21.4.2007).
- RD 1402/2007, 29 October, which modifies RD 1370/2006, of 24 November, which approves the National Plan for Assigning Emissions Trading Rights, 2008–2012. (BOE 30.10.2007).

- RD 227/2006 of 24 February, complementing the legal regime on emissions limits for volatile organic compounds in certain paints and varnishes and for vehicle refinishing products for vehicles. (BOE 25.2.2006).
- RD 61/2006 of 31 January, determining specifications for gasoline, diesel, fuel oil and liquefied petroleum gases and regulating the use of certain biofuels (BOE 17.2.2006), amended by RD 1027/2006, of 15 September regarding sulphur content of marine fuels (BOE 28.9.2006) and by RD 1088/2010, of 3 September, concerning the technical specifications for gasoline, diesel, biofuel use and sulphur content of marine fuels (BOE 4.9.2010).
- RD 100/2011, of 28 January, which updates the catalogue of activities that are likely to cause air pollution and establishes basic implementing provisions.
- RD 101/2011, of 28 January, which establishes the basic legal provisions applying to the schemes for the accreditation and verification of the emissions of Greenhouse gases, the tone-kilometre data from aviation activities, and regulating the transitional free allocation of emission allowances from the stationary installations within the scope of the Act 1/2005 on trading of greenhouse gases emissions allowances.
- RD 102/2011, of 28 January, on the improvement of the air quality (BOE 29.1.2011).

IV. Waste Management and Noxious Substances

- Act 11/1997 of 24 April, Packaging and Packaging Waste (BOE 25.4.1997).
- Act 22/2011, of 28 July, on waste and contaminated soils (BOE. 29.7.2011), as modified by Act 11/2012, of 19 December, which incorporates urgent measures in environmental matter (BOE 20.12.2012), and Act 5/2013, of 11 June 2013 (BOE 12.6.2013).
- RD 833/1988 of 20 July, Regulation Developing Act 20/1986, Basic Act on Toxic and Dangerous Waste (BOE 30.7.1988), amended by RD 952/1997 of 20 June (BOE 5.7.1997) and partially abolished by the Act 10/1998 of 21 April (BOE 22.4.1998).
- RD 1310/1990 of 29 October, Use of Sludge for Agricultural Purposes (BOE 1.11.1990).
- RD 2088/1994 of 20 October, Implementation of the 92/3/EURATOM Directive on the Monitoring and Control of Shipments of Radioactive Waste within, into and out of the European Community (BOE 26.11.1994).
- RD 782/98 of 30 April, Regulation for the Implementation and Enforcement of Act 11/1997 of 24 April (BOE 1.5.1998).
- RD 783/2001, of 6 July, Regulation on Sanitary Protection against Ionizing Radiation. (BOE 26.7.2001).
- RD 1481/2001 of 27 December, on the elimination of wastes by means of their disposal in rubbish dumps.
- RD 255/2003, of 28 February, Regulation on the Classification, Packaging and Labelling of Dangerous Preparations.

- RD 653/2003 of 30 May, on Waste Incineration.
- RD 9/2005 of 10 January, which establishes the list of potentially soil contaminating activities and the criteria and standards for the declaration of contaminated soil.
- RD 1619/2005, of 30 December, on management of used tires (BOE 3.1.2006).
- RD 252/2006, of 3 March, of reviewing the recycling and recovery targets set out in Act 11/1997 of 24 April, on packaging and packaging waste, and amending the Regulations for its execution, approved by RD 782/1998 of 30 April (BOE 4.3.2006).
- RD 679/2006, of 2 June, on management of used industrial oils (BOE 3.6.2006).
- RD 228/2006, of 24 February, by amending the RD 1378/1999, of 27 August, laying down measures for the disposal and management of Polychlorinated Biphenyls (PCBs), Polychlorinated Terphenyls (PCTs) and equipment containing (BOE 25.2.2006).
- RD 1802/2008, of 3 November, which modifies the Regulations regarding the notification of new substances and the classification, packaging and labelling of dangerous substances, approved by R D 363/1995, of 10 March, with the aim of adapting its provisions to the European Council and Parliament Regulations (CE) 1907/2006 (REACH Regulations) (BOE 4.11.2008).
- RD 105/2008, of 1 February, regulating the production and management of construction and demolition waste (B.O.E. 13.2.2008).
- Decision of the Council of Ministers of 20 January 2009, which approves the Integrated National Plan on Waste –Period 2008-2015 (BOE 26.2.2009).
- RD 1304/2009, of 31 July, which regulates waste disposal through landfill (BOE 1.8.2009).
- RD 1436/2010, of 5 November, amending various RD for transposing Directive 2008/112/EC amending several directives to adapt them to Regulation (EC) 1272/2008, on classification, labelling and packaging of substances and mixtures. (BOE 9.11.2010).
- RD 106/2008, of 1 February 1, on batteries and accumulators and environmental management of their wastes (BOE 02.12.2008), amended by RD 943/2010, of 23 July 23 (BOE 5.8.2010).
- RD 243/2009, of 27 February, which regulates the supervision and control of shipments of radioactive waste and used nuclear fuel between Member States or from or outside the European Community (BOE 2.4.2009).

V. Noise Pollution

- Act 37/2003 of 17 November, on Noise (BOE 18.11.2003).
- RD 2028/1986 of 6 June, Implementation of the European Directives Regarding the Type Approval of Vehicles, Trailers, Semi-Trailers and their Parts and Components (BOE 2.10.1986), amended and developed by Order of 4 February 1988 (BOE 16.2.1988), Order of 10 April 1988 (BOE 22.4.1989), Order of 24 November 1989 (BOE 16.12.1989), Order of 16 July 1991 (BOE 27.7.1991), Order of

24 January 1992 (BOE 11.2.1992), Order of 12 July 1992 (BOE 5.8.1992), Order of 29 December 1992 (BOE 11.1.1993), Order of 10 June 1993 (BOE 28.6.1993), Order of 15 October 1993 (BOE 26.10.1993), Order of 22 February 1994 (BOE 15.3.1994), Order of 29 April 1996 (BOE 10.5.1996).
- RD 873/1987 of 29 May, Limitations of Noise Emissions from Subsonic Aeroplanes (BOE 3.7.1987).
- RD 245/1989 of 27 February, Determination and Limitation of the Permissible Sound Power Level of Construction Plant and Equipment and Lawnmowers (BOE 11.3.1989), amended and developed by the Order of 17 November 1989 (BOE 1.12.1989), Order of 18 July 1991 (BOE 26.7.1991), RD 71/1992 of 31 January (BOE 6.2.1992).
- RD 1316/1989 of 27 October, Protection of Workers from Risks Related to Exposure to Noise at Work (BOE 2.11.1989, 9.12.1989 and 26.5.1990).
- RD 1256/1990 of 11 October, Limitations of Noise Emissions from Civil SubsonicJet Aeroplanes (BOE 18.10.1990, 30.10.1990 and 27.4.1991).
- RD 1422/1992 of 27 November, Limitation of the Use of Civil Subsonic Aeroplanes, amended by RD 325/1995 of 3 March (BOE 24.3.1995).
- RD 212/2002 of 22 February, which regulates noise emissions in the environment due to certain machines used in the open air.
- RD 1513/2005, of 16 December, which implements the stipulations of Act 37/2003, 17 November, on Noise, regarding the evaluation and management of environmental noise(BOE 17.12.2005).
- RD 1367/2007, 19 October, which implements the stipulations of Act 37/2003, of 17 November, on Noise, regarding acoustic zoning, quality targets and acoustic emissions (BOE 23.10.2007).

VI. Nature Conservation and Management

- Act of 20 February 1942, River Fishing (BOE 8.3.1942).
- Act 37/1966 of 31 May, National Game Preserves (BOE 2.6.1970).
- Act 81/1968 of 5 December, Forest Fires (BOE 7.12.1968).
- Act 1/1970 of 4 April, Hunting Act (BOE 6.4.1970).
- Act 3/1995 of 23 March, Livestock Trails (BOE 24.3.1995).
- Act 3/2001, of 26 March, on Marine Fishing by the State.
- Act 31/2003 of 27 October, on the conservation of wild fauna in zoological parks (BOE 28.10.2003).
- Act 43/2003 of 21 November, on Forests (BOE 22.11.2003).
- Act 10/2006, on 28 April, which modifies Act 43/2003, of 21 November, on Mountains (BOE 29.4.2006).
- Organic Act 12/1995 of 12 December, Repression of Smuggling (BOE 13.12.1995). – Act 14/1998 of 1 June, Monitoring System for the Protection of Fishing Resources (BOE 2.6.1998, amendment of mistakes BOE 5.6.1998).
- Act 5/2007, of 3 April, on the National Parks Network (BOE 4.4.2007).

- Act 42/2007, of 13 December, on Natural Heritage and Biodiversity (BOE 14.12.2007).
- D of 6 April 1943, Regulation on River Fishing (BOE 2.5.1943).
- D 485/1962 of 22 February, Regulation on Mountains (BOE 12.3.1962, 13.3.1962, 19.3.1962 and 21.5.1962).
- D 506/1971 of 25 March, Regulation on Hunting (BOE 30.3.1970).
- D 3769/1972 of 23 December, Regulation on Forest Fires (BOE 13.2.1972 and 21.3.1972).
- RD 3181/1980 of 30 December, Protection of Certain Wild Fauna Species.
- RD 2994/1982 of the 15th of October, Restoration of Natural Spaces Affected by Extraction Activities (BOE 15.11.1982).
- RD 1095/1989 of 8 September, which defines the species eligible for hunting and fishing and establishes norms for their protection (BOE 12.9.1989).
- RD 1118/1989 of 15 September, which defines the marketable species of fish and game (19.9.89) (BOE 19.9.1989).
- RD 2071/1993 of 26 November, Protection Against the Introduction and Diffusion in the National or European Community Territories of Organisms Noxious for Vegetal Forms or Products. Measures on Exports and Transits of these Organisms to Third Countries. Modified by the Order of 18 March 1998 (BOE 24.3.1998) and Order of 22 May 1998 (BOE 27.5.1998).
- RD 439/1990 of 30 March, National Catalogue of Fauna and Flora Threatened Species (BOE 5.4.1990).
- RD 2488/1994 of 23 December, on the National Commission for the Protection of Wildlife (BOE 18.1.1995).
- RD 1997/1995 of 7 December, Measures for Protecting Biodiversity by Means of Habitats, Flora and Fauna Preservation (BOE 28.12.1995), amended by RD 1193/1998 of 12 June (BOE 25.6.1998).
- RD 1739/1997 of 20 November, on the means of application of the International Agreement on Endangered Species of Wild Fauna and Flora (CITES) and Regulation CE/338/97 of the Council (BOE 28.11.1997).
- RD 1803/1999 of 26 November, National Parks Network Director Plan (BOE 13.12.1999).
- RD 435/2004 of 12 March, which regulates the national inventory of wetland areas (BOE 25.3.2004).
- Order ARM/2444/2008, 12 August, which approves the National Action Programme against Desertification, in accordance with the United Nations Convention in the Fight against Desertification (BOE 19.8.2008).

VII. Subsoil and Minerals

- Act 22/1973 of 21 July, Mining Act (BOE 24.7.1973), Articles 5 and 6, amended by Act 54/1980 of 5 November.
- Act 6/1977 of 4 January, Promotion of Mining (BOE 8.1.1977).

- Act 54/1980, of 5 November, which modifies Act 22/1973, of 21 July, on Mines (BOE 21.11.1980).
- RD 2875/1978 of 25 August, General Mining Regulation (BOE 11 and 12.12.1978). – RD 1389/1997 of 5 September, Minimum Health and Safety Requirements for the Protection of Workers in Mining Activities (BOE 7.10.1997).
- RD 975/2009, of 12 June, regarding the management of waste from extractive industries and the protection and rehabilitation of areas affected by mining activities (BOE 13.6.2009).

VIII. Energy

- Act 25/1964 of 29 April, on nuclear energy.
- Act 15/1980, of 22 April, Creation of the Nuclear Security Council (BOE 25.4.1980), amended by Act 33/2007, of 7 November (BOE 8.11.2007).
- Act 82/1980 of 30 December, on Energy Conservation (BOE 27.1.1981).
- Act 34/1998, of 7 October, Hydrocarbons Sector (BOE 8.10.1998), amended by Act 12/2007, 2 July, in order to adapt it to Directive 2003/55/EC of 26 June 2003 concerning common rules for the internal market in natural gas (BOE 3.7.2007)
- Act 22/2005, of 18 November, which incorporates into the Spanish legal system various EU directives regarding the taxation of energy and electricity products and the common tax regime applied to the parent and subsidiary companies of different Member States, and which regulates the tax regime for cross-border contributions to pension funds in the EU (BOE 19.11.2005).
- Act 54/1997, of 27 November, on Electricity Sector (BOE 28.11.1997), amended by Act 25/2009, of 22 December, on modification of several regulations in order to update them to the Act on free access to professional activities and their exercise (BOE 23.12.2009), and Act 17/2007, of 4 July, amending Act 54/1997, of 27 November, on the Electricity Sector, to adapt it to Directive 2003/54/EC of 26 June 2003 concerning common rules for the internal electricity market (BOE 5.7.2007).
- RLD 4/2006, of 24 February, Modifies the functions of Energy National Commission (BOE 28.2.2006).
- RLD 7/2006, of 23 June, which adopts urgent measures in the energy sector (BOE 24.6.2006).
- RD of 2 April 1984, Promotion of Auto-generation of Electricity (BOE 10.5.1982). – RD 2366/1994 of 9 December, on the production of electric energy by hydraulic facilities, cogeneration facilities and others based on renewable energy sources (BOE 30.12.1994).
- Act 34/1998 of 7 October, on the Hydrocarbon Sector (BOE 8.1.1998 and 3.02.1999).
- Act 40/1994 of 30 December, on the National Electric System (BOE 31.12.1994), developed by RD 404/1996 of 1 March, amending RD 1522/1984 of 4 July,

authorizing the creation of the National Enterprise of Radioactive Waste (ENRESA) (BOE 22.3.1996).
- Act 54/1997 of 27 November, on the Electricity Sector (BOE 28.11.1997).
- RD 1062/1998 of 29 May, Energy Efficiency Requirements for Household Electric Refrigerators, Freezers and Combinations thereof (BOE 5.6.1998).
- RD 2818/1998 of 23 December, Production of Electricity by Plants Using Waste, Co-generation or Renewable Energy Sources (BOE 30.12.1998). Correction of errors (BOE 19.2.1999).
- RD 2819/1998 of 23 December, which regulates transport and electric energy distribution activities (BOE 30.12.1998).
- RD 284/1999 of 22 February, which regulates energy labels on domestic use lighting (BOE 3.3.1999).
- RD 1836/1999 of 3 December, on nuclear and radioactive facilities, amended by RD 35/2008 (BOE 18.2.2008).
- RD 1663/2000 of 29 September, on the connection of photovoltaic facilities to the low tension network (BOE 30.9.2000).
- RD 1955/2000 of 1 December, which regulates the transport, distribution, marketing, supply and authorization procedures in electric energy facilities (BOE 27.12.2000).
- RD 949/2001 of 3 August, which regulates third party access to gas facilities and establishes an integrated economic system for the natural gas sector (BOE 7.9.2001).
- RD 385/2002 of 26 April, which modifies Royal Decree 2018/1997 of 26 December, which passed the regulation of the point of measurement for the consumption and transport of electric energy (BOE 14.5.2002).
- RD 837/2002 of 2 August, which regulates information related to the consumption of fuel and CO2 emissions from new cars on the market or for lease in Spanish territory (BOE 3.8.2002).
- RD 838/2002 of 2 August, which establishes the energy effectiveness requirements for fluorescent light ballasts (BOE 4.8.2002).
- RD 841/2002 of 2 September, which regulates certain obligations of reporting production forecasts and acquisition by marketers of electric energy produced by electric energy production facilities in the special incentive system for participation in the production market (BOE 2.9.2002).
- RD 436/2004 of 12 March, which establishes the methodology for the updating and systemization of the legal and economic system of electric energy production activity under a special scheme (BOE 27.3.2004). Correction of Errors (BOE 8.4.2004).
- RD 616/2007, of 11 May, regarding the promotion of cogeneration (BOE 12.5.2007).
- RD 1027/2007, of 20 July, which approves the Regulations governing Thermal Installations in Buildings (BOE, 29.8.2007).
- RD 1440/2010, of 5 November, Statute of Nuclear Security Council (BOE 22.11.2010).

IX. Agricultural Resources

- Act 45/2007, of 13 December, on sustainable rural development (BOE 14.12.2007).
- RD 1852/1993 of 22 October, Organic Production of Agricultural Products and Indications Referring Thereto on Agricultural Products and Foodstuffs (BOE 26.11.1993), developed by Order of 28 December 1993 (BOE 8.1.1993).
- RD 1201/2002, of 20 November, which regulates the integrated production of agricultural products, modified by RD 108/2010, of 5 February (BOE 30.11.2002).
- RD 824/2005, of 8 July, on fertilizers, modified by RD 108/2010, of 5 February (BOE 19.7.2005).
- RD 1614/2005, of 30 December, which modifies RD 1852/1993, of 22 October, regarding organic farming and labelling in agricultural and food products (BOE 3.1.2006).
- RD 1203/2006, of 20 October, which modifies the Royal Decrees 3482/2000, 29 December, which regulates compensation in certain disadvantaged areas; 4/ 2001, of 12 January, which establishes a grants system for the use of agricultural production methods that are compatible with the environment; 6/2001, of 12 January, on the promotion of the forestation of agricultural lands; and 708/2002, of 19 July, which establishes measures within the Rural Development to Programme that are designed to complement the support measures of the Common Agricultural Policy (BOE 8.11.2006).
- RD 108/2010, of 5 February, which modifies the royal decrees regarding agriculture and farming businesses in order to adapt them to Act 17/2009, of 23 November, regarding free access to service, which incorporates Directive 2006/123/CE of the European Council and Parliament, 12 December 2006, regarding services in the internal market (BOE 6.2.2010).
- RD 752/2010, 4 June, which approves the first programme for sustainable rural development for the 2010–2014 period, in accordance with Act 45/2007, of 13 December, regarding sustainable rural development (BOE 11.6.2010).

X. Industrial Activities

- Act 21/1992 of 16 July, Industry (BOE 23.7.1992).
- Act 34/1998 of 7 October, Hydrocarbon Sector (BOE 8.10.1998).
- Act 16/2002 of 1 July, on IPPC (BOE 2.7.2002).
- D 2183/1968 of 16 August, Application of the Regulation on Unpleasant, Unhealthy, Noxious and Hazardous Activities both in Public Domain Areas and in Activities Directly Carried Out by Official Bodies (BOE 20.9.1968 and 8.10.1968).

- RD 886/1988 of 15 July, Prevention of Major Accidents in Certain Industrial Activities (BOE 5.8.1988 and 28.1.1989), amended and improved by RD 952/1990 of 29 June (BOE 5.8.1988).
- RD 2200/1995 of 28 December, Regulation of the Infrastructures of Industrial Quality and Safety (BOE 6.2.1996 and 6.3.1996), amended by RD 411/1997 of 21 March (BOE 26.4.1997).
- RD 387/1996 of 1 March, Basic Guidelines for Planning Civil Protection Actions Regarding Risks Related to Accidents in the Transport of Dangerous Substances by Rail and Road (BOE 22.3.1996).
- RD 1254/1999 of 16 July, Measures for the Control of Risks Related to Major Accidents Involving Dangerous Substances (BOE 20.7.1999), amended by RD 948/2005, of 29 July (BOE 30.7.2005).
- RD 393/2007 of 23 March, approving the Basic Self-Protection Regulation for centres, institutions and agencies engaged in activities that may give rise to emergency situations. (BOE 24.3.2007), amended by RD 1468/2008, of 5 September (BOE 10.3.2008).
- RD 903/2010, of 9 July, Flood risk assessment and management (BOE 15.7.2010).

XI. Environmental Impact Assessment

- Act 21/2013, of 9 December, on Environmental Assessment (BOE 11.12.2013).

XII. Eco-Audits and Eco-Labelling

- RD 234/2013, of 5 April, which establishes provisions for the implementation of the Regulation (EC) 66/2010 of the European Parliament and the Council, of 25 November 2009, on a EU Eco Label Award Scheme (BOE 24.4.2013).
- RD 85/1996 of 26 January, Voluntary Incorporation of the Industrial Sector Enterprises into an Environmental Management and Audit Community System Established by EEC Regulation 1836/93 (BOE 21.2.1996).

XIII. Public Participation and Information

- Act 30/1992 of 26 November, on the Legal Regime of the Public Administrations and Common Administrative Procedure (BOE 19.8.1994), modified by Act 4/1999 of 13 January (BOE 14.1.1999).

- Act 27/2006, of 18 July, which regulates freedom of information, public participation and access to justice regarding environmental issues (BOE 19.7.2006).
- RD 1771/1994 of 5 August, Adapting the Administrative Procedures Regarding Waters, Coasts and Environment to Act 30/1992 (BOE 19.8.1994).

Part I. Pollution Control

Chapter 1. General Law

§1. Environmental Impact Assessment

62. As in the other Member States of the EU, the Spanish legal system incorporates this technique – which first emerged in the United States (section 102 of the National Environmental Policy Act of 1969) – from the double perspective of the environmental impact assessment (EIA), which evaluates activities and infrastructure projects, and the assessment of the effects of certain plans and programmes on the environment (commonly called a Strategic Environmental Assessment (SEA)). Both techniques are regulated by European law through two different Directives: Directive 2011/92/EU of 13 December 2011 (which codifies the initial Directive 85/337/EEC and its amendments) and Directive 2001/42/EC. As has been mentioned in other Chapters, the Spanish legal regime on environmental assessment must take into account the system of distribution of powers between the State and the Autonomous Communities. Roughly speaking, this system is based on Article 149.1.23 of the Spanish Constitution. According to this article, the State is responsible for drafting basic legislation, while the Autonomous Communities may enact additional and implementing legislation.

63. The basic State regulation that currently applies to environmental assessment in Spain is the Act 21/2013, of 9 December on environmental assessment. It is worth noting that the Act 21/2013 unifies into a single legal text the legal regime applying both to the environmental impact assessment of projects and the strategic environmental assessment of plans and programmes. In this sense, the said Act replaces the RDL 1/2008 (regarding EIA of projects) and the Act 9/2006 (that formerly regulated the strategic environmental assessment of certain plans and programmes).In any case, it is necessary to underline that, according to the EU Law provisions, the Act 21/2013 specifically establishes that an environmental assessment carried out under the SEA provisions shall be without prejudice to any requirements under the legal regime applicable to EIA of projects.

Act 21/2013 establishes certain provisions in the form of basic State legislation (i.e., they are applicable to environmental assessment procedures whether at State or Autonomous Communities' level), and also adds a series of provisions that are only applicable to the environmental assessment of State projects, plans and programmes. The Act establishes a common terminology for EIA and SEA and sets up similar procedures for both environmental protection instruments. In this sense, the

Act foresees four basic types of procedures: (a) general ordinary EIA procedure; (b) simplified EIA procedure; (c) general ordinary SEA procedure and (d) simplified SEA procedure. It is worth noting at this point that the Act regulates EIA and SEA procedures in such a detailed way, that there is no need to elaborate implementing regulations.

64. As specifically regards to the EIA of projects, it has to be mentioned that the model established by the Act 21/2013 incorporates the minimum requirements that establishes the Directive 2011/92/EU into Spanish law. Likewise, the text of the Act 21/2013 includes the specific decisions adopted by the basic State legislator within the margin of discretion that the said Directive concedes to the Member States in terms of submitted projects and in terms of questions regarding the structure and phases of the procedure and of the administrative bodies that have the competencies to carry out EIA.

More specifically, as regards to the EIA screening provisions, Article 7.1 of the Act 21/2013 foresees that public and private projects consisting of works, installations or any other activity listed in Annex I, among other cases, must be subject to the general ordinary EIA procedure. This generally refers to those types of projects that are likely to cause the highest environmental impacts: projects relating to agriculture, forestry, aquaculture, animal husbandry, the extractive industry, the energy industry and the iron and mineral industries; metal production, the chemical, petrochemical, textile and paper industries, certain infrastructure projects, certain hydraulic engineering and water management projects, certain waste management and treatment projects, other projects relating to changes in land use and activities listed in Annex I. Finally, it is necessary to take into account that certain projects included in Annex II of the Act 21/2013 (below) must follow a general ordinary EIA procedure if the competent administrative environmental body so decides after carrying out an screening procedure in a case by case basis. In this cases, the competent environmental body adopts the mentioned decision by relying on the criteria established by Annex III of the Act.

On the other hand, the Act foresees that certain projects which are not likely to cause so severe environmental impacts must follow a simplified EIA procedure. These projects are, among others: (a) public or private projects consisting of works, installations or any other activity listed in Annex II; and (b) public or private projects not included in Annex I and Annex II that may directly or indirectly affect areas of the Natura 2000 Network.

However, in accordance with Article 8, the Act does not apply to 'projects regarding national defence if such an application would have negative repercussions on national defence. The Act will also not be applied to projects specifically approved by a State Act', or when the 'Council of Ministers (...) and the body determined by each Autonomous Community (...)' decide 'under exceptional circumstances and by means of a fully explained agreement to exclude a given project from EIA'.

65. Within the Spanish legal system, the EIA is a procedure included within the main authorization procedure of a project. In order to determine who is the competent authority, we should distinguish between the body that authorizes (the substantive body) and the one that has environmental competence (this is the Ministry of Agriculture, Food and Environment if the project has to be authorized by the State, or the administrative body designated by the Autonomous Communities' legislation for projects that must be authorized by the Autonomous Communities or local authorities). In accordance with Article 33 of the Act 21/2013, the general ordinary procedure of EIA of projects has the following phases: (a) scoping, (b) the environmental impact study, public information and consultation, and (c) the environmental impact declaration (statement). Regarding the initial stages of the environmental assessment, it is worth noting that, by contrast with the former Spanish basic legislation on EIA –RDL 1/2008-, scoping is not a mandatory stage of the EIA procedure under the Act 21/2013.

The EIA procedure also includes consultation to the public, interested persons and administrative authorities. The environmental impact study should include, at least, the following points: a description of the project and its activities; an analysis of the technically feasible alternatives as well as a justification of the alternative chosen; an environmental inventory and a description of the key environmental or ecological interactions; the adoption of correction and prevention measures; an environmental monitoring programme and a synthesis document. It is should be mentioned that the Act establishes some provisions regarding the expiry of the EIA whereby the assessment cannot be completed if a certain period has elapsed between when the EIA was drawn up and when it was submitted for public information and consultation.

The final phase is when statement on the environmental impact statement is made and published, thus bringing an end to the process. The environmental impact statement is an administrative decision that must be adopted into the framework of every authorization procedure of projects submitted to EIA. The lack of an environmental impact statement renders the whole procedure completely null and void (Article 62, 1.e of Act 30/1992 of 26 November on the Legal Regime of the Public Administrations and Common Administrative Procedure).

66. Regarding the legal nature of the environmental impact statement, it should be noted that traditionally one of the most debated subjects in the literature was whether or not such a statement could be challenged separately from the decision of the administrative procedure for the substantive authorization of the project. Courts and administrative legal doctrine gave different answers to this question depending on whether the environmental impact statement was considered as a definitive decision in itself or not. If it was regarded as only a part of the wider authorization procedure, then the statement could not be separately challenged in court. But if it is regarded as a definitive decision, then the environmental impact statement could be challenged separately either by administrative remedy before the administration or by a judicial review of administrative decisions in court.

This debate makes no longer sense. Article 41.4 of the Act 21/2013 provides a clear solution for this problem by establishing that the environmental impact statement cannot be challenged separately from the administrative decision that finally authorizes the project.

Finally, it should be taken into account that the RLD establishes an expiry period for the environmental impact statement that aims to prevent projects from being carried out on the basis of outdated assessments.

67. Under Spanish law, the administrative body with substantive competence monitors the environmental impact statement. This body can ask for all information regarding the statement and make the necessary checks to verify that all the requisites have been fulfilled. The administrative body's follow-up and monitoring should not interfere with those carried out by the environmental bodies which can, at any moment, ask for the necessary administrative help to obtain information or to perform the necessary verifications.

The Act 21/2013 contains a list of violations and specific sanctions regarding this matter (ranging from EUR 24,040.44 to EUR 2,404,148.42). It should be noted, however, that the special nature of the EIA procedure means that it is subject to the specific sanction system of the authorization procedure. The legislation establishes a series of measures that can be taken when an EIA procedure has not been carried out or has been improperly executed. These are:

- Suspension of the activities. If a project has been started before the compulsory EIA (and therefore environmental impact statement) has been completed, it will be suspended by order of the environmental body (ex officio or at the petition of an interested party) without affecting the responsibilities that the initiation of the project may have incurred. Suspension of the works can also be agreed in any of the following circumstances: (a) the intentional withholding of information or falsification of or tampering with data during the evaluation procedure, (b) the non-compliance with or violation of the project's environmental requirements.
- Restitution of the environment to its original state before it was altered by projects that had not followed the compulsory EIA procedure.
- Compensation of losses and damages. In all cases, the promoter of the project in which the compulsory EIA was omitted will be forced to compensate any losses and damages that may arise, as estimated by the environmental body.

68. Finally, it should be noted that most Autonomous Communities have also regulated the EIA procedure in accordance with their powers to legislate for matters concerning the environment and the regulation of administrative procedure. There has been a series of important changes in the legal system governing the use of EIAs in the Autonomous Communities. These changes are the result of a raft of new legislation that has progressively replaced the legislation that was previously in force. Of particular note are the regulations approved by Navarre, Andalusia, Aragon, Cantabria, the Balearic Islands, Castile-La Mancha and, most recently Catalonia. The main characteristic of these reforms is that they all aim, albeit in greater or lesser detail and with different approaches, to resolve the problems caused by applying EIA, SEA and IPPC in conjunction. Nevertheless, it should be made clear that the reforms introduced by the Autonomous Communities vary in their scope; for example, some go for full regulation of EIA, SEA and IPPC together (as in Navarre and Andalusia), while others only regulate EIA and SEA or EIA and IPPC (as is the case with Act 20/2009 on prevention and environmental control of activities in Catalonia).

69. The previous paragraphs refer to the application of EIA to projects; however, as pointed out at the start of this chapter, this should now also involve a global strategic environmental assessment (SEA). European Parliament and Council Directive 2001/42/EC of 27 June 2001 regarding the assessment of the effects of certain plans and programmes on the environment was first incorporated into Spanish law through Act 9/2006 of 28 April on the assessment of the effects of certain plans and programmes on the environment. Currently, as explained before, the main general provisions regarding SEA are established by the Act 21/2013 on environmental assessment. In this regard, and in accordance with the structure of environmental assessment in European law, Act 21/2013 applies environmental assessment to the earlier and more general stages of the decision-making process (planning and programming). This is in contrast to EIA Directive and its transposing domestic legislation, which only apply environmental assessment to the final stage, that is, specific projects. Act 21/2013 is basic state legislation drafted under the aegis of Article 149.1 23ª of the Spanish Constitution. In addition, various sectorial regulations have been added to the basic state legislation, such as Act 42/2007, of 13 December, on Natural Heritage and Biodiversity, RD 907/2007, of 6 July, which approves the Regulations on Water Planning, and, most importantly, RLD 2/2008, of 20 June, which approves the Redrafted Text of the Land Act.

The environmental assessment defined by Act 21/2013 is applied to a series of plans and programmes listed in Article 6 of the Act (these coinciding substantially with Articles 2 and 3 of Directive 2001/42/CE, with a few additions), and follows a process that is generally in keeping with Directive 2001/42/CE and that therefore has many similarities with the Spanish transposition of the EIA of projects. It is worth noting that the new Act 21/2013 establishes two different procedures for carrying out a strategic environmental assessment: the general ordinary SEA procedure (applicable to those plans and programmes of Article 6.1 of the Act –which basically coincides with Article 3.2 a and 3.2 b) of Directive 2011/42/EC) and the simplified SEA procedure (that applies to the rest of the plans and programmes that fall within the scope of the Act). In this regard, special emphasis must be placed on the requirement that strategic environmental assessment in Spain must involve an environmental body along with the promoter and the competent authority if a plan or programme is to be definitively approved. The phases of the procedure are screening, scoping, the drafting of an Strategic Environmental Report, the publishing of the Environmental Report for public information and consultation by the interested parties and public administrations affected, the drafting of an strategic environmental statement, the approval of the plan or programme, and monitoring.

The environmental report must contain the elements specified in Annex IV of Act 21/2013. It should also be added that in this general context the Redrafted Text of the Land Act (which is also applied alongside Act 9/2006 to the environmental assessment of territorial and land development planning mechanisms) also requires the elaboration of an economic sustainability report, which must be submitted for public information and consultation alongside the environmental report, as well as a particular consultation to the water, coastal and transport infrastructure administrations, Act, whose findings are to be regarded as decisive.

Special mention must be made of the strategic environmental statement, given that it is one of the system's most novel elements of the Act 21/2013 In this regard, and in accordance with Article 25:

once the consultation phase has finished, the environmental administrative body must elaborate the strategic environmental statement. This statement is an administrative decision that has the nature of a preceptive administrative report that analyses the evaluation process and the strategic environmental report, evaluates the results of the consultation phase and how these have been taken into consideration and it will analyze the predicted impact of the plan or programme.

The strategic environmental statement, is compulsory and will be taken into account before the definitive approval of the plan or programme. It cannot be challenged separately from the final administrative decision that approves the plan or programme.

70. Finally, we should take into account a long series of regulations passed by the Autonomous Communities. These regulations share the basic elements of the basic state legislation, but diverge in certain aspects, in particular the modifications to plans and programmes and the configuration of the environmental report. In this last regard, differences can be seen in the configuration of the environmental report, whereby some communities regard it as an administrative action to be undertaken jointly between the promoter and the environmental body, and other communities regard it as action to be undertaken exclusively by the environmental body. Of particular note are the Autonomous Community of Madrid's Act 2/2002 of 19 June on Environmental Assessment, Catalonia's Act 6/2009 of 28 April on the Environmental Assessment of Plans and Programmes and Navarre's Act 4/2005, on 22 March on Interventions for the Protection of the Environment.

§2. Integrated Pollution Prevention and Control

71. The transposition into the Spanish legal system of Council Directive 96/61/EC of 24 September 1996 concerning IPPC has been mired in difficulties. Spain took too long in adapting the 1996 Directive and was consequently censured by the European Court of Justice (ECJ) in its judgment of 7 March 2002. The transposition finally took place through Act 16/2002 of 1 July on Integrated Prevention and Pollution Control which was later modified by Acts 1/2005, on Emission Trading, 27/2006, of 18 July, which regulates the rights of access to information, public participation and justice in environmental matters, and 42/2007, of 13 December, on Natural Heritage and Biodiversity. Act 16/2002 was implemented by RD 509/2007, of 20 April, which covers the technical-administrative measures for processing Integrated Environmental Authorizations of installations. To conclude this review of the transposition of European regulations regarding IPPC to the Spanish legal system, it should be mentioned that Spain also failed to adopt in time the modification made by Directive 2008/1/CE on 15 January, which includes the modifications made over the years to the EU regulations. In its ruling of 18 November 2010, the Court of Justice of the EU condemned Spain for not having adopted the measures specified in the Directive for establishing and updating the authorizations system before 30 October 2007.

In accordance with the Spanish legislation, the Integrated Environmental Authorization included in Directive 2008/1/CE was introduced by Act 16/2002 and substitutes the existing environmental authorizations and establishes a set of conditions regarding the functioning of industrial complexes. The Act defines an 'integrated authorization' as a 'resolution passed by the competent body of the Autonomous Community in which the facility is located that has the sole purpose of protecting the environment and the health of the population and that allows the complete or partial use of the facility under certain conditions in order to ensure that it meets the objectives and the resolutions of this Act. Such an authorization may be valid for one or more facilities or parts of facilities which share the same location and are used by the same owner'. Article 3 on the granting of integrated environmental authorization is compatible with Act 30/1992, of 26 November, on Common Administrative Procedures. Under that Act, a procedure is established which involves analysing the documentation; making the information public; requesting reports and issuing a declaration of environmental impact; proposing a resolution; consulting the interested parties; notifying the competent bodies in order to send linked reports on previous proceedings; and finally passing, notifying and publishing the resolution.

72. Such a process necessitates coordination between the different administrations (national, autonomous, local) that are involved in the authorization concession procedure and that will subsequently ensure that the requirements specified in the authorization are being met.

This coordination is implemented by means of the 'single window' system which dramatically simplifies the proceedings for opening establishments that are affected by the Act.

73. The Act is applied to publicly or privately held facilities in which any of the activities listed in Annex 1 of the Act are carried out, and includes combustion facilities, facilities for the production and transformation of metals, mineral industries, chemical industries, waste management facilities, paper and cardboard facilities, the textile industry, the leather industry, agricultural industries, livestock farming and the coal industry. In accordance with Act 42/2007, existing installations were able to continue functioning provisionally for a maximum period of six months, provided that they had submitted their Integrated Environmental Authorization request before 1 January 2007. The Act does not apply to facilities or parts of facilities which are used for the research and development of or experimentation with new processes.

74. Furthermore, the law requires the integrated environmental authorization to use the best techniques available and to take into account the technical characteristics of the facility and its geographic location when determining the emission limits for contaminating substances. At any rate, it is possible that national sectorial plans may also be taken into consideration when determining emission limits, and that authorization may be given for the statutory establishment of emission limits and of parameters or technical means that are equivalent to those they replace for certain substances or for specific categories of facilities.

75. It should be remembered that the State's late incorporation of the EU Directive meant that it was first transposed at a regional level by some of the Autonomous Communities. Catalonia's Act 3/1998 of 27 February on Integral Intervention of Environmental Administration deserves particular mention (although it is no longer in force). It should be remembered that the general trend at Autonomous Community level has been to draft legislation that covers (either partially or as a whole) the procedure for integrated environmental authorization and the assessment of the environmental impact of activities (but not infrastructures). Particularly interesting in this regard are the provisions of Act 7/2007 on the Integrated Management of Environmental Quality in Andalusia, and Act 20/2009, of 4 December, on prevention and environmental monitoring of activities in Catalonia.

76. Catalonia's Act 20/2009 has the following main characteristics: first, the simplification and decentralization of the administrative procedures, by establishing the integration of authorization and environmental control systems, the setting up of unified environmental management bodies, the reduction and acceleration of the procedure and the integration of other sectorial procedures. Consequently, the Act integrates the EIA of activities listed in Annex I into the procedure for environmental authorization; second, from a territorial perspective, the Catalan Act applies only to the Catalan autonomous administration and local entities, whereas from a material perspective, its provisions apply to all public or private activities listed in its Annexes I, II and III that can affect the environment, security or the health of the population.

Finally, the Catalan Act establishes a new preventive control system with three different procedures. The economic activities that it covers are classified in three different groups depending on their environmental effects. Annex I includes activities with far-reaching effects, which are submitted to an EIA and to an environmental authorization regime. Annex II includes activities with moderate effects which require an environmental license. Finally, Annex III includes activities with minimal effects which will be only subject to a regime of prior communication. When compulsory, EIA is also integrated into the procedure.

77. Several environmental management tools, such as eco-labelling, eco-management and eco-audits are linked to integrated pollution prevention and should also be mentioned.

78. Regarding eco-labelling, RD 234/2013, of 5 April, establishes provisions for the implementation of the EU Regulation 66/2010 on an EU Eco-labelling Award Scheme (which replaced the Regulation 1980/2000). This RD confers powers on eco-labelling management to the Autonomous Communities, that must appoint the specific competent bodies for awarding the eco-label. Finally, it must be pointed out that many regulations have been introduced regarding the listing of environmental qualities on product labelling, and there is other sectorial legislation regarding the eco-labelling of the following products: soil treatment products, toilet paper, clothing detergents, paints and varnishes, personal computers, mattresses, dishwasher detergents, textiles, footwear, hand-washing detergent, multi-use cleaning products, floor tiles, televisions, tourist accommodation, camping grounds, farming products, soaps and shampoos.

79. Regarding eco-management and eco-audits, RD 85/1996 of 26 January established provisions for the implementation of Regulation (EC) 1836/1993 on an Environmental Management and Audit System (EMAS), which was replaced in 2001 by Regulation (EC) 761/2001 and in 2009 by Regulation(EU) 1221/2009 (EMAS III). This system allows the Autonomous Communities to appoint the competent authorities. They are responsible for the registry of the firms which partake in the EMAS. Several Autonomous Communities have created Registers of entities that adhere to the system and they are also competent to receive the validated environmental statements. At national level, the National Certification Entity (ENAC) is the entity designated by the state administration to certify independent verifiers so they can validate declarations according to the EMAS Regulation. AENOR is an environmental verifier currently certified by ENAC in the framework of the EMAS Regulation, as well as the entity certified by ENAC to certify environmental management systems according to the provision ISO 14001.

Chapter 2. Air Pollution Control

§1. Act 34/2007 on Air Quality and Protection of the Atmosphere

80. Act 38/1972 of 22 December and D 2414/1961 on Unpleasant, Unhealthy, Noxious and Hazardous constituted the basic legislation regarding the protection of the atmosphere for more than forty years. Both became clearly outdated in important areas, and, for this reason, the Spanish Parliament passed the Act 34/2007, of 15 November, on air quality and protection of the atmosphere. The new Act, which replaces the old Act 38/1972 and the D 2414/1961, is aimed to provide Spain with a basic legal framework that meets current circumstances and demands. The Act, is based upon the precautionary and preventive action principles, as well as applies the principles that environmental damage should be rectified at source and that the polluter should pay. The Act also encourages co-responsibility with an integrated and integrating focus. In this sense, the Act gives co-responsibility a transcendental role in the fight against pollution and reflects the importance of this concept on three basic levels. First, it involves not just the public powers in the protection of the atmosphere, but also society as a whole. Second, it involves the public administrations and finally, it encourages the public administrations to consider air quality and the protection of the atmosphere in its planning, execution and implementation of various sectorial policies and to make efforts to achieve sustainable development. Furthermore, RD 833/1975, which has been modified on various occasions, and the Order of 18 October 1976 are still partially in effect and apply supplementary provisions, unless the Act 34/2007 provides otherwise.

81. Act 34/2007 aims to prevent, monitor and reduce atmospheric pollution in order to prevent the harm that it can cause to people, the environment and any other kind of asset (Article 1). 'Air pollution' shall refer to 'the presence of substances or energy in the air which implies risk, harm or serious inconvenience for the population and goods'. In order to achieve the objectives of the Act, the public administration will fix air quality standards and emission limits for each industrial activity, as well as establish the most suitable technology for reducing the emission of pollutants into the air. The public administration will also create a list of industrial activities that are likely to cause air pollution (Article 4).

82. Under the section 'Prevention and control of emissions', Chapter II of Act 34/2007 regulates measures for controlling air quality and protecting the atmosphere, these including the establishment of administrative control procedures and of emission limits and other substantive requirements regarding the various sources of pollution. Article 12 of the Act fixes the emission regulations (i.e., the 'emission limits for pollutants, in particular those named in Annex I, and for those activities with the potential to pollute the atmosphere as named in Annex IV of the Act'. It also fixes the regulations on products (i.e., 'specific obligations for the manufacture, importation, inter-regional acquisition, transport, distribution, sale, use and management throughout their lifecycle of those products that can cause atmospheric pollution').

83. According to Article 3 of the Act 'activities with the potential to pollute the atmosphere' are 'those that by their own nature, location or the technological processes they involve constitute a source of pollution that should be subject to a stricter monitoring and control regime'. These articles are listed in Annex IV of the Act and the control and monitoring regime is established in Article 13. Furthermore, Annex I of the Act lists the pollution sources that are governed by the Act, these being: sulphur oxides and other sulphur compounds; nitrogen oxides and other nitrogen compounds; carbon oxides; ozone; volatile organic compounds; polycyclic aromatic compounds and persistent organic compounds; metals and metal compounds; particulate matter (including PM 10 and PM 2,5); asbestos (suspended particles and fibres); halogens and halogen compounds; cyanides; polychlorodibenzodioxines and polychlorodibenzofurans; substances and preparations which have been demonstrated or indicated as having carcinogenic, mutagenic or xenoestrogenic properties or that may affect reproduction; and substances that deplete the ozone layer.

84. According to Article 5 of the Act, the State is responsible for updating the list of pollutants and the list of activities with the potential to pollute the atmosphere. The State must also define the air quality targets, the warning, information and emission limit thresholds, the minimum standard requirements for installations, networks, methods and other air quality evaluation systems and methodologies used to estimate natural sources. It must also define the procedures used to determine their presence in the data recorded for certain pollutants. Likewise, the State must create national action plans and Spanish emissions inventories and coordinate the Spanish information, monitoring and prevention system regarding atmospheric pollution and the adoption of inter-regional measures to protect the atmosphere or ensure air quality. All of this is carried out with the participation of the Autonomous Communities. Furthermore, the Autonomous Communities are responsible for evaluating air quality, and can establish stricter air quality targets and emission limits. They will also adopt the action plans within their geographical limits, and will exercise legal authority. Finally, the local authorities will execute the air quality and atmospheric protection measures assigned to them within the ambit specified by the law.

Section VI of RD 833/1975, still partially in force, sets up the special legal regime for the settlement, enlargement, modification, start-up authorization, operation, control, inspection and monitoring of these activities. The industrial plants carrying out any of the listed activities must previously obtain an administrative license from the competent local authority. In addition, RD 833/1975 requires an administrative permit from the Autonomous Communities' competent authorities for installing, enlarging or initiating these industrial activities. Since the adoption of Act 16/2002 of 1 July on IPPC, all authorization procedures are governed by the 'integrated authorization' system provided for in that Act, except when special sectorial requirements are applied (Articles 5.b, 12.1.c and e, 19.3, 22.1.g, 26.1.d and e, 31 of Act 16/2002).

The local authority shall verify whether measures regarding the limitation of air pollution have been adopted, as well as whether the necessary technical proceedings have been carried out before the Autonomous Communities' competent authorities. Monitoring, control and inspection activities are carried out by the Autonomous Communities' authorities – without prejudice to the competence of the local entities. Some non-public entities specifically set up for the purpose of carrying out some delegated administrative functions assist the administration. Thus the responsibility for administrative authorization and monitoring the functioning of these industrial activities fell to the Ministry of Industry. However, the Act makes the Autonomous Communities responsible for the substantive regulation of industrial activities with the potential to pollute the atmosphere, by virtue of the constitutional and statutory rules regarding the distribution of environmental competencies. To date, those Autonomous Communities which have their own regulations regarding atmospheric pollution are: Catalonia (Act 22/1983, of 21 November, on the Protection of the Atmosphere, modified Act 6/1996, of 18 June, and D 322/1987, of 23 September, on the execution of the said Act, partially modified by D 158/1994, of 30 May); Andalusia (D 74/1996, of 20 February, which approves the Air Quality Regulations, whose Articles 11, 12 and 13 have been supplanted by Act 7/2007, on the Integrated Management of Environmental Quality); Navarre (D 6/2002, of 14 January, which establishes the conditions for implementing and carrying out activities that emit pollutants into the atmosphere); Galicia (Act 8/2002, of 18 December, on the Protection of the Atmosphere, and Act 34/2007) and Cantabria (D 50/2009, of 18 June, which regulates industrial atmospheric pollution).

85. Articles 5 and 7 of RD 833/1975 foresee the possibility of establishing more stringent limits for the so-called Air Polluted Areas (ZAC). This concept refers to those areas in which the concentration of pollutants in the air exceeds any of the air quality limits during a specified period (even though the emission limits are not exceeded). More stringent limits can also be established for Emergency Areas (ZSE), which are the areas in which the air quality limits are notably exceeded as a result of accidental or meteorological causes. Regarding this aspect, it must be pointed out that the Constitutional Court has decided that declaring an area as ZAC or ZSE falls within the competence of the Autonomous Communities.

86. An area will be declared as ZAC in those cases in which the air quality limits fixed in Annex I for certain pollutants are reached, or the air quality limits (twenty-four hours) fixed for the rest of pollutants are exceeded during fifteen days within a one-year period, or during ten days within a semester. The special regime established in Articles 25–32 of RD 833/1975 will apply to these areas.

The following measures will be adopted, among others: measures setting up a service for combating air pollution, which will integrate the Air Pollution Analysis Centres; measures regarding the use of less-pollutant fuels or energy sources in permanent installations; and other measures within the affected area.

87. An area will be declared as ZSE in those cases in which the air quality limits fixed in Annex I are reached. Articles 37–40 of RD 833/1975 foresee specific measures to be taken in accordance with the seriousness of the situation. Among others, the suspension or limitation of the operation of the polluting activities or facilities can be ordered, as well as the limitation or suspension of the use of motor vehicles.

88. RD 833/1975 effectively settled up a network of permanent and mobile ground stations for monitoring air pollution. Section II of this RD details the functions of the network, outlines its organization (National Monitoring and Control Centre, Data Reception Centres, and Air Pollution Analysis Centres), as well as lays down the different parameters to be measured. In addition, the Spanish network is integrated within the EMEP Programme (European Monitoring Evaluation Programme) created subsequent to the Geneva Convention of 1979 on Long-Range Cross-Boundary Air Pollution, as well as in the BAPMoN Network (Background Air Pollution Monitoring Network) and in the CAMP Programme (Comprehensive Atmospheric Monitoring Programme) created under the Oslo and Paris Conventions. Likewise, Spain is currently participating in the development of the AIRBASE information system, as well as in the Europe-wide air quality monitoring and information network (EUROAIRNET), within the framework of the European Environmental Agency.

§2. The Emission of Pollutants into the Atmosphere

89. Article 3 of Act 34/2007 defines the concept of 'emission' in the following terms: 'the continuous or intermittent discharge into the atmosphere of materials, substances or energy sources that come, directly or indirectly, from any source that can cause atmospheric pollution'. It also defines the concept of emission limits as 'the maximum level of emissions of one or more pollutants that can not be exceeded under certain circumstances and within one or several periods, with the aim to prevent or reduce the effects of atmospheric pollution'. According to RD 833/1975, the 'emission level' (or 'emission limit') can also be fixed 'on the basis of the maximum weight of each pollutant that is systematically released into the atmosphere during a specified period or by production unit'. Annex IV of RD 833/1975 establishes the limits for emissions from plants that are likely to cause air pollution. In addition, Article 7.2 of Act 16/2002 of 1 July on IPPC establishes that the Government, without undermining additional protective regulations laid down by the Autonomous Communities, will be able to establish emission limits for contaminating substances and for industrial activities that fall within its scope of application. Article 12 of the 2007 Act states that the Government has the legal authority to establish emission limits for pollutants, in particular for those listed in Annex I and for those activities with the potential to pollute the atmosphere listed in Annex IV

I. Industrial Plants

90. Two modes of administrative intervention are established regarding the activities with the potential to pollute the atmosphere included in Annex IV of Act 34/2007. On the one hand, authorization is required by those who wish to 'construct, assemble, exploit, transport or substantially modify' installations used for any of the activities included in Groups A or B of the List activities with the potential to pollute the atmosphere (Article 13.2). On the other hand, those who wish to carry out any of the activities listed in Group C need only notify the authorities when constructing, assembling, exploiting, transporting, substantially modifying or 'closing' the installations needed for these activities (Article 13.3). The Act recognizes the Autonomous Communities as the competent authorities both to authorize the installations in Groups A and B and to receive notifications regarding the installations in Group C (Article 13.2 and 3). By the same token, the Act makes no stipulations regarding the devolution of control of the installations from the Autonomous Communities to local entities, and leaves it to the Autonomous Communities to decide whether or not they wish to do this (Article 2.2 of the Act governing the Guidelines for Local Legislation.

RD 646/1991 of 22 April, and RD 430/2004 of 12 March which partially modifies RD 833/1975, appear to be especially relevant. RD 646/1991, currently partially derogated, established provisions on limitation of emissions of certain pollutants into the air from large combustion plants and it transposed into domestic law Directive 88/609/EEC on combustion plants whose rated thermal input is equal to or greater than 50 MW. RD 430/2004 which establishes new standards on atmospheric emissions restrictions of certain contaminating agents originating in large combustion facilities, and which fixes certain conditions for the control of atmospheric emissions from petroleum refineries, transposes into Spanish Law Directive 2001/80/CE, on emissions restrictions on certain pollutants into the air from large combustion plants. Although the adoption of RD 430/2004 replaces the former, few Articles of RD 646/1991 were applicable to facilities approved before 21 March 2004 (the date that RD 430/2004 went into effect) until 1 January 2008. Those regulations mainly refer to electric plants and refineries (other industrial sectors are dealt with to a lesser extent). Following the Directives, the RDs make a distinction between 'new plants' and 'existing plants', irrespective of the type of fuel used. On the basis of this distinction, the Annexes of the RDs fix the emission limits and the reduction objectives both for SO2 and NOX.

91. Measurement and assessment of emission methods, as well as procedures for determining the total annual emissions are also established. RD 1800/1995 of 3 November later modified by RD 646/1991 in so far as it related to emissions from combustion plants with rated thermal inputs of between 50 MW and 100 MW, and oil refineries. It fixed new limits for emissions of SO_2 into the air from new plants (adapting the Spanish legislation to the 94/66/EEC Directive). In addition, Chapter III of RD 430/2004 replaces the existing general regulation on SO_2 emissions from combustion facilities with one with a more global treatment of the issue. It modifies the RD 833/1975 in what concerns combustion facilities, and regulates SO_2 emissions from facilities other than combustion ones, such as the regeneration of catalysts in fluidized bed catalytic cracking units (FCC) and sulphur recovery units, in the same way as RD 1800/1995 does for the performance of the former.

Finally, RD 430/2004 establishes a national plan for the reduction of emissions in existing large combustion facilities higher than fifty thermal megawatts. It affects electricity generation plants, the fuels they use and other industrial sectors such as petroleum refineries. According to the RD, by no later than 1 January 2008, they had to achieve reductions in the total annual emissions of nitrogen oxides (NOX), sulphur dioxide (SO_2) and particles from existing facilities, similar to those which would have been achieved if the emission limits established for new facilities had been applied. The plans constitute action programmes aiming to reduce emissions from plants that are likely to cause air pollution. They are generally conceived as voluntary instruments by which an enterprise commits itself to implementing the necessary modifications for reducing the emission of pollutants into the air within a specified period to some predetermined quality standards. Voluntary agreements between the administration and groups of enterprises or employers' associations should also be mentioned.

92. As for the Autonomous Communities, in addition to their specific legislation, they may also approve General Plans for the Reduction of Emissions.

II. Household and Hazardous Waste Incineration Plants

93. After Spain was condemned by the EU Court of Justice in its judgment of 1 July 2002, RD 1088/1992 of 11 September on the Emission of Pollutants into the Air from Municipal Waste Incineration Plants (transposing the former Directives 89/369/EEC and 89/429/EEC) and RD 1217/1997 of 18 July on the Limitation of Emissions from Hazardous Waste Incineration Plants (transposing the former Directive 94/67/EEC) were finally replaced by RD 653/2003 of 30 May, on Waste Incineration, which transposes Directive 2000/76/EC.

RD 653/2003 applies to facilities in which only wastes specified in Article 2 are incinerated or co-incinerated, and to experimental facilities used for research and development and for the carrying out of tests in order to improve the incineration process which incinerate or co-incinerate fewer than 50 tonnes of waste per year. The RD also determines the authorization system in these facilities (Articles 4, 5 and 6). It adopts several requirements relating to the delivery and reception of wastes in the facilities (Article 7), such as provisions on their construction and use in those facilities in which it is determined that incineration or co-incineration are also carried out (Article 8), and which become stricter when dealing with hazardous wastes.

It fixes common atmospheric emission limits for different types of wastes that are incinerated (Annex V) or co-incinerated (Annex II). The standards of RD 1073/2002 of 18 October on Air Quality Evaluation and Management in relation to sulphur dioxide, nitrogen dioxide, nitrogen oxides, particles, lead, benzene and carbon monoxide are also applicable here. It also adopts emission limits for certain contaminants which are to be enforced in waste water discharges originating from the purification of exhaust gases in incineration and co-incineration facilities. It establishes requirements for measurement and monitoring (Articles 14–18) and it establishes a transitional system for existing incineration and co-incineration facilities, to which the RD system will be applicable as from 28 December 2005.

Finally, these activities are also affected by the environmental restrictions stipulated in Act 10/1998 of 21 April on Waste, as well as with Act 16/2002 of 1 July on Integrated Prevention and Pollution Control, which includes under its scope of application hazardous waste incineration facilities with a capacity of more than 10 tonnes per day and urban or municipal waste incineration facilities with a capacity of more than three tonnes per hour.

III. Motor Vehicles

94. RD 2204/1975, modified on several occasion, regulated for the first time the characteristics, qualities and conditions for the use of the different types of fuel (with regard to 90, 96 and 98 – octane petrol, and diesel oil – A, B, C). The sulphur content specified in this RD was successively updated (RD 2482/1986 of 25 September and RD 1485/1987 of 4 December, which transposes the technical specification for oil products of Directive 87/219/CEE. RD 2616/1985 of 9 October regulates the homologation of ignition motor vehicles with regard to the emission of polluting gases. The Order of 3 September 1990 on Emissions of Air Pollutants from Motor Vehicles (in the terms of the 88/1976 EEC Directive), as well as the Order of 16 October 1992 (transposing the 91/441/EEC Directive) on Emissions from Motor Vehicles, can also be mentioned. The maximum contents of lead in petrol are currently established by RD 1513/1988 of 9 December.

RD 2028/1986 of 6 June on norms for the application of European Community Directives related to the standardization of types of vehicles, trailers, semi-trailers and their parts and pieces, incorporates the specifications on the standardization considered in Directives 78/315/CEE, 78/547/CEE, 80/1267/CEE for automotive vehicles and 79/694/CEE and 82/890/CEE for agricultural tractors. Their Annexes I and II have been updated by the Order of 29 December 1992. Order CTE/3216/2002 of 12 December 2002 transposed in national law EC Decision 1753/2000/CE concerning the adoption of a plan to monitor specific emissions of CO2 from newly registered cars. It is nevertheless worth mentioning RD 837/2002 of 2 August which regulates information concerning fuel consumption and CO2 emission from new cars on the market or cars offered for rent in Spanish territory.

§3. Air Quality Standards

95. Prior to Act 38/1972 and RD 833/1975, D 2414/1961 on Unpleasant, Unhealthy, Noxious and Hazardous Activities simply established air quality standards for indoor atmospheres. Act 38/1972 and RD 833/1975 establish quality objectives for air pollutants, measuring criteria, as well as the levels for admissible situations and ZAC and ZSE declarations.

96. Article 3 of Act 34/2007 defines air quality standards as 'the amount of each pollutant in the atmosphere, in isolation or in association with others, which, once reached, invokes obligations in accordance with conditions determined for each one of them'; that is to say, the permitted quantity of polluting substances per unit volume of air. According to Article 9 of the Act:

> in order to prevent or reduce atmospheric pollution and its effects, the Government, with the participation of the Autonomous Communities, will review the

list of pollutants in Annex I every five years and, if necessary, will update it taking into account the directives in Annex II and will define and establish the air quality targets and the conditions and time limits for achieving them in accordance with the factors in Annex III.

Article 4 of RD 833/1975 refers to Annex I, which establishes not only air quality standards (for sulphur dioxide, airborne particulates, NOX and compounds), but also weighting criteria and air quality levels for acceptable situations.

A substantial corpus of specific complementary legislation exists, setting air quality standards for each type of pollutant and taking into account the specific period considered. In this sense, different categories of air quality standards are established, that is, guide values (concentrations of pollutants in the air which are considered acceptable for health and the environment on a long-term basis), and limits (concentrations of pollutants in the atmosphere that should not be exceeded during a specified period for the purpose of protecting public health).

I. Sulphur Dioxide and Airborne Particulates

97. Spain has been traditionally one of the most important emitters of SO_2. Since the 1970s, SO_2 emissions grew mainly due to the increasing demand for energy and the lack of control measures in industrial production processes. In addition to being subject to RD 833/1975, this issue is also controlled by RD 1613/1985 of 1 August on Quality Values for SO_2 and Smoke, modified on several occasions. This RD (which transposes the 80/779/EEC Directive into domestic law) sets air quality standards with regard to air pollution from SO_2 and airborne particulate. It sets limits (Tables A and B), guide values (Tables C and D), and reference values for the declaration of emergency situations (section 3). RD 1321/1992 of 30 October later modified RD 1613/1985. It included the new standards fixed in the 89/427/ EEC Directive. Such RDs have been partially abolished by RD 1073/2002 of 18 October on Air Quality Evaluation and Management related to sulphur dioxide, nitrogen dioxide, nitrogen oxides, particles, lead, benzene, and carbon monoxide.

The RD includes standards on Air Quality Evaluation and Management which affect, in a general way, various contaminants, as well as particular rules related to each of those contaminants, and establishes air quality and limit value objectives. The RD establishes the values which apply as of 1 January 2005: the annual limit value for SO_2 is 20 µg/m3. For suspended particles the annual limit value is 40 µg/m3 (20 µg/m3 by 1 January 2010). The RD also stipulates the mechanisms for the reciprocal exchange of information and data from networks and isolated measurement stations, such as the development of a questionnaire that must be used to present annual information. Finally, it is worth mentioning that the Resolution of 11 September 2003 establishes the publication of the Government's Decision of 25 July 2003, in which a national programme for the progressive reduction of national emissions of sulphur dioxide (SO_2), nitrogen oxides (NOX), volatile organic compounds (COV) and ammonia (NH3) is approved.

II. Nitrogen Dioxide and Lead

98. Nitrogen oxides are considered important air pollutants by RD 833/1975, which fixes air quality standards determining acceptable situations and declarations of ZAC and ZSE. The air quality values with regard to nitrogen dioxide and lead in the terms of the 82/203/EEC and 82/884/EEC Directives are established by RD 717/1987 of 27 May (which partially modifies RD 833/1975). However, that RD has been partially abolished by RD 1073/2002 of 18 October on Air Quality Evaluation and Management in what concerns to sulphur dioxide, nitrogen dioxide, nitrogen oxides, particles, lead, benzene, and carbon monoxide.

RD 1073/2002 establishes an annual limit value for nitrogen dioxide of 40 μg/m3 after 1 January 2010 (until then, the values of RD 717/1987 apply: annual limit value of 200 μg/m3; annual guide value of 50 μg/m3) and an annual limit value for lead of 0.5 μg/m3 as of 1 January 2005.

III. Ozone

99. RD 1494/1995 of 8 September (which transposed Directive 92/72/EC) was abolished and replaced by RD 1796/2003 of 26 December that regulates air pollution caused by ozone (it transposes Directive 2002/3/EC). It defines 'threshold values' and fixes the values beyond which adverse effects associated with the presence of O3 in ambient air are deemed to occur. It sets a health protection threshold (120 μg/m3, which must not exceed more than an average of twenty-five days for each calendar year over a period of three years) and a vegetation protection threshold (18.000 μg/m3 h on average over a period of five years), that must be reached in the three-year period beginning in the year 2010, as well as stricter objectives that will have to be achieved in the long-term. The fulfilment of these values must be assured through the development of a series of plans or programmes which will be coordinated with the National Programme on National Ceilings for Emissions. A population information threshold (180 μg/m3 over a one-hour period), and a population warning threshold (240 μg/m3 over a one-hour period) are also established. As for the evaluation of concentrations, it establishes the standards and criteria which must be acknowledged for the measurement of ozone concentration and of its precursory substances, nitrogen oxides, and volatile organic compounds, with a specific regulation on the number and location of measuring stations and the reference methods that must be used for the analysis of ozone and for the calibration of the measuring equipment.

EC Regulation 1005/2009, of 16 September on Substances that Deplete the Ozone Layer came directly into force in Spain on 1 January 2010. The general requirements of RD 1073/2002 of 18 October on Air Quality Evaluation and Management related to sulphur dioxide, nitrogen dioxide, nitrogen oxides, particles, lead, benzene, and carbon monoxide are also applicable.

IV. Volatile Organic Compounds

100. RD 2102/1996 of 20 September regulates the emissions of volatile organic compounds resulting from the storage of petrol and its distribution from terminals to service stations. It transposes the 94/63/EC Directive into Spanish legislation. It was completed with RD 1437/2002 of 27 December, which regulates the Adaptation of Petrol Storage Tanks.

Later, RD 117/2003 of 31 January, on Emission Restrictions on volatile organic compounds due to the use of solvents in certain activities (which transposes Directive 119/12/EC) was adopted. It was later modified by RD 227/2006 and completed by RD 1436/2010. RD 117/2003 sets the requirements which must be fulfilled by new facilities which use certain quantities of solvents on their activities, either in order to be authorized under the Act 16/2002, or if they deal with registered activities included within its scope of application, or if they deal with activities which require prior notification of the competent authorities. Activities included in Annex 1 of the RD are: adhesive coatings, coating activities, spool coating, dry clearing, shoe manufacturing, coating manufacturing, varnishes, dyes and adhesives, the manufacture of pharmaceutical products, printing works, conversion of natural or synthetic rubber, surface cleaning, vegetable oil extraction and vegetable oil and fat refining activities, refinishing of vehicles, coating of spooled barbed wire, saturation of wood fibres, and wood or plastic laminating. For existing facilities an adaptation period has been set which ended on 31 October 2007.

The authorization system for these facilities is also subject to Act 16/2002 on IPPC, which affects facilities for the treatment of the surfaces of materials, objects, or products using organic solvents whose consumption capacity exceeds 150 kg of solvent per hour or 200 tonnes per year.

It is worth mentioning, finally, the adoption of the Resolution of 11 September 2003, which published the Government's Decision to approve the National Programme of Progressive Reduction of National Emissions of sulphur dioxide (SO2), nitrogen oxides (NOX), volatile organic compounds (COV) and ammonia (NH3).

V. Other Pollutants

101. RD 833/1975 establishes annual limits for carbon monoxide, total hydrocarbon content, hydrogen sulphide, chlorine, and hydrogen chloride.

102. RD 61/2006, of 31 January determines the specifications regarding petrol, diesel and liquid petroleum gases and regulates the use of certain biofuels. This RD has been modified by RD 1027/2006 and RD 1088/2010 with the aim of transposing EL Directive 2009/30/CE of 23 April 2009. According to Article 2 of RD 61/2006, 'the sale of leaded petrol is prohibited except for petrol with a lead content lower than 0.15 g per litre, which is to be used in old special vehicles and whose sale may not exceed 0.03% of national petrol sales'. Metallic additives are limited to 6 mg of manganese per litre from 1 January 2011 and 2 mg of manganese per litre from 1 January 2014. The specifications for petrol are listed in Annex I of RD 1088/2010.

The RD states that:

> from 1 January 2011, the maximum authorized sulphur content in diesel will be 10 mg/kg, although deliveries to final users may contain up to 20 mg/kg of sulphur to take into account the possibility of contamination in the supply chain. Diesel with a maximum of 1,000 mg/kg can be sold for railway vehicles and tractors provided that this limit does not place the adequate functioning of the emission control systems at risk.

The specifications for diesel are listed in Annex III of RD 1088/2010.

103. As for asbestos, RD 108/1991 of 1 February, on the Prevention and Reduction of Environmental Pollution Caused by Asbestos should be taken into account. It transposes Directive 97/217/EC.

§4. Climate Change

104. The EU context frames the Spanish policy on climate change. Nonetheless, Spain has traditionally appeared reluctant to face the social and economic consequences that establishing extra taxes on fossil fuel consumption would likely bring about. In the EC Decision 2002/358, Spain was allocated a share of 15% of greenhouse gases emissions. However, it soon became evident that Spain had overestimated its capacity to reduce those emissions. Shortly after accepting this commitment, it was clear that it would be very difficult for Spain not to exceed this +15%, given that the figures for recent years showed significant growth in emissions. Emissions caused by all the activities covered by international agreement in 1995 already passed this limit by 10.8%; in 2000 this rose 33.8%, and in 2005 reached 53.3%, although this fell to 50.6% in 2006.

The first national measure was the adoption of RD 569/1992 which settled up the National Commission on Climate, which tried to elaborate a National Plan on Climate. Subsequent institutional measures have been adopted: the Coordinating Commission for Climate Change Policy was created as a consultative body designed to ensure coordination between the central, regional and local administrations that are responsible for approving the National Plan for Adapting to Climate Change. The Delegated Governmental Commission on Climate Change was also created. It is made up of representatives from the different ministries. This Commission has identified a series of strategic lines that affect various sectors such as transport, waste, private homes, energy, forestry and innovation. These actions have up to now led to the adoption of specific strategies such as: the Sustainable Mobility Strategy, the National Integrated Waste Management Plan, the Animal Waste Management Plan, and the Strategy regarding Energy Saving and Performance in Central Administration Buildings. In addition to this, the Spanish Climate Change Office is the administrative body responsible for coordinating the participation of the different administrations and social sectors involved, and the Inter-Ministerial Group on Climate Change is responsible for coordinating the different Departments of the central administration. Finally, the National Climate Council has been created to ensure collaboration between the public administrations, social agents, Non-Governmental Organizations (NGOs) and others in the creation of proposals and strategies for adapting to climate change.

105. Concerning emissions trading, Directive 2003/87 was first implemented in Spain by RDL 5/2004 of 27 August. As such, the RDL was only justified by the urgency to implement the Directive, taking into account that the transposition period had already expired. The RDL was later validated by Parliament and a few months later Act 1/2005 of 10 March, which established a scheme for greenhouse gas emission trading rights, was adopted. This is the basic legal framework for emissions trading in Spain. Act 1/2005 has recently been modified by Act 13/2010, of 5 July, to improve and expand emissions trading and to include aviation in the system. It thus transposes Directive 2009/29/UE. The modifications introduced by the new Act focus on including the aviation sector in the emissions trading system, on modifying the authorization system regarding greenhouse gas emissions, and on modifying the nature and contents of the national allocation plan to adjust them to the provisions of Directive 2009/29/UE.

The Act applies to activities listed in its Annex I, which includes big emissions centres in sectors such as electricity generation, refining, production and transformation of ferrous metals, cement, lime, glass, ceramics, paper pulp, and paper and cardboard and aviation amongst others. In the area of energy activities, the scope of application is limited to the facilities with a nominal thermal power of more than 20 MW, including those of cogeneration combined with any other type of activity.

Operators of any of such activities must obtain specific authorization granted by the Autonomous Community, and a greenhouse gas emission permit which identifies the rights allocated and the applicable obligations. Allowances are granted by the central Government. Once the allowance has been granted, the facilities' operators must complete periodic reports, which are to be verified by external entities (duly authorized consultancy firms). Verified reports are to be checked by the Autonomous Community. If a verified report complies with applicable legal and technical requirements, the Autonomous Community forwards it to the Ministry of the Environment, which adds the information to the National Register.

Penalties are of an administrative nature, imposed by the Ministry of the Environment or the Autonomous Community's authorities. A firm that pollutes more CO2 than allowed must pay EUR 100 for each tonne of CO2 emitted in excess.

106. Apart from that, the main goal of such regulation was to establish an operating framework for the National Emissions Allocation Plan (NAP). Spain adopted its first NAP for the 2005–2008 period by RLD 5/2004, of 27 August, which regulates emissions trading, and RD 1866/2004, of 6 September, which approves the NAP 2005–2008. The list of installations covered was approved by RD 60/2005, of 21 January 2005 and Act 1/2005. Moreover, during this first period, several of the Act's provisions were implemented by RD 1264/2005, of 21 October, which regulates the National Emissions Register, RD 1315/2005, 4 November, which established the guidelines of the systems for monitoring and verifying greenhouse gas emissions, and the resolution of 8 February 2006, which approved the regulations for recording, evaluating and reporting on greenhouse gas emissions trading. For the

2008–2012 commitment period, according to Kyoto Protocol, Spain adopted the RD 1370/2006, of 24 November, which approves the NAP for 2008–2012, which has been modified by RD 1030/2007, of 20 July, the RD 1402/2007, of 29 October and Order PRE/2827/2009, of 19 October. The difficulties regarding compliance with international commitments have led to the adoption of a National Plan which aims to limit Spain's greenhouse gas emissions to no more than 37% above 1990 levels during the aforementioned period. According to the Ministry's provisions, in addition to the reduction resulting from the Kyoto Protocol (+15%), Spain acquired carbon credits to the value of 20% by means of the flexibility mechanisms and an additional 2% through carbon sequestration.

107. The process of incorporating EU climate change regulations into Spanish law has continued with the partial replacement of Directives 2008/101/CE and 2009/29/CE, by means of RD 341/2010, of 19 March, which implements certain obligations to provide information regarding activities that form part of the emissions trading scheme, and which modifies Act 1/2005. The most significant change, however, has been brought by Act 13/2010 of 5 July, which again modifies Act 1/2005.

108. In accordance with EU Directives, some Autonomous Communities have approved strategic documents which define the guiding principals and lines of action of their climate change policies. In this regard, the Spanish Climate Change and Clean Energy Strategy (Horizon 2007–2012–2020) of 2007, points out that the 'Autonomous Communities and Local Entities are key to identifying and implementing climate change measures, especially through Regional Strategies which are due to be drafted this year.' The Regional Strategies follow criteria approved by the Coordinating Commission on Climate Change Policy, which are as follows: they must be in place up to a horizon of 2012, they must include measures both for mitigating emissions and for adapting to the effects of climate change, they must affect the same sectors covered by the Spanish Strategy, and they must incorporate a monitoring system based on the existing indicators of the Spanish Strategy to prevent problems of double accounting. To date, thirteen Autonomous Communities have implemented a Climate Change Plan (Andalusia, Asturias, the Balearic Islands, Cantabria, Catalonia, Galicia, La Rioja, Madrid, Murcia, Basque Country, Valencia, Aragon and Castile-Leon). Likewise, most of the Autonomous Communities currently have their own structure for implementing climate change policies in the own areas of jurisdiction. For example, in the case of Catalonia, Decree 573/2006 of 19 December 2006, led to the important creation of the Interdepartmental Commission on Climate Change and the Catalan Office of Climate.

Chapter 3. Water Pollution

§1. Sea and Ocean Protection

109. The length of Spain's coast is 8,000 km, 24% of which is beaches. The coastal zone suffers from a significant population growth as well as from the intensification of the uses (tourist, industrial, transport) to which it is subjected. Historically, Spain has suffered from a lack of control of urban development and infrastructure policies. This handicap, together with the lack of any policy for the protection against pollution has led to a very significant coastal degradation.

110. The legal framework in this matter is currently the Coasts Act 22/1988 of 28 July (implemented by RD 1471/1989 of 1 December and 1112/92 of 18 September, and complemented by the Constitutional Court Decisions 149/91 of 4 July and 198/91 of 17 October). Act 22/1998 addresses the general degradation scenario and establishes a complex legal regime in order to achieve its main objective: i.e., 'the delimitation, protection, use and police of the marine public domain and especially of the seashore'. Notwithstanding, it has to be taken into account that the Act 22/1988 has been recently modified in depth by the Act 2/2013 of 29 May, on the protection and sustainable use of the Coastal zone (BOE 30.5.2013). The said Act 2/2013, which has deserved rather critical comments from legal experts and environmental protection associations, brings about certain substantial changes mainly as regards to the extension up to a seventy-five-year period of the concessional rights granted by the Transitory Provisions of the Act 22/1988, as well as to the possibility of transmitting the said concessional rights. In addition, the Act 2/2013 also modifies the legal regime regarding the use of the beaches (by making a distinction between urban and non-urban beaches), and finally, excludes certain urban areas from the State Maritime public Domain.

According to Article 3 of the Act 22/1988, the marine public domain includes, the seashore, the shore from the low tide line as well as beaches, dunes, cliffs, marshes and other wetlands, the territorial sea and inland waters, and the natural resources in the exclusive economic zone and the continental platform.

Basically, the general aims of the Act are, on the one hand, to subject any projected action to environmental criteria and, on the other hand, to restore the marine public domain. In order to fulfil these objectives, the Act foresees three possible ways of protection.

111. First, the Act provides for direct protection actions within the strip qualified as marine public domain. Regarding this strip, the Act specifically declares its imprescriptibility and inalienability, as well as the administrative power of ex officio restoration.

The fact that the coasts are public domain subjects their use to some special requisites. Thus, in order to achieve a better protection of the marine public domain, the Act and its complementary regulations establish limitations and prohibitions. Among them are limitations on the existence of properties other than public properties (Article 9 of the Act); limitations on the construction of facilities and services, and subjection of projects to environmental criteria (Articles 33 and 39 of the

Act; Articles 64 and 65 of the Regulation); and the restoration actions related to the marine public domain (Article 17 of the Act). In any case, it is important to note that the specific regime applying to the use of the beaches (included in the State public maritime domain) may vary depending on the particular type of beach considered (whether urban beach or non-urban natural beach –Article 33.3 of the Act 22/1988).

According to Article 31, the common general use will be the in accordance with the nature of the seaside (swimming, sailing and walking). The uses that involve specific danger, intensity or profit, or that require execution of works, require an assignment, authorization or concession. According to Article 37 of the Act, these permits should be registered in the Register of uses of the marine public domain. Finally, the Act prescribes the adoption of specific measures of protection regarding the discharge of waste waters and solid waste (Articles 32, 56 and 57 of the Act), extraction of solid matters and dredging (Article 63 of the Act) and navigation (Article 69 of the Regulation).

112. The Act foresees preventive and corrective action in the private properties adjacent to the marine public domain, thus permitting the adoption of control measures for the uses and activities that are likely to affect the environment.

Two types of areas can be distinguished: (a) areas affected by protection easement (Articles 23–26 of the Act), and (b) areas of influence on non-urban land (Article 30 of the Act).

Regarding areas affected by the protection easement (100 m–200 m from the inner limit of the seaside –except in some cases where extent of these areas may be reduced up to a maximum of 20 m), several measures have been passed:

– a general prohibition (Article 45 of the Regulation) on residential housing, roads, dry land exploitation, overhead cables, unpurified solid and liquid waste and publicity;
– a specific prohibition, regarding an area not larger than 20 m from the inner limit of the seaside (Articles 24 and 44 of the Act and 44–46 and 65 of the Regulation), on embankments, levelling and illegal clearings, beach services, closets and drainage facilities and parallel rubbish disposal;
– authorization of the Peripheric Coastal Services will be compulsory for the uses (marine industries, restaurants, and sport facilities) that, due to their nature, cannot be located elsewhere, and for necessary or convenient services within the marine public domain (Articles 46 and 65 of the Regulation);
– an administrative authorization or permit from the Council of Ministries is required for any new residential housing, industries not linked to the sea, roads and railways and high tension lines (Article 25 of the Act);
– even though the installation of hoardings of any other means of publicity are generally prohibited, Article 25.4 of the Act 22/1988 foresees that a future administrative implementing regulation will establish the conditions that may make possible to authorize the installation of means of publicity;
– easements of transit (Article 27 of the Act) and access to the sea in urban areas (Article 28 of the Act).

Regarding the zone of influence on non-urban land (up to 500 m counting from the inner limit of the seaside), the Act imposes important limitations on private properties, establishing basic conditions for urban planning, which have a direct impact on the dry land in the final stretches of river beds (Article 29 of the Act); parking areas outside transit zones (Article 30 of the Act); architectonic shields (Article 30 of the Act); license or authorization requirements for waste discharges into the marine public domain (Article 30 of the Act); authorization requirements for discharging industrial wastes (Articles 61 and 62 of the Act); and deprivation, right of first refusal and right of repurchase at the same price as dry land (Article 29 of the Act).

113. In the third place, the quality of coastal waters can be protected through the setting of water quality standards related to the uses to which they are destined as well as the establishment of waste water emission limit values.

Article 108*bis* of the RLD 1/2001 of 20 July which passes the rewritten text of the Water Act (introduced in section 33 of Article 129 of Act 62/2003 of 30 December, of Fiscal and Administrative Actions and Social Order) establishes that the objective of sea water protection is to 'gradually abate or eliminate spills, emissions and hazardous substance leaks, with the ultimate aim being to achieve concentrations similar to the basic values for natural substances and near zero for artificial synthetic substances in the marine environment'. It should be noted that the Coasts Act and RD 1471/1989 do not specify any quality standards for sea water. Neither do they specify emission limit values for discharges of pollutants, contrary to the case for inland waters. However, the Act does establish the scope of the notion of discharge, which according to Article 56 covers both liquid and solid discharges, irrespective of the coastal public domain. Article 57 of the Act also requires express permit or authorization of the competent administration (State administration or autonomous administration) to proceed to any kind of discharge that will be granted pursuant to the applicable legislation. The Act also establishes a general prohibition on discharges of solid waste and debris to the sea and seaside as well as to the protection easement zone, except when those solid wastes and debris can be used as filling material and their use is properly authorized.

The absence of quality objectives has been redressed by the final fifth Provision of Act 42/2007, of 13 December, on Natural Heritage and Biodiversity, which adds a new ninth additional provision to Act 22/1988, 28 July, on Coasts, regarding the reduction of pollution caused by spills of dangerous substances in the marine environment. The act establishes quality targets for an environment which has been affected by spills on land that have reached coastal waters and which may contain one or several of the dangerous substances included in an annex to the Act. It also establishes measurement methods and control procedures both of which are specified in two more annexes.

Nevertheless, this area of law should be noted for Directive 2008/56/EC, of 17 June 2008, which establishes a European action framework for marine environment policy that will be incorporated into the Spanish regulations and which includes coastal waters. The Directive means that each Member State must create a marine strategy applicable to its own marine waters in cooperation with other States in the same region or sub-region (in the case of Spain, the Atlantic, the Bay of Biscay and the Iberian coast, the Macaronesian bio-geographic region, defined by the waters around the Azores, Madeira and the Canary Islands, and the western Mediterranean). This strategy will involve an initial assessment of the state of the environment which must be completed at the latest by 15 July 2012; a description of these waters when they are in a good state, completed at the latest by 15 July 2012; the establishment of a series of environmental objectives and associated indicators, completed at the latest by 15 July 2014; the creation and application of a monitoring programme to permanently assess and periodically update the targets; and the creation, by 2015 at the latest, of a programme of measures designed to reach or maintain a good environmental state, to be implemented by 2016 at the latest. The Marine Environment Protection Act, which adopts this Directive, is being processed by the Spanish Parliament and establishes five marine areas (the north Atlantic, the south Atlantic, the Straits of Gibraltar, the Levante-Balearic area and the Canary Islands). These will be implemented through regional maritime agreements, which in the case of Spain include the Barcelona Convention for the protection of the marine environment and Mediterranean coast and the OSPAR Convention for the Protection of the north-eastern Atlantic marine Environment. There is no Convention regarding cooperation to establish a marine strategy for the Macaronesian sub-region, which means that bilateral cooperation with Portugal will be needed. In the last days of 2010, the Marine Strategy Framework Directive (Directive 2008/56/EC) has been transposed into Spanish law as Act 41/2010, of 29 December 2010, on Protection of Marine Environment.

Regarding the quality control of bathing waters, the applicable legislation is RD 1341/2007 of 11 October, which transposes Directive 2006/7/EC. This regulation affects both marine and inland bathing zones, insofar they are included in the Census on Bathing Zones. Its application requires the setting up of a series of monitoring parameters and allows waters to be classified in terms of their aptitude for their destined use. Furthermore, the public must receive sufficient and appropriate information regarding the quality of bathing zones, the corrective and preventative measures which are applied to them and all aspects that affect bathing zones and that may pose a risk to the health of swimmers.

114. The General Directorate of Coasts of the Ministry of the Environment and Rural and Marine Affairs promotes several actions in order to implement a conservationist coastal policy.

Among those actions are the mandatory and binding obligation that the coastal administration be informed about any plans or regulations on territorial or urban planning undertaken by any other administration; the coastal public domain demarcation plans (the Act imposes the demarcation of all Spanish coasts); the opening of paths, reuse of dunes, restoration of salt marshes and rehabilitation of beaches.

The application of this policy based on an integrated vision of the coast has been strengthened at the community level with the celebration of the First European Forum on Community Strategies for the Integrated Management of Coastal Areas, held in Spain (Vila Joiosa, Alicante) in April 2002. As agreed in that Forum, Spain has the responsibility of leading the start-up of National Strategies to coordinate all of the activities which are carried out on the European coastline, in the framework of the European Strategy for Sustainable Development and the VI Environmental Action Programme.

115. Finally, another aspect that should be considered is the participation of Spain in several international conventions of regional character related to the protection of the sea. Specifically, Spain has been party to the Barcelona Convention for the Protection of the Mediterranean Sea and some of its Protocols since 1978.

Among others, Spain is also a party to the Convention on the prevention of marine pollution caused by waste and other substances (1972) and its Protocol of 1996, the Convention on the prevention of marine pollution caused by spills from Shipping and Aircraft (15 February 1972), the Convention on the prevention of marine pollution originating on land (11 June 1974), the Convention for the Protection of the Marine Environment of the North-east Atlantic (OSPAR), the International Convention for the Prevention of Pollution from Ships (MARPOL 73/78) and its Protocol of 1978, the Protocol on intervention in cases of marine pollution by non-hydrocarbons (2 November 1973), the Protocol on Preparedness, Response and Cooperation to Pollution Incidents by Hazardous and Noxious Substances (London, 15 March 2000) and the Convention on the Conservation of Cetaceans of the Black Sea, Mediterranean and Contiguous Atlantic Area (24 November 1996).

§2. Inland Water Protection

116. The physical and biotic characteristics of Spain are defined by its diversity of climates, pluvial regimes and water environments, as well as by its heterogeneous water distribution. The aforementioned heterogeneity can be explained by:

- significant variations in the annual rainfall levels throughout the national territory;
- irregular distribution of the water variations in the territory (in the Guadiana river basin, the maximum and minimum values of the annual contributions can differ by a factor of thirty, while in other areas they differ by a factor of around three);
- uneven territorial use of underground waters.

Even with these peculiarities, the main problems regarding water resources management identified in the aforementioned White Paper are probably very similar to those affecting other EU Member States: deterioration of the quality of surface waters, inadequate treatment of industrial wastes, pollution from diffuse sources and eutrophication, pollution caused by nitrates and heavy metals and salinization. We should also mention draught, which is becoming a severe environmental problem due to its consequences for the aquatic ecosystems and landscapes, as well as the greater risk of floods.

117. In general terms, the basic legislation on inland waters protection is RLD 1/2001 of 20 July, which approves the Rewritten Text of the Water Act (Water Act) (later modified by Acts 24/2001 of 27 December on Fiscal and Administrative Actions and Social Order; 16/2002 of 1 July on IPPC; 53/2002 of 30 December on

Fiscal and Administrative Actions and Social Order; 13/2003 of 23 May Regulating Concessionary Public Works Contracts; 62/2003 of 30 December on Fiscal and Administrative Actions and Social Order which transposes the WFD to Spanish legal ordinance; Act 11/2005 of 22 June which modifies Act 10/2001 of 5 July on the National Hydrologic Plan, RLD 4/2007, of 13 April, Act 42/2007, of 13 December, on Natural Heritage and Biodiversity, and Act 25/2009, of 22 December, which incorporates into Spanish Law Directive 2006/123/CE, of 12 December 2006, on services in the internal market.) which replaces the former Act 29/1985 of 2 August on Water. This RLD therefore constitutes the pillar on which the legal regime on inland waters is built.

Article 1 states that the Water Act aims to 'establish the legal regime ruling the hydrological public domain, the use of water resources and the exercise of the powers that the State administration holds in relation to the hydrological public domain'. It is also the purpose of this act, according to the precept, 'to establish basic norms for the protection of continental, coastal and transitional waters, without detriment to their legal description and the specific legislation that applies to them'. With this stipulation, the establishment of basic norms for the protection of coastal and transitional waters is incorporated as an objective in the Water Act and takes an important step toward common global regulations for all types of community waters, as provided for in the WFD. However, it neither replaces their legal description, nor the specific legislation that governs them. In accordance with these stipulations, the Water Act now includes the river basin district (defined in Article 16*bis* as 'the land and marine zone composed of one or various neighbouring river basins and the subterranean and coastal transitional waters associated with those basins') as the main unit of river basin management.

Sections I and IV to VII of this Water Act have been implemented by RD 849/1986 of 11 April on the Hydrological Public Domain, which has been the object of several modifications; the most recent by means of RD 995/2000 of 2 June that also lays down quality standards for specific polluting substances and of Royal Decree 606/2003 of 23 May, Royal Decree 9/2008, of 11 January and Act 25/2009, of 22 December, on the prevention of floods and other accidents and the security of dams and reservoirs. Sections II and III of the Act were implemented by RD 927/1988 of 29 July on Water Public Administration and Hydrologic Planning (as last amended by RD 2068/1996 of 13 September, RLD 4/2007, of 13 April, on desalination activities and the National Water Council, and Royal Decree 907/2007, of 6 July, which approves the Regulations regarding Hydrological Planning, and Royal Decree 1383/2009, of 28 August, on the National Water Council).

118. Water Act establishes the legal regime regarding the hydrological public domain, in accordance with the constitutional provisions related to the distribution of powers between the different public administrations (as understood by the Constitutional Court Decision 227/1988 of 29 November). As a matter of fact, pursuant to Article 149 of the Spanish Constitution, the State only has exclusive powers regarding the legislation, regulation and concession of water resources and projects when the waters run through more than one Autonomous Community. For the purpose of ensuring the full management of the water basins, Article 21 of the Water Act creates the Water Basin Authorities. These are public law entities, endowed with their own legal personality and functional autonomy, and for administrative purposes attached to the Ministry of the Environment. Furthermore, to ensure sufficient cooperation in the application of water protection norms, the Water Act creates the Committee of Competent Authorities for river basin districts in inter-community basins. This Committee is made up of representatives of the General Administration of the State who have competencies related to the adequate use, protection and monitoring of the waters that are the subject of this Act; and the bodies of the Autonomous Communities and local institutions whose territory falls completely or partly within the river basin district and which have competencies related to the adequate use, protection and monitoring of the waters that are the subject of this Act.

119. The Autonomous Communities shall exercise the powers regarding water basins entirely located inside their territories, according to their respective Statutes of Autonomy. The Autonomous Communities can adopt additional provisions on environmental protection, and in this sense more stringent requirements regarding water quality may be established (as stated by the Constitutional Court Decision 227/1988).

Notwithstanding the reforms introduced by the Statutes of Autonomy of different Autonomous Communities, such as that of Andalusia, in recent years certain conflicts have emerged because some of these new Statutes allow the Autonomous Communities to take on competencies that break with the traditional principle regarding the united management of drainage basins and bring into question again the principle established by the Water Act, whereby the State is responsible for basins shared by two or more Autonomous Communities and the Autonomous Communities are responsible for those that fall solely within their boundaries, if they possess such a basin.

I. Water as Public Good

120. According to the preamble to the Water Act, 'water constitutes a scarce natural resource, indispensable for life and most economical activities, irreplaceable, not susceptible of enlargement at human's will, irregular in its presentation in space and time, easily vulnerable and capable of successive uses', therefore justifying its public nature. In the Act, the management of inland waters, considered as a natural resource and environmental vector, is based on several principles contained in Article 14: consideration of water as an unitary resource (consideration of the hydrologic cycle); public character of the resource (included in the State public domain); unitary management (water basin authority); rational use of water (hydrological planning); and citizens' participation (role of user communities).

121. Article 2 of the Water Act, modified by Acts 62/2003 of 30 December, on Financial, Administrative and Social Order Measures, and 11/2005 of 22 June, states that the hydrological public domain is made up of:

- inland waters, both surface waters and underground renewable waters;
- beds of permanent or intermittent natural streams;
- beds of lakes and dams in public basins;
- aquifers, according to the regulations for disposing of or allocating water resources;
- waters resulting from the desalinization of sea water.

122. This hydrological public domain can be subject to different kinds of use: common general use, common special use, and private use.

The Water Act refers to common uses in its Article 50. Everybody is entitled to freely use surface water resources which run through their natural basins, for normal purposes in accordance with the laws and regulations. The Water Act describes as general common uses: bathing, drinking, domestic uses and watering cattle.

Common special uses require an administrative license that gives the authorized person or entity permission to use the resource in a more intense, dangerous or profitable way than described above. Granting the license does not confer any private ownership of the public good, because the other common general uses persist. Article 100 of the Act bans, in general, 'direct or indirect discharge of waters and of waste products liable to contaminate continental waters or any other water element of public domain without previous administrative authorization'. According to Article 51 of the Act these uses will be the following: navigation, flotation, ferry-boats and piers, and all uses not included among the common general uses.

Finally, the so-called private uses require an express and special administrative permit called 'concession' or otherwise, set up by an express legal provision.

Thus, Article 54 of the Water Act provides that the owner of a plot of land can use the rain water running over it, stagnant waters within its limits and waters coming from springs or underground waters located under its soil to up to 7,000 m3 per year. By administrative concession, and according to Articles 59–66 of the Act, temporal uses will be possible for a period not longer than seventy-five years, and with prior registration in the Water Registry. Nevertheless, the concession does not ensure the availability of the water and is subject to several limitations: the granted water will be limited to the specified use, and an order of priority can be established by the Hydrologic Plan of the specific water basin considered.

If no provisions on this matter were specifically adopted in this Plan, the order of priority established by Article 60 of the Water Act will apply: public supply uses; irrigation and agricultural uses; electric power generation; other industrial uses not included in the previous ones; fish hatcheries; recreational uses; navigation and transport uses; other uses.

123. The regulatory modifications that have been undergone in recent years with respect to waters have introduced a significantly more flexible concession regime, thus permitting the possibility of total or partial transfer of private uses of water use through a new kind of transfer contract. In fact, the point discussed here, and that has also been the topic of long debates in Spain these last years, is the difficult coexistence of a legal regime that declares the water resources to be public domain and therefore excluded from commerce, with the setting up of a so-called 'water market'.

Although it has been severely criticized for establishing a questionable privatization of water rights far beyond what the concessional regime requires, The Rewritten Text of the Water Act sets out a system of transmission of water use rights, if a previous public authorization has been granted, and regulated by a contract of transfer.

Article 67 states that the concessionaires and title-holders of any right to the private use of waters will be able to temporally cede to other concessionaires or title-holders of equal or higher rank – according to the order of priority established in the hydrological plan or, in its absence, in Article 60 – the whole or part of the rights of use to which they are entitled.

Therefore, the cession is subject to the authorization of the water basin authority (or autonomous hydrological authority in case of basins located inside a single Autonomous Community). It can only take place among title-holders of rights to private use and have as its object the whole or part of the rights of use of the transferor (in any case, the annual water volume cannot exceed the volume effectively used by the transferor). Finally, the cession takes place in exchange for an economic compensation, fixed by agreement by both parties as stated in the contract and whose effects will be the transfer of all the obligations as to the public administration regarding the water use.

II. Hydrologic Planning

124. According to Article 1 of the Water Act, any action taking place in the hydrological public domain shall be submitted to hydrological planning, as has been usual in Spain since the last century. Article 40 of the Act defines the objectives pursued by the plan as follows: to accomplish the satisfactory condition and adequate protection of water courses of public domain and of the waters which are the subject of this Act, among which include coastal and transitional waters in addition to continental waters; to satisfactorily meet the existing water demands; and to promote a harmonically and balanced sectorial and regional development, increasing the resource availability, protecting its quality, as well as economizing and rationalizing its use according to the circumstances of the environment and natural resources.

125. The Water Act foresees the elaboration of two different types of plans, which will be public and binding and shall be coordinated with the different sectorial plans that may affect them. These two plans are the Water Basin Hydrologic Plans and the National Hydrologic Plan. The territorial scope of every river basin hydrologic plan will coincide with the corresponding demarcation of its river basins. This is an important new development, introduced due to the transposition of the WFD in the Spanish legal system, through Act 62/2003 of 30 December which modified The Rewritten Text of the Water Act. Previously, the territorial scope of river basin hydrologic plans coincided with the river basin itself, and not with the river basin district. The National Hydrologic Plan, as its name implies, is instituted at a national level.

126. The Water Basin Hydrologic Plans are prepared by the river basin Authority or by the hydrological authorities of the competent Autonomous Communities in cases of intra-communitarian basins, and approved by the State government, by RD. Despite the relevant role played by these plans in the management of the hydrological public domain, it was not until 1998, thirteen years after the approval of Act 29/1985 of 2 August on Water, that the preparation process of the Water Basin Hydrologic Plans was concluded with RD 1664/1998 of 24 July. Now, the transposition of the WFD into the Spanish legal system makes it necessary to revise those plans in order to meet the new stipulated regulations.

127. With the approval of Act 62/2003 of 30 December, which modified the Water Act in order to incorporate that directive into Spanish law, several important new points were introduced in the Spanish hydrological planning process. There are four main changes.

In the first place, the necessary inclusion of coastal and transitional waters in Hydrological Plans, following the tendency of global regulation of all waters, is introduced at the community level. This leads to a substantial new point: the territorial scope of river basin hydrological plans changes from being the river basin itself to the river basin district, as we saw above. It states:

> programmes related to coastal and transitional waters which have been produced by the General Administration of the State or by the Autonomous Communities which participate in the Committee of Competent Authorities of demarcation and have a coastline must be expressly integrated in the Hydrologic Plan. (Article 41.2 of the Water Act).

In the second place, as we will see later, the articles of the Water Act which govern the objectives, criteria, contents and procedures for the realization of Water Basin Hydrological Plans have been redrafted.

Third, it states the measures which must be established for each river basin district (Article 92 quarter of the Water Act), with the aim being to achieve the environmental objectives laid out in Article 92*bis* of the Water Act itself, and which will be coordinated and integrated in River Basin Hydrological Plans. These programmes are made up of basic actions (minimum requirements which must be fulfilled in each demarcation and which will be periodically re-established) and complementary actions (those which must be applied additionally to achieve environmental objectives or for additional protection of waters) which are approved by the competent administrations for the protection of waters.

These programmes must be approved before 31 December 2009 and they must be updated in the year 2015 after which they will be revised every six years. In any case, all of the actions included in the programmes must be in operation by the year 2012.

Finally, it incorporates programmes for the monitoring of water condition, which must be established in every river basin district and which will give a coherent and complete overview of the condition. These programmes will be incorporated in the action programmes and must be in operation by 31 December 2006.

128. According to Article 42 of the Water Act, the minimal compulsory content of the basin plans must include the general description of the river basin district; the general description of the uses, pressures and significant human incidents on the water; the identification and maps of protected zones; the tracking networks established for the monitoring of the status of the surface water, of subterranean water and of protected zones and the results of this monitoring; the list of environmental objectives for surface water, subterranean water and protected zones, including the forecasted terms for their achievement, the identification of conditions for exceptions and extensions, and complementary information; a summary of the economic analysis of water use, including a description of the situations and reasons which may allow exceptions in the application of the cost recovery principle; a summary of the Action Programmes adopted in order to reach the stipulated objectives; a more detailed registry of hydrological plans and programmes related to river sub-basins, sectors, specific questions or water categories, along with a summary of its contents; a summary of the incidences involving the giving of public information and of consultations received, their results and the consequential changes effected in the plan; a list of the designated competent authorities; and the contact points and procedures to obtain documentation basic information and the information required for public enquiries.

In addition, the first action of the Hydrological Plan and all the subsequent actions must include a summary of all of the changes or updates made since the publication of the first version of the plan; a report on the progress made toward the achievement of the environmental objectives; a summary and explanation of the actions planned in the former river basin Hydrological Plan that never came to fruition; and a summary of all additional transitional measures adopted since the publication of the first version of the River basin Hydrological Plan, for the water masses which will probably not reach their forecasted objectives.

These new stipulations, as indicated, will require the current Hydrological Plans to be revised. The revision will have to come into effect on 31 December 2009, and must be revised every six years after that date.

129. The National Hydrologic Plan is prepared by the Department of the Environment and Rural and Marine Affairs together with the other concerned ministries, informed by the National Council on Water and approved by the Parliament.

The mandatory content of the National Plan is stated in Article 45 of the Act. First, the Plan should contain the necessary measures to coordinate the Water Basin Plans. According to the White Paper on Water of 1998, these measures have a three-fold impact: the setting up of unique systems of exploitation for each Water Basin Hydrologic Plan; the identification and delimitation of Hydrogeological Units shared by two or more basins, and the fixation of consolidated demands and balance of resources with homogeneous criteria. Regarding environmental protection, the way in which the restrictions should influence the traditional natural resources use should be determined, as well as the addition of other parameters (physical and chemical characteristics of the water, protection parameters and measures addressed to the preservation and recovery of the resource, forestry hydrologic plans and land preservation, plans for the protection and recovery of aquifers). Second, the Plan should provide a solution to the possible alternatives presented in the Water Basin

Hydrological Plans. Third, the Plan must foresee and establish the conditions for the hydrological resource transfers among the territories affected by the different Water Basin Hydrological Plans.

In that sense, the transfer question, which in fact does not appear in the Act, requires considering three relevant aspects (cf. White Paper on Water, Ministry of Environment, 1998, 36): cost-benefit analysis, the aim pursued by the water transfer and urban planning. Transfer requirements must necessarily include a positive EIA, determination of the economic-financial regime of the works, and the compensation and agreement of the transferor basins.

Finally, the National Plan shall incorporate the necessary modifications in the resource use planning which may affect existing uses aimed at population supply and irrigation.

130. After a delay of several years and wrapped in huge controversy, the National Hydrological Plan was approved through Act 10/2001 of 5 July. The plan culminates the planning process through the coordination of previously approved River basin Hydrological Plans, but it also opens a great debate in Spain on the direction in which water policy should go. The National Hydrological Plan, opted, preferentially, for a policy calling for the construction of big water projects in order to confront the shortage of water resources in certain river basin regions.

To this effect, it stipulates and regulates certain transfers, limited to 'those supposed justified for reasons of national interest, in response to situations of accredited structural lacks in the weather'. The transfers treated in Article 13 of the Act (it also includes small quantity one in Article 14), which authorize subject to the fulfilment of the conditions laid out in the rule itself, are up to 1,050 cubic hectometres (hm3) per year from the Lower Ebro, in the province of Tarragona. The destination and the volume of such transfers were the internal river basins of Catalonia (Barcelona), up to 190 hm3 annually; the river basin of Júcar, up to 315 hm3 annually, the river basin of Segura, up to 450 hm3 annually; y the river basin of the south (Almeria), up to 95 hm. The provision of this transfer in the Plan has been, without doubt, one of the most controversial decisions, based on the reaction it caused, on a political level, a social level, a legal level, etc. The change in government after the general elections of April 2004, has caused significant changes in this area. The reorientation of the water policy in Spain which has been undertaken by the new government motivated the revocation of those articles of the Act which refer to the transfer of water from the Ebro. That reform was contained in Royal Decree 2/2004 of 18 June, by which it modified Act 10/2001.

131. The regulatory process concluded with the recent approval of Act 11/2005 of 22 June, which modifies Act 10/2001. This new regulation either partially or entirely revokes certain articles of Act 10/2001 which are basically related to the provision for new ordinary transfers, their technical conditions, the destinations of the transferred water, the conditions of organization of the users in the catchment basins, the management condition of the authorized transfers, the effects of the authorized transfers, the financial-economical system of the transfer, the compensations of environmental character to the receiving river basins and the investment programme. Furthermore, they add new annexes to the text of the Act and they relate them to the various actions themselves. In part, they incorporate new general interest actions by river basin, and they include and reorder the combination of priority and urgent actions in Mediterranean river basins. All together, more than a hundred actions are dealt with, of which more than twenty are new sea water desalination plants, and the rest are aimed at the conservation, better management and reuse of water.

This new water policy has been complemented by the AGUA (*Actuaciones para la Gestión y Utilización de Agua* – Actions on Water Management and Use) programme which was introduced by the Ministry of the Environment on 2 September 2004. The programme combines all the investment activities stipulated by the Ministry in order to increase the availability of water resources. This programme also includes acts in the whole national territory which affect all policies and areas directly and indirectly linked to the availability and sustainable management of water.

III. Water Quality Protection

132. Article 93 of the Water Act defines 'pollution' as:

> The act or effect of depositing materials or forms of energy in water, or of inducing conditions which either directly or indirectly cause a harmful alteration in its quality in relation to its previous uses, to human health, or to aquatic ecosystems or the terrestrial ecosystems which are directly linked to them; of damaging goods; or detracting from or hampering its leisure time and environmental uses.

This is a very similar definition to that provided in Directive Water Framework.

133. According to Article 92 of the Water Act, modified by Acts 62/2003 of 30 December and 11/2005 of 22 June, modified by Act 62/2003, the objectives of the protection of water and hydrological public domain are:

(a) to prevent deterioration, to protect and improve the condition of aquatic ecosystems as well as the terrestrial ecosystems and wetlands which directly depend on them, in relation to their water needs;
(b) to develop the sustainable use of water by protecting available water resources and ensuring a sufficient supply in good condition;
(c) to protect and improve the aquatic environment through the establishment of specific measures to progressively reduce spills, emissions and priority substance leaks, as well as to gradually eliminate or suppress spills, emissions and harmful priority substance leaks;
(d) to ensure the progressive reduction of subterranean water pollution and avoid further polluting;
(e) to alleviate the effects of floods and droughts;

(f) to achieve, through the application of the corresponding legislation, the objectives established in international treaties in order to prevent and eliminate the contamination of the aquatic environment;
(g) to avoid any accumulation of toxic or harmful compounds in the subsoil or any other accumulation that may cause degradation of public waters;
(h) to ensure that water of the best existing quality in an area or region is assigned to population centres.

In Article 92*bis*, added by Act 62/2003, of 30 December, the Water Act also establishes a series of environmental objectives to be reached in order to achieve adequate water protection. These environmental objectives are established both for surface waters (to prevent the deterioration of the condition of surface water masses; to protect, improve and regenerated all surface water masses with the aim of achieving their good ecological status; and to progressively reduce pollution originating from priority substances and to gradually eliminate or suppress spills, emissions and harmful priority substance leaks) and for subterranean waters (to avoid or limit the entrance of contaminants in subterranean waters and avoid the deterioration of the condition of all subterranean water masses; to protect, improve and regenerate subterranean water masses and ensure a balance between extraction and recharging in order to achieve good ecological status of subterranean waters; and to reverse the long-term tendencies in the increase of the concentration of whatever contaminant stemming from human activity in order to progressively reduce the contamination of subterranean waters), protected areas (to fulfil the requirements and achieve the specific environmental objectives of protection regulations which are applicable in the area), artificial and very modified water masses (to protect and improve artificial and highly modified water masses in order to accomplish good ecological potential and a good chemical condition of surface waters).

134. According to data from the Spanish Government:

> Thus, in 2005 a diagnosis was made of the characteristics and environmental and socio-economic circumstances of water masses (as established in article 5 of the WFD), identifying as superficial water masses some 4,000 rivers and 300 lakes, 129 in transition, 224 in coasts and 700 masses of water. This typification was accompanied by an evaluation of their state, having studied the pressures that affect these masses and the impacts they suffer, to finally analyze the risk of not reaching the environmental objectives. This analysis concludes that there are a high number of masses at risk, as a result of the pressure of human activity, with the presence of urban nuclei, agricultural and industrial activities, production of hydroelectric power and hydro morphological alterations. As for underground masses, the most important pressures come, on the one hand, from diffuse pollution (nitrates and biocides) fundamentally originated by non-sustainable fertilizer use in the agricultural sector, that has caused pollution by nitrates in many aquifers, as well as by excessive use of pesticides. On the other hand, a regime of non-sustainable extractions, a circumstance that is aggravated n the coastal areas by the phenomena of saline intrusion. Concretely, the most important cases of over-exploitation of aquifers occur in La

Mancha aquifers, in aquifers of the Mediterranean coastal area, in the Vinalopó area, in the river basin of the Segura River, and the Adra aquifer. (Spanish Sustainable Development Strategy, Madrid, 2007).

135. We should also note that one of the objectives of the Water Basin Plans is to achieve, 'good ecological status and adequate protection of public waters and of all waters cited in this Act' and to protect its quality, 'rationalizing its use according to the environment and the rest of natural resources' (Article 40 of the Water Act). Likewise, the aim of discharge permits is to 'attain the good ecological status of waters, in accordance with quality standards, environmental objectives and the emission and immission characteristics statutorily established by the application of the current Act'. In this respect, Article 100 of the Act defines the 'good ecological status of waters' as that determined from 'biological quality, physical and chemical and hydromorphological criteria inherent to the natural conditions of any hydrologic ecosystem in the way and with the evaluation criteria specified in the regulations'. Article 42 enumerates, as compulsory content of those plans, the list of environmental objectives for surface waters, subterranean waters and protected areas, including the forecasted terms for their completion, the identification of conditions for exceptions and delays, and complementary information as well as a summary of the Action Plans adopted to meet the planned objectives. Also, to the prohibitions already imposed on the owners of private intermittent river courses (as the undertaking of any work that could alter the natural course of waters), Article 5 of the Act modified by Act 46/1999 has added the prohibition of any activity that may alter the quality level of the waters involved.

136. In order to achieve these objectives, the Water Act foresees two different kinds of actions.

First, the tables of the Annexes 1–4 of RD 927/1988 fix the quality objectives for inland waters, which reproduce the values established by the EU Directives (waters destined for drinking water production, bathing waters, fishing waters).

The specific quality levels are specified in other complementary regulations, such as RD 1341/2007 of 11 October, establishing quality standards of bathing waters; Royal Decree 345/1993 of 5 March which establishes the quality norms required for the breeding of molluscs and other marine invertebrates. the Order of 16 December 1988 on analysis or inspection methods and their frequency for inland waters requiring protection or improvement for the good development of fishing life; the Order of 11 May 1988 on the basic characteristics that should be maintained for surface waters flows destined to produce drinking water (modified by the Orders of 15 October 1990 and 30 November 1994); and the Order of 8 February 1988 on measurement methods and sampling frequency for the analysis of surface waters destined to produce drinking water.

Special mention must be made of Royal Decree 140/2003 of 7 February which establishes the sanitary criteria for water quality for human consumption, which revokes the former Royal Decree 1138/1990 of 14 September. This regulation establishes the sanitary criteria which water for human consumption must meet. It also lays out the criteria for water supply facilities encompassing the entire process from collection of the water to the tap of the consumer and the monitoring of these in order to ensure the healthfulness, quality and cleanliness of public water with the aim of protecting public health from the adverse effects derived from any and all types of water contamination. Annex II of the decree has been modified by Order SAS/1915/2009, of 8 July.

137. Second, the Water Act, the Regulation of Public Waters and Order 1873/2004 of 2 June approve the official models for declaring discharge and develop some aspects of authorizing discharges and paying the fee for monitoring discharge. They provide general regulations for discharges in public waters and, in particular, discharge permits.

The Water Act in its Article 97 as modified by Act 46/1999, creates a general prohibition of discharges capable of producing pollution or degradation of the inland waters. Specifically, the new wording of Article 100 of the Act repeats this limitation, stating the general prohibition of direct or indirect discharge of waters and waste products to inland waters or any other element of the hydrological public domain.

Nevertheless, this prohibition comes with a reservation of authorization. Thus, the discharge of several polluting substances is permitted as long as, according to Article 100 of the Act, this is carried out after the an express administrative permit has been obtained. This must be read together with the broad concept of discharge supplied by Article 100 of the Act, which includes all substances directly or indirectly poured into inland waters as well as into the rest of the hydrological public domain, whatever the procedure or technique used.

138. The regional or local competent authority will authorize the discharge of polluting substances where this is to take place in any part of the sewer network or the collection networks managed by the regional or local authorities or by entities dependent on these (Royal Decree 4/2007, of 13 April, Act 42/2007, of 13 December). In the remaining cases, the responsibility of granting discharge authorization corresponds in the case of direct discharge in surface water to the State (the river basin Organizations) or autonomous regional Water Administration, depending on whether the river basin in question is shared by Autonomous Communities or located within the boundaries of an Autonomous Community. Indirect discharges into surface water are authorized by local competent or autonomous regional authorities as established by the Regulation of Hydrological Public Domain. With respect to authorization for indirect discharges with special effects on the quality of recipient, these must be favourably reported by the river basin Organization before the granting of official authorization (Article 245.2 and 4, modified by Royal Decree 606/2003 of 23 May).

To determine whether the responsibility of the granting of direct or indirect discharge authorizations in subterranean water is that of the State or that of the autonomous region, the criteria of the river basin is applied in terms of whether it is shared by Autonomous Communities or located within the boundaries of an Autonomous Community.

139. The absence of delimitation of the polluting substances requiring an administrative permit or authorization should be noted. The Water Act demands the authorization generically, regarding all potentially polluting discharges. In effect, the requirement for authorization is quite loose and irresolute, not only because of the breadth of the concept of discharge, but also because of the terms with which requirements and authorizations are set. This extends to all discharges that contain whatever substance or material liable to contaminate, even if they are not 'harmful substances' in the sense used by the WFD. However, our ordinance does not set clear standard terms for when a discharge is liable to contaminate. Although, as previously stated in this text, the Rewritten Text of the Water Act defines the term contamination, it deals with a relative concept linked to the uses the water is meant for, human health, etc. It is incumbent upon the administration to assess its agreement with the prescribed definition and the execution of this task is largely at their discretion, although in the process, it must take into account certain qualitative parameters – represented by the emission and immission regulations and environmental objectives.

140. Discharge authorizations allow the exception to the general ban on discharges liable to contaminate continental waters or any other element of hydrological public domain. However, it does not constitute a free ticket to pollute, but they remain subject to a series of limits in relation to contaminating substances, both in terms of the types of substance they can discharge and in the establishment of the maximum admissible values that they must adhere to. In this way, the requirement of previous authorization complements the establishment of limit values for the substances which negatively affect water quality. Discharge authorizations 'are granted taking into account the best available techniques and in accordance with environmental quality norms and regulatory emission limits' (Article 100.2 Water Act). The discharge authorization regime requires that the authorization itself prescribes the conditions under which the discharges may be carried out.

Aside from the necessary depuration facilities and the operation control systems, it should specifically state the quantitative and qualitative limits of the effluent, as well as the total amount of the discharge control fees that must be paid to the administration as defined by Article 105. This prescription is repeated, regarding quantitative and qualitative limits, in Article 251 of RD 849/1986, modified by Royal Decree 606/2003 of 23 May. Thus, according to Article 251, the discharge authorization will establish the conditions by which these must be carried out, specifically stating, among other points, the flow and the emission limit values of the effluent. To determine emission limit values, river basin organizations will have to follow the regulations stipulated in the Regulation of Hydrological Public Domain [Article 251.1(b)]:

– 'The characteristics of discharge emissions will meet the environmental quality norms of the recipient. A gradual application of those norms can be established until they have been completely achieved'. We see a combined focus (emission characteristics/environmental quality norms) in the monitoring of discharges in this provision, as is the present tendency in the latest environmental directives.

– 'Emission limit values are required for the characteristic parameters of the activity causing the discharge'.
– 'Emission limit values may not be reached through dilution techniques'.

With these regulations, the prevailing system until the approval of Royal Decree 606/2003 of 23 May, which fixed uniform emission limit values for strict application in all river basins, is abandoned for another in which the river basin organization must indicate limit values case by case, ensuring at all times their adherence to the recipient's quality objectives. It allows, then, the adaptation of discharge authorizations to the specific case of each river basin, but it leaves a wide margin of discretion in the hands of the hydrological administration. The Regulation of Hydrological Public Domain includes, in compensation, some regulations which allow a reduction in the discretionary power of the hydrological administration in the execution of this task. In effect, the discharge authorizations must limit the harmful substances coming from the activity that causes the discharge, to insure compliance with the emission limits for specifically regulated hazardous substances and existing or future environmental quality regulations. Measures will also be considered to progressively reduce or eliminate the hazardous substances listed in Annex IV and in particular those in priority list II, as specified by Royal Decree 907/2007, of 6 July, which approved the Hydrological Planning Regulations.

141. The harmful substances that are referred to in the Regulation of Hydrological Public Domain are those laid out in sections I and II of Annex IV of that Regulation – they basically coincide with the substances in Annex X of Decision 2455/2001/CE of the European Parliament and Council of 20 November 2001 which approves a list of priority substances in the scope of water policies, and which modifies the WFD.

Furthermore, the Regulation of Hydrological Public Domain now includes as Annex II, a list of contaminants which is defined as 'any substance that can cause contamination and in particular that is listed in Annex II' [Article 245.5.c].

142. With respect to discharges of harmful substances into subterranean waters, the hydrological administration will adopt the necessary means to deter the introduction of the substances which appear in section I of Annex III into subterranean waters as well as limit the introduction of the substances which appear in section II of the same Annex. To these effects, it maintains the absolute prohibition of all direct discharges of the substances from list I except 'if it was the subject of a previous hydrological study which demonstrated that the subterranean waters into which the substances of section I are intended to be discharged are permanently unsuitable for any use, particularly agricultural or domestic', in which case discharge authorization can be granted for those substances (Article 257.3 of Royal Decree 849/1986, modified by Royal Decree 606/2003 of 23 May). The substances of list II can only be discharged when a hydrological study has demonstrated their innocuousness, and any necessary technical precautions are subsequently adopted in the list of conditions.

143. Concerning discharges from treatment facilities, Royal Decree 509/1996 of 15 March, which clarifies RLD 11/1995 of 28 December establishing norms applicable to urban waste water treatment, laid out the minimum requirements that must be met. To these effects, it fixes concentration values and reduction percentages (it allows a choice between the two) for three parameters (biochemical oxygen demand, chemical oxygen demand, and solids suspension) for discharges from secondary treatment facilities or facilities of an equivalent process. Nevertheless, discharge authorizations can impose stricter requirements when necessary in order to ensure that the recipient water meets the quality objectives set in current regulations. For discharges from treatment facilities in sensitive zones, Royal Decree 509/1996 of 15 March also allows the choice between concentration values and reduction percentages which are fixed in this case for five substances (in addition to the three previously mentioned it also applies to phosphorous and nitrogen). In any case, stricter requirements can be imposed if necessary to insure that quality objectives are met.

144. As of 31 December 2009, 23,296 authorizations had been issued for discharges into the public water system, these amounting to a total volume of 10,070,432,235 m3. Of these 17,165 were urban discharges, with a volume of 3,167,500,942 m3; 5,870 were industrial discharges, with a volume of 6,902,063,888 m3. Also, 647 authorizations were issued by the Autonomous Communities for discharges from land to sea with a volume of 14,647,737,211 m3.

145. The authorizations are given, according to of the Act, for a maximum term of five years (except discharge authorizations of harmful substances into subterranean waters, which are granted for a term of four years – Article 259.2 of Royal Decree 849/1986, modified by Royal Decree 606/2003), successively renewable as long as the quality regulations and environmental objectives required at each moment are satisfactorily met. The Act also foresees, in its modified Article 104, the revision of already granted discharge authorizations, and insists on the possibility of their modification due to drought or extreme hydrological circumstances in order to ensure the quality objectives. Finally, regarding the administration's role in cases of non-authorized discharges or when the authorization requirements are not met, Article 105 provides for the initiation of sanction proceedings and determination of the damage done to the water's quality; and the liquidation of the discharge fee. In addition, the administration can agree to initiate procedures for the revocation of the authorization in case there was any whose requirements were not met or the initiation of the authorization proceedings if there was none and the discharge was susceptible of legalization; and the lapsing declaration of the water concession, in those cases where the non-compliance with the requirements or the lack of authorization resulted in great damage to the public domain. Accordingly, revocations and agreed expiry declarations do not give the right to indemnity.

IV. Urban Waste Waters

146. Directive 91/271/EEC regarding urban waste water treatment was transposed to the Spanish legal system by RLD 11/1995 of 28 December which establishes the rules applying to urban waste water treatment. This RD was implemented by RD 509/1996 of 15 March, basically intended to complete the norms on collection, depuration and discharge of urban waste water. This RD has recently been modified by RD 2116/1998 of 2 October, which transposes to the Spanish legal system the Commission Directive 98/15/EC amending Directive 91/271/EC.

Prior to all that, in 1992, an Inventory of Waste water Depuration Facilities (EDAR) had been completed in Spain and in 1995, the Spanish Government adopted the National Plan for Depuration and Cleaning-up of Urban Waste water 1995–2005, directed to facilitate the implementation of the obligations included in the Directive, through the setting up of new cleaning and depuration infrastructures and the adoption of a whole set of complementary actions. According to the studies carried out for the Plan's preparation, in 1994 an estimated national total polluting burden of 85 million of equivalent inhabitants could be established, distributed as follows: 69.5% in normal areas, 9% in sensitive areas and 21.5% in less sensitive areas, according to the criteria contained in Annex II of Directive 91/271/EEC (cf. Ministry of Environment, Medio Ambiente en España 1997, 1998, 70).

147. The aforementioned Plan also determined, for the first time, the sensitive areas on a national level, in compliance with RDL 11/1995 and RD 509/1996.

According to both dispositions, the sensitive areas can be classified into four groups: water masses with scarce water renewal in which nutrients accumulation can take place; estuaries, bays and other sea waters with scarce water exchange or which receive a great amount of nutrients; surface waters destined for potable water production; and areas of high environmental value, in which any polluting discharge should be avoided. By means of a resolution of the Secretary of State of Waters and Coasts (Ministry of the Environment) of 25 May 1998, sensitive zones of inter-Autonomous Community river basins were declared. This declaration delimited the treatments that waste water in certain urban agglomerations must undergo before it can be discharged into continental or marine waters. It is the responsibility of the autonomous communities to carry out this task in waters that fall within their own boundaries, and also to officially designate less sensitive zones in its marine waters.

148. Both the Directive and RDL 11/1995 establish specific time limits to carry out the treatment and depuration infrastructures works. The first of them, regarding agglomerations with more than 10,000 equivalent inhabitants whose waste waters are discharged in sensitive areas, terminated on 31 December 1998.

The second time limit runs up to 31 December 2000 and affects urban agglomerations with more than 15,000 equivalent inhabitants whose waste waters are discharged in less sensitive areas. The deadline for other agglomerations was set at 31 December 2005, also the date on which the agglomerations with between 10,000 and 15,000 equivalent inhabitants, as well as the agglomerations with between 2,000 and 10,000 equivalent inhabitants whose waste waters are discharged into estuaries or inland waters, should have treatment and depuration systems. The remaining agglomerations should also have a treatment system for their waste waters.

The first plan enabled Spain to obtain a compliance level of 77%, which will increase over the next two years to 91% if new infrastructures under construction are included. In 2007, Spain had more than 2,500 waste water treatment plants, which treated more than 3,375 hm3 of waste water annually. Of this, it is estimated that around 450 hm3 are reused each year, which is more than 13% of the total. With the new National Water Quality Plan, the aim is to facilitate the reuse of treated water, thus increasing the water resources available.

149. On 8 June 2007, the Government approved the National Water Quality Plan: Cleaning and Treatment 2007–2015. The new Plan aims to cover both the objectives not achieved under the previous plan and the new objectives specified in the Framework Water Directive and the A.G.U.A. Programme. The National Water Quality Plan forms part of a set of measures designed to ensure full compliance with Directive 91/271/CEE and the good ecological state required by the Framework Water Directive for 2015.

The new National Water Quality Plan will continue to promote research into natural resources and in particular the cleaning, treatment and quality of water, and biodiversity and associated ecosystems. The total investment is to be EUR 19,007 million, of which EUR 6,233 million will come from the Ministry for the Environment and the rest from the Autonomous Communities.

150. Generally, the treatment facilities are of municipal title, and the same municipal body that provides the drinking water supply normally assumes their direct management. Indirect management, either through mixed entities or by administrative contracting with a private firm, is less frequent.

V. Water Quality Control Networks

151. In order to control and track the surface waters, to proceed to quality diagnosis and to comply with the quality objectives, several control networks have been created. The oldest of them, the so-called COCA Network (Water Quality Official Control) which controls a total of forty quality parameters, was created in 1962. In 1993, an integrated network of control stations, known as ICA Network (Water Quality Information System) was designed, in order to control the whole of the river stretches with the frequency and intensity demanded by their respective existent uses. The COCA Network (currently with more than 500 stations), the COAS Network (Drinking Water Control) and the monitoring network of fish life (ICTIO-FAUNA) are integrated into it. For its part, the SAICA Network (Automatic Water Quality Information System) has set up 185 automatic alert stations in the nine Spanish water basins. All of these are centralized in the General Water Management Department (ministry of the Environment). Currently, a water quality information system (SICA) is being set up for the monitoring, diagnosis and evaluation of quality, which will clarify monitoring and control functions of waters through the ICA and SAICA networks, subterranean waters, etc.

Some of these networks are being integrated into the new control programmes created to apply the Framework Directive on Water. These programmes are as follows:

Monitoring Programme. This programme aims to generate the information needed for an overall view of the state of each drainage basin in order to assess long-term changes in natural conditions and to assess long-term changes caused by extensive human activity. It includes several sub-programmes: the Evaluation of the general state of surface waters and of long-term trends caused by anthropogenic activity; the Evaluation of long-term trends caused by changes in natural conditions; the Exchange of information with the EU; and the control of discharges into the sea and across borders. It also includes, among others, the COCA Network, the RID (Riverine Inputs and Direct Discharges) – OSPAR programme, and the Eionet –Water Programme of the European Environment Agency.

Operational control programme for bodies of surface water. This programme provides the necessary information to determine the state of those bodies of water that may not meet the environmental objectives. It is also used to determine the efficacy of the measures implemented to return these bodies of water to a good state.

Research control programme for bodies of surface water. This programme consists of taking samples over a period of time to study the effect of occasional pollution on the environment and to investigate the causes of problems detected in the environment. It includes the SAICA. Network.

Protected zones control programme. This programme aims to control bodies of water used for drinking water. It includes the COAS Control Network for Water Supplies.

152. We should also mention here the National Control Network of Environmental Radioactivity in Surface Waters, functioning since 1978. Moreover, the Department of the Environment and Rural and Marine Affaire is completing the setting up of the SAIH Network (Automatic Hydrologic Information System) for flood prevention and hydrologic resource management in the different basins. SAIHs are used in the Hydrographical Confederations of Júcar, Segura, Guadalquivir, Tajo, Ebro, Guadiana and what used to be known as Norte I (nowadays Miño-Sil and part of the Hydrographical Confederation of Cantabria, previously known as Norte II and III; the latter is currently in the process of being put out to tender) and are being implemented in the short term in the Duero Drainage Basin (to be finalized by October 2010). In this respect, we must note that it is also working on a map of easily flooded areas, identifying 'black points' or areas of potential flood risk. Moreover, several actions are directed at improving the available information, among them the White Paper on Water of 1998, a technical and scientific tool which analyses the hydrological situation of Spain. Other actions are also taken in order to improve the available information, such as the White Paper on Underground Waters of 1995, which foresees sixteen action plans, among them a programme for a uses census and a programme of integration of the Hydrogeological Units in the exploitation systems.

153. Regarding the creation of surveillance and control networks aiming to achieve a better knowledge of the characteristics and evolution of the underground waters, the setting up by the Geological and Mining Institute of Spain (IGME) of the Underground Waters Control Networks, which evaluates the evolution of several physical and chemical parameters, must be mentioned. According to the objectives pursued, these networks are classified as Piezometry Water Network (AGPZ) for the control of water levels in the aquifers; Chemical Analysis Water Network (AGAQ) for the control of the status and the evolution of the chemical characteristics of underground waters; Hydrometer Water Network (AGHD) for flow measurement by stations set up at wells and waterbeds, including aquifers drainage, and finally, the Intrusion Water Network (AGIN) created to evaluate the salt-water invasion of the coastal aquifers.

Chapter 4. Waste

§1. Urban Waste

154. The total quantity of waste generated in Spain grew by 95.9% in the period between 1990 and 2007. In 2007, 25,584,000 tonnes of waste was produced in Spain, and 537 kg/per person of waste was produced in 2006. Spain recycles 14% of its urban waste and decomposes 20% (Eurostat).

155. From a legal perspective, D 2414/1961 on Unpleasant, Unhealthy, Noxious and Hazardous Activities (now replaced) constituted the first national regulation on urban waste, together with Act 42/1975, of 19 November. Act 42/1975 aimed to establish the legal system for planning and controlling the collection and processing of urban waste. Among the objectives of the Act was to promote the reuse of waste. Nevertheless, political changes and the lack of any regulation meant that Act 42/75 was never fully applied. It was thus necessary to update and improve the Act's content.

156. Act 42/1975 was later replaced by the Waste Act 10/1998 of 21 April, which established a common general regulation on waste excluding gaseous effluents emitted into the atmosphere, radioactive waste and discharges into water bodies. That Act was later modified by RDL 4/2001, of 16 February on the Administrative System applicable to the Energy Assessment of flour of animal origin obtained by the transformation of the remains and cadavers of animals, Act 62/2003 of 30 December, on Tax, Administrative and Social Measures, Act 34/2007, of 15 November, on air quality and the protection of the atmosphere, and Act 25/2009, of 22 December, on free access to the activities and execution of services.

157. By the end of the first decade of the twenty-first century, it became clear that the Spanish legislation on waste had to be revised to a certain extent, mainly in order to incorporate into the Spanish Legal System the new requirements established by the Directive 98/2008/EC (Waste Framework Directive). The Ministry of Environment and Rural and Maritime Affairs elaborated the Draft of the new general Act on this matter, and finally, the Spanish Parliament passed the Act 22/2011 on waste and contaminated soils, which substituted the former act 10/1988 on waste. It is worth noting that the process of elaboration of the said Act 22/2011 followed the participation principles set out in Act 27/2006, of 18 July, on access to information, public participation and access to justice in environmental matters, in addition to the provisions on participation specified in Act 50/1997, of 27 November. The Act 22/011 has been modified by Act 5/2013, of 11 June, and Act 11/2012, of 19 December, which establishes urgent legislative provisions on environmental matter. The aim of the Act is to establish measures designed to protect the environment and human health by preventing waste and reducing the adverse impact of waste production and management. It will also introduce measures to reduce the global impact resulting from the use of resources and to improve the efficiency with which these resources are used.

158. The legal concept of 'waste' in the current Act 22/2011 is based upon the definition made by Article 3.1 of the Directive 2008/98/EC. Thus, Article 3 a) of the Act 22/2011 defines waste as 'any substance or object which the holder discards or intends or is required to discard'. By contrast to the former Act 10/1998, the Act 22/2011 currently in force does not make any express reference to the European List of Waste when defining the concept of waste. At this point, it is necessary to take into underline that Article 3 of the Act is consistent with Article 7 of the Directive 2008/98/EC, which foresees that the list of waste established by Decision 2000/532/EC only shall be binding as regards to the determination of the waste which is to be considered as hazardous waste. On the contrary, the inclusion of a substance or object in the list shall not mean that it is waste in all circumstances: i.e., a substance or object shall be considered to be waste only where the elements of the definition of the aforementioned Article 3 are met. This means that the concept of waste is mainly defined with regard to the final destination of the substance or object. In this sense, waste is not only any discarded substance or object, but also any substance or object resulting from any production process or whatsoever whose holder discards or intends to discard it, whether on a voluntary or compulsory basis. The concept of waste thus encapsulates two specific aspects: (a) a subjective aspect, which is related to the final decision of the holder; (b) an objective or regulatory aspect, in that these regulations aim to safeguard a specific general interest.

In general terms, the Act 22/2011 distinguishes among different types of waste, and, at this point, it is worth noting that the Act does not make any particular and express reference neither to the concept of 'urban waste' nor to the concept of 'municipal waste'. In this sense, the Act incorporates the following types of waste: (a) 'Household waste' (b) commercial waste and (c) industrial waste. Therefore, Article 3 of the Act defines household waste as waste resulting from household activities. This concept includes waste resulting from the cleaning of public ways, green areas, recreation areas and beaches; dead domestic animals; furniture, household equipment and abandoned vehicles; and waste from minor domestic repair and construction jobs. The Act thus defines household waste on the basis of its origin or the activity from which it is produced.

As regards to hazardous waste produced in households, Article 19 of the Act 22/2011 provides that the legal regime regarding hazardous waste shall not apply to separate fractions of hazardous waste produced by households until they are accepted for collection, disposal or recovery by an establishment or an registered undertaking entitled for the collection and management of hazardous waste.

Finally, it is important to note that the Act 22/2011 incorporates the concepts of by-product (in the terms of Article 5 of the Directive 2008/98/EC) and end of waste -EOW- (i.e., waste that shall cease to be waste when it has undergone a recovery (including recycling) operation and complies with specific criteria –Article 6 (1) and (2) of the Directive 2008/98/EC-). As regards to by-products, it is important to underline that the Spanish Legislation has not totally developed the criteria applicable to consider a specific product as by-product. These criteria will be issued through Ministerial Orders of the Ministry of Environment, following a technical assessment carried out by a Coordination Committee of waste. As regards the EOW criteria, they will be also established by Ministerial Order.

159. Regarding waste management, Act 22/2011 incorporates into the Spanish legal system the EU's rules established by Directive 2008/98/EC. In this sense, for the purposes of this Act, 'management' shall mean collection, transport and treatment of waste, including the supervision of such operations and the after-care of disposal sites, and including actions taken as a dealer or broker (Article 3).

The Act 22/2011 updates the hierarchy of principles concerning the management of waste. These principles, that are applicable to the public administrations and the economic agents, were introduced in the Spanish law for the first time by the Act 10/1998. Thus, Act 10/1998 brought about the necessary adaptation of the Spanish legislation to the existing principles of the EU, and implied a relevant 'updating' of the traditional practices. Currently, under the Act 22/2011, the prevention of waste production, as well as the reuse, recycling or other means of waste recovery, and safe disposal principles are expressly mentioned in Article 8.

160. Hierarchy of waste management implies, as a starting point that every economic agent who commercializes any product that can become waste, must handle these products in such a way that favours the prevention of waste production. Waste should be handled in an environmentally safe manner. In this regard, according to Article 17 of the Act, original waste producers or others holders are obliged:

> a) to carry out the treatment of waste himself or has the treatment handled by a dealer or an establishment or undertaking which carries out waste treatment operations or arranged by a private or public waste collector in accordance with the provisions of the Act; b) to provide all the information necessary for the proper treatment and disposal of waste to the authorised undertakings; c) to provide adequate information to the local entities in cases where the special characteristics of the waste may cause disruptions in transport, collection, recovery or disposal; d) to separate waste by types of materials, if such a requirement is established by an administrative regulation applicable to the specific stream of waste considered.

Furthermore, production, storage and management of waste activities are in certain cases subjected to a previous administrative control that may imply the need of obtaining an administrative permit as well as to comply with certain registration requirements. Articles 27, 28 and 29 of the Act 22/2011 deal with this specific matter, and, in general terms, reduce the number of cases where an administrative permit was required under the Act 10/1998. More specifically, for instance, producers of hazardous and non-hazardous waste exceeding 1,000 tonnes/year amount are subject to the requirement of prior notification in the Autonomous Community where they are located. This means to replace in these cases the previous system of authorization (under the Act 10/1998) by the current communication.

Article 17 establishes that the holder must put the waste at the local authorities' disposal for its recycling, recovery or disposal (in the terms of the applicable local ordinances). In any case, the collection, transport and disposal of waste constitute a public service within the jurisdiction of the local authority. Moreover, it has to be taken into consideration that the Act 10/1998 foresaw that since 1 January 2001, systems of selective collection of waste had to be implemented in towns whose population exceeds 5,000 habitants. This constituted a provision that enlarged the powers regarding waste management that the local authorities formerly held pursuant to Act 7/1985 on Basics of the Local Regime.

Article 3 n) defines 'manager' as any public or private person that carries out any operation involving waste management, whether a waste producer or not. In both cases, management operations should be carried out without endangering the public health and without using processes or methods that could harm the environment. Urban waste can be privately managed through a particular system, through participation in an existing management system (semi-private or semi public), or through economic contributions to public management systems. Delivery of domestic household waste for treatment will occur in the terms established by local ordinances. On the other hand, as far as non-hazardous commercial waste is concerned, Article 17.3 of the Act establishes that, in case that the treatment of waste is carried out by the producer itself, it must be demonstrated that the waste management operations are properly performed. In any case, the initial producer or other holder of non-hazardous commercial waste can manage waste treatment operations by using a public waste management system, if exists, in the terms established by the ordinances of the Local Authorities. The treatment of urban waste in Spain has traditionally been limited to landfill and incineration, with far less emphasis given to recycling, recovery and minimization. The concepts related to the production and management of urban waste have gradually changed, but, as a matter of fact, landfill, incineration and composting appear to be the common practice regarding waste.

The classification of the activities of landfills is established in RD 1481/2001 of 27 December which regulates the disposal of waste in landfills, modified by RD 105/2008, of 1 February, which in turn regulates the production and management of construction and demolition waste; RD 1304/2009, of 31 July, which regulates waste disposal by means of landfill; and RD 367/2010, of 26 March, which adapts the various environmental regulations to Act 17/2009, of 23 November, on free access to the activities and execution of services, Act 25/2009, of 22 December, which adapts various acts to the Act on free access to the activities and execution of services, and Ministerial Order AAA/661/2013, of 18 April, which modifies Annexes I, II and III of the RD 1481/2001.

This activity is excluded from the specific administrative authorization system. Disposal of urban waste by local entities in landfills is regulated under Act 16/2002 on IPPC. Nonetheless, the Spanish legislation regarding incineration has significantly progressed by applying the emission limit values of dioxins and furans established for the incineration of hazardous waste and for the incineration of urban waste by RD 653/2003 of 30 May, on Waste Incineration and Co-incineration, partially modified by RD 367/2010, of 26 March, and which transposes Directive 2000/76/EC.

161. Act 22/2011 imposes on the public administration the obligation of elaborating reliable statistics on the basis of the basic data on produced or managed waste all over the national. Title VI of the Act deals with information issues regarding waste. This article requires that the information, authorizations and registers provided by the Autonomous Communities should be incorporated into a single Waste Production and Management Register which will cover the whole of Spain. Even though the National Plan on Urban Waste does not lay down quantitative objectives for the reduction of waste production, it has at least included quantitative aims related both to waste recovery and the reduction of the amounts destined for final disposal. Article 25 establishes that by means of adequate financial, economic and fiscal measures, the prevention of waste production and the promotion of clean technologies, reuse, recycling and recovery activities should be furthered. In the same sense, Article 26 refers to setting up systems for the collection and recovery of waste as well as the promotion of markets for recycled products.

162. Finally, there are two aspects that have to be specially taken into consideration: On the one hand, together with the proximity principle which consists of disposing waste at the nearest appropriate installations, there is the self-sufficiency principle, that is, the establishment of an integrated and adequate network of disposal facilities. In this sense, the Act 22/2011 foresees the adoption of appropriate measures to establish an integrated and adequate network of waste disposal installations and of installations for the recovery of mixed waste collected from private households, including where such collection also covers such waste from other producers, taking into account best available techniques (Article 9.1). On the other hand, the public administration had to elaborate waste management plans at national, autonomous and local levels.

163. To understand what these aspects properly mean in the context of the Act 22/2011, it is necessary to have in mind that provisions regarding the planning of waste management were established for the first time by the Act 10/1998. Within the former legislation (Act 72/1975) there was no such provision regarding the planning of waste management.

Later, RDL 1163/1986 expressly obliged the State administration to elaborate a National Plan on Waste. However, this plan was never adopted.

164. The Act 10/1998 required the State administration to elaborate the National Plans, integrating the respective plans adopted by the Autonomous Communities. These National Plans (which are approved by the Council of Ministers) had to be revised every four years.

Likewise, Article 5 of the Act 10/1998 established the compulsory contents of the Autonomous Communities' plans as well as gives the local administrations the opportunity to elaborate their own urban waste management plans.

165. Pursuant to these provisions, the Ministry of Environment created the first National Plan on Urban Waste, approved by the Resolution of 13 January 2000, and which constitutes 'an aggregated synthesis of the existent Autonomous Communities' plans, complemented with national objectives' (cf. Ministry of Environment, National Plan on Urban Waste 2000–2006, 4).

The main goals pursued by the first National Plan can be summarized as follows: the closure of uncontrolled landfill sites; the adaptation of the waste management facilities to the requirements established by the Directive on landfill sites; the closure of incineration plants that do not recover energy; the reduction of waste production by up to 6%. Finally, it must be noted that the Ministry of Environment has also adopted national plans for certain specific urban waste: Waste from Construction and Demolition Works, End-of-Life Vehicles, Used Tyres, and Decontamination and Disposal of PCBs, PCT and the equipment that Contain them. The Spanish government finally approved the Resolution of 20 January 2009 regarding the Integrated National Waste Plan (PNIR) for the 2008–2015 period, which initially received a fund of EUR 23 million. This plan promotes the reduction, reuse and recycling of waste and sets out the following objectives: to stop the current growth in waste generation, to completely eliminate illegal tipping, to reduce dumping, to encourage the prevention, reuse and recycling of waste that can be recycled, to develop other mechanisms that give value to waste that cannot be recycled, to provide the country with new waste management infrastructures, to improve existing waste installations, and to eliminate waste that contributes to climate change. The second National Plan covers the same wastes that were defined in the first one and complements the other national waste plans. The following waste substances are included: hazardous household waste (certain glues, adhesives, paints, varnishes, solvents, insecticides, electrical and electronic waste, etc.), these substances being also included in the second National Hazardous Waste Plan (Annex 2); and batteries and accumulators for domestic use, these being included in the National Used Batteries and Accumulators Programme (Annex 8).

The Act 22/2011 establishes certain provisions concerning plans and programmes on waste management (whether at National, Autonomous Communities' or Local level). In this sense, Article 14 foresees the elaboration of a National Framework Plan regarding waste management, which will contain the General Strategy in waste policy, as well as the guidelines and basic structure of the Autonomous Communities' Plans. The National Framework Plan will establish the minimum objectives regarding prevention, preparation for reuse, recycling, recovery and disposal of waste. The provisions of the National Framework Plan (as well as the Autonomous Communities' Plans) must be consistent with the aims and objectives of the Strategy on the limitation of emissions of greenhouse gases, and the international commitments regarding climate change assumed by Spain. Plans and programmes must be assessed and revised at least every six years.

§2. Hazardous Waste

166. The exact quantity of industrial waste generated in Spain is unknown. Information supplied by the Autonomous Communities indicates that of the 60.4 million tonnes of industrial waste generated in 2005, almost 2.2 tonnes were classified as hazardous waste according to EU regulations. However, the handling of hazardous waste fell by almost 28% in 2009, according to a study carried out by the Association of Waste Handling and Specialist Resources Companies (ASEGRE).

Nevertheless, Spain had no specific legislation on hazardous waste management or a national policy on this matter until the middle 1980s. This matter was regulated for the first time by Act 20/1986 on Toxic and Hazardous Waste (except in the Autonomous Community of Catalonia, which has had its own legislation since 1983: Act 6/1983 of 7 April on Industrial Waste).The content of Act 20/1986 was supplemented by RD 833/1988 of 20 July, as modified by RD 952/1997 of 20 June.

which modified the Regulations for the Execution of Act 20/1986, of 14 May, on Toxic and Hazardous Waste, approved by Royal Decree 833/1988, of 20 July. Act 10/1998 on Waste completely replaced Act 20/1986 and partially replaced RD 833/1988, which is still applicable in some of its articles. RD 833/1988 has also been modified by RD 367/2010, of 26 March, which adapts various environmental regulations to Act 17/2009, of 23 November, on free access to the activities and execution of services, and by Act 25/2009, of 22 December, which adapts various acts to the Act on free access to the activities and execution of services.

167. Until the promulgation of Act 10/1998, Act 20/1986 defined 'hazardous waste' as 'any solid or sludge material, as well as liquid or gaseous materials in containers, resulting from any production, transformation, using or consuming process whose producer intends to discard, that contains any substance set out in the Annex in such quantity or concentration as could endanger human health, natural resources or the environment' (Article 2). The scope of Act 20/1986 was defined on the basis of the origin, form and state of the hazardous waste. Two criteria were established: qualitative (the waste should contain a substance listed in the Annex), and quantitative (the substance had to be present in such quantities or concentrations that could endanger human health, natural resources or the environment). However, Annex I of this Act did not contain any criterion to determine whether a certain quantity or concentration implied risk. RD 833/1988 partially solved this question by defining hazardous waste as waste that because of its content, presentation or other characteristics could be considered as hazardous waste in terms of the criteria now established in Annex I of RD 952/1997. As a last resort, waste could be classified as hazardous waste if and only if, it contained any of the substances listed in Table 4 and met any of the characteristics set out in Table 5. The Order of 13 October 1989 on Technical Methods for Classifying Waste completed the contents of this regulation. Later, RD 952/1997 also established a new dual system in order to characterize dangerous waste, and included the first five tables of RD 833/1988 and the Hazardous Waste European List (HWEL).

168. Act 10/1998 characterized dangerous waste on the basis of objective criteria. Finally, in the terms of Article 3 e) of the Act 22/2011, 'hazardous waste' is, first, the waste which displays one or more of the hazardous properties listed in Annex III of the Act. Waste is also deemed to be dangerous if it is so qualified by the European legislation. Dangerous waste is also any waste that the Government could decide to include in this category, according to the European legislation and the international conventions applying in Spain.

169. Regarding the production and management of dangerous waste, Act 22/2011 establishes certain specific provisions in addition to the general rules on waste production and management.

170. Uncontrolled abandonment, tipping or dumping of dangerous waste are not, of course, allowed. The Act 22/2011 establishes that producers of hazardous waste are subject to the requirement of prior notification in the Autonomous Community where they are located. Small producers of less than 1,000 tones/year are exempted from this obligation.

171. In general terms, producers of hazardous waste are obliged to elaborate and provide to the Autonomous Community's Administrations a report/study of minimization of the production of such type of waste. This report must include a commitment concerning the reduction of the production of dangerous waste. In any case, small producers (in the terms of the applicable administrative regulations) are exempted from this obligation. Producers of hazardous waste may be obliged to constitute financial guarantees in order to ensure eventual civil liability. The Act 22/2011 also imposes certain obligations concerning the information that the producer or holder of hazardous waste must provide in certain cases. In this sense, initial producers or holders of hazardous waste must inform immediately to the competent environmental public administrative authorities in case of disappearance, loss or release of hazardous waste or which by its nature or amount could damage the environment (Article 17). Finally, Article 17.6 of the Act foresees that producers or holders of hazardous waste must comply, additionally, with any other requirement that the administrative regulation on hazardous waste may establish.

172. Pursuant to the Act 21/2013, of 9 December, on Environmental Assessment, authorizing such installations also requires an EIA. RD 1254/1999 of 16 July, on prevention of major accidents in certain industrial undertakings or involving dangerous substances (which transposes Directive 96/82/EC), as modified by RD 119/2005, also applies to some of these installations (particularly to those disposing of liquid or solid substances by means of combustion or chemical decomposition).

173. Article 21 of the Act 10/1998 list the obligations imposed on the producer of dangerous waste. Besides the obligations to not mix and to adequately package and label dangerous waste, the producer must submit an annual report to the administration. This report should state the quantities and types of the waste produced during the one-year period, as well as their final destination. Small producers are exempted from this report obligation. The producer should also record the dangerous waste that is produced or imported. For the purpose of monitoring the disposal or recovery of dangerous waste, the Act establishes the duty to properly fill out the forms on the monitoring and control of transport of dangerous waste. If dangerous waste is managed off-site, the producer should be previously supplied with a written acceptation agreement from the receiving entity. This document should be kept at least for five years (although it is advisable to keep the document and the copies of the aforementioned forms until the closure of the establishment). The producer should also inform both the administration and the undertakings authorized to carry out waste management operations.

174. Pursuant to Article 3 of the Act, 'management' means the collection, storage (for a less than six-month period), transport, recovery and disposal of waste, including the supervision of such operations. In addition to the obligations to not mix dangerous waste and to package and label waste in an adequate way, and to maintain facilities in proper operating conditions, the manager must report its activities to the administration annually. The manager should also record all operations regarding waste management. The manager should also keep the written agreement on the acceptation of the dangerous waste, as well as the documents on the monitoring and control of the transport of dangerous waste. These documents should be kept at least for five years (although it is advisable to keep them until the closure of the establishment).

175. Besides the general duty of planning (materialized in the National Planning on Dangerous Waste 1995–2000, adopted by the Resolution of 28 April 1989), the State administration is responsible for the coordination of the policy on dangerous waste management, both at the national level and in relation to the EU; for the coordination of activities related to dangerous waste that affect more than one Autonomous Community; and for exercising the administration's punishing power. It must be noted that the Ministry of Environment revised the aforementioned National Plan on Dangerous Waste. This process lead to the adoption of the Plan for the period 2001–2006, which integrated different actions to be taken according to the different Autonomous Communities' plans. Finally, the aforementioned Resolution of 20 January 2009 approved the Integrated National Waste Plan for the 2008–2015 period. The Autonomous Communities (Articles 21 and 22 of the Act 10/1998) are responsible for granting administrative permits; for collecting and supervising the annual reports and the annual statements of both waste managers and producers; for keeping administrative waste registers; for monitoring and supervising activities; and for enforcement of the punishing regime.

176. Article 17 of the Act 10/1998 regulates the cross-boundary movement of dangerous waste. It simply contains a twofold reference: to the Basel Convention on the Control of the Disposal and Cross-Border Movements of Hazardous Waste (which came into effect in Spain in 1994), and to Council Regulation 259/93/EEC on the Supervision and Control of Shipments of Waste Within, Into and Out of the European Community.

Pursuant to Article 17 of the 10/1998 Act, both the State and the Autonomous Communities can prohibit shipments of waste into the national territory, when international or European legislation so foresees. The State administration can also limit the quantities of waste that can be imported. However, some problems regarding the distribution of powers between the State and the Autonomous Communities could arise in this framework.

§3. Packaging and Packaging Waste

177. The production, commercialization, using, recycling and refilling of packaging in Spain were formerly regulated by RD 319/1991 of 8 March, which complemented Act 42/1975.

It must be noted that this RD, presently abolished, was approved just a few months before the ECJ declared that Spain had failed to fulfil its obligations arising from Directive 85/339/EEC. The Directive 94/62/EEC brought about the need to establish a new legal regime on packaging and packaging waste in Spain.

The legal framework is currently given by Act 11/1997 of 24 April on Packaging and Packaging Waste (which transposes Directive 94/62/EC), RD 782/1998 of 30 April and the Order of 27 April 1998. Several regulations have later modified Act 11/1997: Act 10/1998, on Waste, and Acts 66/1997 of 30 December, 50/1998 of 30 December and 14/2000 of 29 December, on Tax, Fiscal, Administrative and Social Measures. It has also been affected by the Resolution of 30 September 1998, the Order of 21 October 1999 and the Order of 12 June 2001. The Act has also been modified by RD 252/2006, of 3 March, which reviews the recycling and assessment objectives. The RD also modifies the Regulations approved by RD 782/1998, Order MAM/3624/2006, of 17 November, which in turn modifies Annex 1 of the Regulations for the implementation and execution of Act 11/1997, and Order of 12 June 2001, which specifies the conditions regarding the non-application of heavy metal concentration levels to glass containers established in Article 13 of Act 11/1997. RD 252/2006 also partially adopts Directive 2004/12/CE.

178. Act 11/1997 covers all packaging and packaging waste. Article 2 of the Act 11/1997 defines ‘packaging’ as:

> all products made of any materials of any nature to be used for the containment, protection, handling, delivery and presentation of goods, from raw materials to processed goods, from the producer to the user or the consumer.
>
> Non-returnable items used for the same purpose are also deemed to be packaging. This concept only includes sales packaging or primary packaging, grouped packaging or secondary packaging and transport packaging or tertiary packaging.

Article 2 of RD 782/1998 includes in the concept of packaging ‘non-returnable bags given or purchased at the point of purchase for the user or consumer carrying goods. Non-returnable items used for the same purpose are also deemed to be packaging’. The concept of ‘packaging waste’ is defined in the following terms: ‘any packaging or packaging material which the holder discards or intends or is required to discard pursuant to the applicable legislation’. Act 11/1997 does not cover those items that the Annex I of RD 782/1998 excludes from the concept of ‘packaging’ (bags used for the purpose of collecting urban waste, shopping baskets, wrappers, envelopes, etc.).

179. For the purpose of limiting or reducing packaging disposal as far as possible, Article 1 of the Act 11/1997 establishes that the priority options to be taken regarding this matter shall be the prevention of the formation of packaging waste as well as the promotion of the reuse, recovery or recycling of packaging. Act 11/1997 foresees that both the State and the Autonomous Communities shall adopt the necessary measures on prevention and minimization. The following especially relevant measures should be taken into consideration. First, targets must be established regarding the prevention, recovery and recycling of packaging waste. These recycling and evaluation objectives are updated by RD 252/2006, which states that (a) from the date on which the RD comes into effect (5 March 2006), a minimum of 25% and a maximum of 45% of the total weight of packaging materials will be recycled, with a minimum of 15% of the weight of each packaging material; (b) before 31 December 2008, and in successive years, a minimum of 55% and a maximum of 80% of the total weight of packaging materials will be recycled; (c) before 31 December 2008, and in successive years, the following minimum recycling objectives will be achieved for packaging materials: 60% of the total weight of glass, 60% of the total weight of paper and cardboard, 50% of the total weight of metals, 22.5% of the total weight of those plastics (this referring exclusively to those that can be turned back into plastics) and 15% of the total weight of wood. Second, the contents of heavy metals present in packaging must be limited, and packaging must comply with certain technical requirements (packaging volume and weight shall be limited to the minimum adequate amount, the presence of toxic substances in packaging shall be reduced, etc.). Finally, the administrations should compromise on adopting measures regarding the use of noxious and hazardous substances in packaging materials, as well as on the use of PVC as packaging material.

180. Likewise, Article 17 foresees that within a one-year period from the enactment of the Act 11/1997, the State administration shall elaborate a National Plan on Packaging, Packaging Waste and Used Packaging. However, this Plan was adopted only in January 2000 (integrated into the National Plan on Urban Waste). Until then, the Plans adopted by the Autonomous Communities constituted the only planning activity on this matter.

181. Act 11/1997 sets up a return, collection and recovery of packaging and packaging waste system that follows the overall concepts of the German and French systems. However, the Spanish system appears to be more similar to the French system, which is based upon agreements between the industry and the administration.

It also links recycling to the restructuring and co-financing of the local entities' collection and treatment systems. That implies that the local entities play a major role regarding this subject (it must not be forgotten that they are the competent authorities for managing this service). In the same sense, Act 7/1985 on the Basics of the Local Regime confers on the municipal authorities the administrative powers regarding the collection of waste (which constitutes an essential service in every municipality).

Chapter IV of the Act 11/1997 deals with this matter. As a matter of fact, it outlines two different systems: (a) packaging shall be put on the market in such a way as to permit its return by means of consignment or deposit; (b) the economic agents can however be exempted from this obligation if they assume the responsibility of collecting packaging and packaging waste by means of voluntary agreements leading to integrated management systems.

182. As for point (a), Article 6 of the Act establishes the return and deposit system. Packaging converters and traders should charge the consumer a certain amount of money for every package that they have either put on the market or distributed. Once the package has been used, these economic agents must accept its return and repay the amount previously charged. The Order of 27 April 1998 establishes the symbol identifying the packaging that has been put on the market through a return and deposit system.

Packaging converters and traders for whom a specific legal regime exists are exempted from the system just described. In accordance with the Additional Provision I of the Act 11/1997, the following agents are exempted:

- Packaging converters and traders of commercial or industrial packaging, unless they decide to assume these obligations on a voluntary basis. Article 2 of the Act 11/1997 defines industrial or commercial packaging as those exclusively used and consumed by the industry, trade, services or agricultural and livestock exploitations, so that they are not appropriate for the ordinary use and consumption of households.
- Packaging converters and traders of reusable packaging – neither industrial nor commercial – for whom a specific return and deposit system has been established. Packaging converters and traders within the scope of the Orders of 31 December 1976 and 16 July 1979 (later modified by the Orders of 30 November 1981) regarding compulsory guarantees for packaging of beers, soft drinks and waters are so exempted from this system.

183. Regarding point (b), Articles 7–11 of the Act 11/1997 foresee the development of packaging and used packaging integrated management systems, which should ensure the achievement of the objectives regarding recycling and recovery in the terms of Article 5 of the Act, modified by RD 252/2006. These systems are based upon agreements between the economic agents operating in the specific sector, which should be supervised and approved by the respective Autonomous Community.

The packaging converters contribute financially to these systems for every package put on the market for the first time (depending on the different types of packaging). These systems aim to periodically collect used packaging and packaging waste from households, by means of collaboration agreements. The local entities (or subsidiarily the Autonomous Communities) carry out the selective collection of packaging and packaging waste covered by the system. Packaging covered by the system shall be marked for identification purposes.

The system ECOEMBES (integrating the system ECOACERO) joins together almost every sector involved – packaging converters, traders, distributors, recycling undertakings, etc. – and aims to cover all packaging materials. Likewise, the system ECOVIDRIO was developed in the framework of the glass sector. This system groups packaging converters using glass packaging, producers, distributors and importers of products packaged in glass, and recoveries.

§4. Other Waste

184. This section deals with some regulations transposing other European legislation on waste, and some actions undertaken with respect to the management of certain types of waste.

185. Directive 75/439/CEE, of 6 June 1975, on the management of used oils (subsequently modified by Council Directive 87/101/CEE, of 22 December 1986) was incorporated in the Spanish regulations by means of Order 28 February 1989, which regulates the management of used oils and which was in turn modified by the Order of 13 June 1990. Currently, Act 10/1998, of 21 April, on Waste and RD 679/2006, of 2 June, which regulate the management of used industrial oils provide the legal framework for regulating these waste products.

The RD establishes the regulations regarding the manufacture of industrial oils and stipulates that they must contain the lowest possible quantity of hazardous substances in order to reduce their environmental effect as far as possible. The RD also requires manufacturers to prepare prevention plans and includes measures regarding the production, possession and management of used oils whereby those who produce or own used oils must guarantee to hand them over to an authorized administrator for evaluation and disposal, unless they choose to manage the oils themselves. The RD states that those who own used oils must guarantee to handle them correctly by handing them over to manufacturers, who in turn are obliged to take responsibility for them and hand them over for correct management. To this effect, the RD establishes a series of priorities for the handling of used oils which favour reuse over all other methods, followed by other forms of recycling, the assessment of their energy value, and, finally, their disposal, which can only be carried out when none of the previous options is possible. At the same time, the RD establishes the specific ecological objectives of regeneration and evaluation.

186. As for PCBs, the Order of 14 April 1989 on Management of PCB and PCT transposed the Directive 76/403/EC on this matter. Because of the delay in the implementation of Directive 96/59/EC on the disposal of PCBs and PCTs, Spain was condemned by the ECJ judgment of 3 October 2002. That implied the abolition of the Order by RD 1378/1999, of 27 August on Disposal of PCBs and PCTs, which currently transposes Directive 96/59/EC and which was modified by RD 228/2006, of 24 February. It establishes measures applying to the disposal and management of PCBs and PCTs and any equipment that contains them. RD 1378/1999 made the State Administration responsible for creating the National Plan for the decontamination and disposal of PCBs and PCT, which was approved on 6 April 2001. Both RD 1378/1999 and the National Plan establishes 1 January 2011 as the deadline for decontaminating or eliminating certain transformers and other apparatus containing more than 5 dm3 of PCB. Apparatus containing less than 5 dm3 PCB is to be collected and disposed of as soon as possible. Likewise, RD 1378/1999 introduced measures regarding unused PCBs and apparatus that is in use, required owners to declare apparatus subject to inventory and to provide information on provisions they have made to decontaminate or dispose of it, and made the Autonomous Communities responsible for creating inventories to hold the data provided by owners. In addition, the Spanish Government adopted the Resolution of 9 April 2001, that approves the National Plan for Decontamination and Disposal of PCBs, PCT and the engines that contain them (2001–2010).

187. Of particular note among the modifications incorporated into RD 228/2006 is the requirement for owners to declare any apparatus subject to inventory, a distinction being made between data referring to apparatus made with PCB fluids, apparatus made with non-PCB fluids that have subsequently become contaminated with PCBs, and apparatus that may contain PCBs. The RD also stipulates new requirements for owners whereby they must inform the Autonomous Communities of their action plans and of any quantities that they have decontaminated or disposed of. Likewise, the authorities in charge of power stations and transformers are obliged to analyse dielectrics, oils and any apparatus that may contain PCBs and to pass their results onto the competent authorities of the Autonomous Communities

188. RD 45/1996 of 19 January on Batteries and Accumulators Containing Certain Dangerous Substances, as modified by the Order of 25 October 2000, incorporated the European legislation regarding this matter into Spanish law. This regulation aims to facilitate the evaluation or controlled disposal of used batteries and accumulators by establishing a series of measures, such as organizing effective systems for selective collection, limiting the use of batteries and accumulators to apparatus from which they can be easily extracted imposing labelling regulations, creating programmes and ensuring that consumers are fully informed about such measures. The National Plan on Used Batteries, adopted by Resolution of 25 November 1999 develops the contents of this RD. RD 45/1996 was subsequently replaced by RD 106/2008, of 1 February, regarding batteries and accumulators and the environmental management of waste, which in turn was modified by RD 943/2010, of 23 July.

189. RD 106/2006 implements Directive 2006/66/CE, of 6 September, into the Spanish regulations. This RD applies to batteries and accumulators for domestic, industrial and automotive use, and prohibits the sale of those that contain certain quantities of mercury or cadmium. A system of obligations is established for their sale and a schedule is set for collection targets regarding all three of the aforementioned types of battery and accumulator. Manufacturers of batteries and accumulators that are legally considered to be hazardous once they have been used must guarantee to comply with the RD's requirements by participating in a deposit and return system, an integrated management system or a public management system. The RD also requires the authorized entities to take part in the management of hazardous battery and accumulator waste. The text contains the technical instructions and conditions which must be adopted by treatment and recycling plants and the legal system for the authorization of these installations.

190. The Order of 28 July 1989 on the Prevention of Pollution Caused by Waste from the Titanium Dioxide Industry and the Order of 18 April 1991 establishing provisions for the reduction of pollution caused by waste from the titanium industry, transpose the European Directives regarding this matter.

191. The use for agricultural purposes of waste from waste water depuration plants is regulated by RD 1310/1990 of 29 October. This regulation (which almost literally transcribes the limit values fixed for heavy metals by Directive 86/278/

EEC) creates the National Register of Sludges, and establishes the obligations to be observed by the different economic agents and the administration.

The Order of 26 October 1993 develops the contents of this RD. The National Plan for the Purification of Waste Water Residues 2001–2006 was adopted by the Resolution of 14 June 2001.

192. In general terms, the Ministry of Industry and Energy holds jurisdiction on radioactive waste. This waste is managed by the National Company for Nuclear Waste (ENRESA), whose activities are regulated by RD 1349/2003, of 31 October. Among its functions, the collection, transport, treatment, storage and monitoring of radioactive waste generated in Spain, the dismantling of nuclear and radioactive facilities which are no long in use, the environmental restoration of uranium mines and research and development activities are emphasized.

Aspects related to radioactive waste movements were first regulated by RD 2088/1994 of 20 October (which implemented the 92/3/EURATOM Directive on the supervision and control of shipments of radioactive waste between Member States and into and out of the Community), according to the directives of the AEIA. This RD was replaced by RD 243/2009, of 27 February, which regulates the monitoring and control of the transport of radioactive waste and nuclear fuel between EU Member States or from and to destinations outside the EU. RD 243/2009 adopts Directive 2006/117/EURATOM into the Spanish internal regulations and aims to ensure that Spanish law is consistent with the Convention on the Security of Spent Fuel Management and on the Management of Radioactive Waste (Vienna, 5 September 1997), which Spain joined on 30 June 1998 and which EURATOM joined on 2 January 2006; and with Directive 2003/122/EURATOM, on the control of sealed highly radioactive sources and orphan sources, which was incorporated into Spanish law by RD 229/2006, of 24 February, on the control of encased highly radioactive sources and orphan sources.

193. The management of end-of-life vehicles is regulated by RD 1383/2002 of 20 December, which incorporates Directive 2000/53/CE into Spanish law. It was completed by the Order of 5 February 2004, which regulates the permanent expiration of registration for decontaminated vehicles at the end of their useful lives, which in turn has recently been substituted by the Order of 26 February 2008, which regulates the electronic administration of contaminated vehicles at the end of their useful lives. This Order implements the disposal certificate issued by the centres authorized to dispose of vehicles at the end of their useful lives. Based on the principle of producer responsibility, the RD fixes requirements for the product (Annex II) and return obligations. The Spanish government also adopted a National Plan on End-of-Life Vehicles (ELV) (2001–2006) by Resolution of 25 September 2001. Prior to this Plan several Autonomous Communities had already approved their own regional plans on ELV, namely Andalucía, Basque Country and Navarra.

194. It should also be pointed out that RD 1619/2005, of 30 December, on the management of used tyres, requires tyre manufacturers to create company plans which identify manufacturing processes that prolong the useful life of tyres and that help used tyres to be reused and recycled at the end of their useful lives. Manufacturers are required to take responsibility for managing the waste derived from their products and for ensuring that it is collected and handled in accordance with the principles established in Act 10/1998. The RD also determines the legal system for managing such waste, in particular collection, transport and storage, in conjunction with RD 1383/2002. Furthermore, the application of RD 1481/2001, which regulates the disposal of waste through landfill, prohibited the disposal of shredded tyres in landfills from 16 June 2006.

195. As for electric and electronic waste, RD 208/2005 of 25 February has transposed Directives 2002/95/EC, 2002/96/EC and 2003/108/EC in the Spanish legal system. The RD establishes some restrictions measures from 1 July 2006. The RD establishes preventative measures aimed at limiting the use of hazardous substances in the design and manufacturer of electric and electronic apparatus. It also specifies that electric and electronic apparatus should be managed to minimize the effect of these substances on the environment, placing particular emphasis on those occurring in household waste given that this forms the highest percentage of all electrical and electronic waste. The RD has been modified by RD 1436/2010, of 5 November, which adapts various RD to Directive 2008/112/CE, and RD 367/2010, of 26 March, which adapts various environmental regulations to Act 17/2009, of 23 November, on free access to the activities and execution of services, and Act 25/2009, 22 December, which adapts various acts to the Act on free access to the activities and execution of services.

Chapter 5. Soil Pollution

§1. Preventive Action

196. The Spanish administration has only recently developed policies concerning the protection of soil against pollution caused by industrial activities, uncontrolled landfills or accidental discharges. Articles 27 and 28 of Act 10/1998 of 21 April on Waste constituted the first piece of legislation that outlined the basics upon which the policies regarding soil pollution might be based. This regulation was completed with the adoption of RD 9/2005 of 14 January, which establishes the list of activities that could potentially contaminate the soil and the criteria and standard for the declaration of contaminated soils. Finally, the Act 22/2011 on waste and contaminated soils, which implements Directive 2008/98/ CE, establishes a new legal framework for the management of contaminated land, and specifies the distribution of competencies between the State and the Autonomous Communities.

There are several reasons – such as the lack of a long-term vision – that could explain why Spanish policies on this matter have been adopted so late. As a matter of fact, the low awareness of these problems shown by the administration from the 1960s to the latter 1980s as well as the preponderance of the economic development objectives over the environmental concerns is likely reasons for this persistent delay. These elements led to an anarchic industrial growth with no care shown to the problems that could arise in the long-term.

In the late 1980s, the State and Autonomous Communities began to pay more attention to soil pollution. Since then, the protection of soils against pollution as well as the restoring of polluted soils has been the main target of the national plans on toxic and hazardous waste. The Autonomous Communities also have enforcement powers regarding actions on polluted soils located in their respective territories. Thus, for example, the Basque Government has adopted Act 1/2005, of 4 February, on the prevention and correction of contaminated land, and Decree 165/ 2008, of 30 September, on the creation of an inventory of land that is used or has been used for potentially contaminating activities or installations, and the Government of the Canary Islands passed Decree 147/2007, of 24 May, which established the legal system for contaminated land and created the Inventory of Contaminated Land of the Canary Islands.

197. Article 3 of Act 22/2011 defines polluted soils as those soils whose physical, chemical or biological characteristics have been degraded by dangerous compounds from human origin, which are present in such concentrations as to endanger the human health or the environment in accordance with the standards and criteria to be determined by the Government. Article 2 of RD 9/2005 sets the definition of contaminated soil and makes reference to the presence of harmful chemical substances and substances of human origin that can alter the chemical, physical or biological characteristics of the soil that may imply a risk having to be quantified in order to estimate the possible damage that they may cause to human health and the environment.

In addition, it is worth noting that RD 9/2005 has set general reference levels, a basic parameter used for the assessment of soil contamination by certain substances which are grouped by harmfulness to human health (in Annex V) and to ecosystems (in Annex VI). In its Annex VII, the criteria for calculating reference levels of those substances not included in Annexes V and VI are specified as well as for the valuation of contamination by metals.

However, the provisions of Act 22/2011 concerning polluted soils (Title V) mainly refer to the applicable legal regime and liability questions rather than to preventive actions. It is therefore necessary to turn to other provisions contained in different Titles of the same Act, as well as to other directly or indirectly linked environmental legislation aiming at a higher level of soil protection, in the planning and regulating of human activities affecting the soil.

198. Act 22/2011 prohibits the uncontrolled abandonment, tipping or dumping of wastes, as well as requires the adoption of the appropriate measures addressed to preserve and restore soils if soil pollution was either suspected or proved. The Act also establishes that waste management operations should be carried out in such a way as to ensure that the final destination of wastes does not endanger the soil. Regarding this precise purpose, the Act establishes that any installation or enterprise producing or managing wastes should previously obtain an administrative authorization from (or carry out a communication procedure in front of) the competent authority of the Autonomous Community.

199. In particular, it is necessary to turn to the legal regime applying to dangerous waste management facilities, as explained before. Article 17 of the Act also requires to contract compulsory civil liability insurance and to deposit a guarantee for the purpose of securing all the administrative obligations deriving from these activities. The civil liability insurance shall at least cover compensations for death, damage or disease caused to human persons. Compensations for damages to goods, as well as the costs of reparation and recovery of environmental damages, should also be covered by this civil liability insurance. The administration sets the quantitative limit of civil liability when granting the permit. The guarantee deposit at least allows the administration to partially recover any costs deriving from restoring actions.

Pursuant to the Act 21/2013, of 9 December, on Environmental Assessment, authorizing such installations also requires an EIA. It constitutes one of the most efficient ways to prevent environmental damage, since this legal proceeding takes into consideration every effect that the projected activity or installation is likely to cause.

200. The legislation applying to surface and underground watercourses also has an indirect impact on the preservation of the quality of the soil, given that it contains provisions on discharges of certain dangerous substances into the waters. Act 29/85 of 2 August on Water, and RD 849/1986 of 11 April on the Hydrological Public Domain substantially affect soil protection, since they include among their objectives the prevention of the subsoil accumulation of toxic or dangerous compounds capable to cause underground water pollution. These norms also aim to impede any other action that could cause water degradation. For these purposes, the following actions are prohibited: the accumulation of solid wastes or substances, irrespective of their nature and the place where they are dumped, that implies or could imply risk of pollution of the waters or their surroundings; activities in the physical or biological environment linked to the waters (hydrological public domain) which will degrade or threaten to degrade it; and carrying out certain activities within protected areas declared in the respective Hydrological Plan, where such could imply a risk of pollution or degradation of the hydrological public domain.

201. Urban planning also constitutes a suitable framework within which an appropriate policy regarding the protection of the quality of the soil can be developed, by means of establishing an adequate legal regime in accordance with the social function of the soil. For the purpose of protecting the quality of the soil, RDL 1/1992 of 26 June on the Legal Regime of Land and Urban Planning, establishes the legal regime applying to the soil on a twofold basis: the situation and the land use (urban land, land that may be urbanized, and land that may not be urbanized). According to this RDL, land-use planning should mark the location and the characteristics of the centres and services of public interest, as well as ensure that land uses are in accordance with the public interest and the social function of property rights. The action of the public administration has to prohibit and prevent those land uses that do not match the provisions established by the plans. Properly planning land uses and strictly controlling the fulfilment of the provisions of the plans, both constitute an appropriate way to protect the quality of the soil.

§2. Corrective Action

202. Pursuant to Article 35 of Act 22/2010 on Waste and contaminated soils, the Autonomous Communities are responsible for the identifying and elaboration of an inventory of polluted areas, as well as for adopting administrative decisions declaring an area to be an 'area affected by soil pollution' (Article 34). In principle, an area could be declared as affected by soil pollution if any activity that is likely to cause soil pollution had been carried out within it. A list of activities liable to cause soil contamination is included in Annex I of RD 9/2005. In addition, Article 3 of the RD requires the holders of those activities to send a preliminary report for each of the soils affected by the activity to the competent body of the Autonomous Community within a period of no more than two years (February 2007). However, soils of public holding on which military installations are located or on which military activities are carried out are excluded from the scope of application of the RD.

According to RD 9/2005, soil will be declared contaminated through the express resolutions of the Autonomous Community, if in accordance with the standards and criteria established in Annexes III, IV, V, VI, VII and VIII, that risk is considered unacceptable for human health and the environment. Likewise, the Autonomous Communities should define a list of priority actions to be undertaken as well as determine the terms and the way in which cleaning-up and restoring operations will be carried out. Once the success of these last operations are assessed, the Autonomous Communities may declare that the area has become non-affected by soil pollution area.

203. Some Autonomous Communities had undertaken certain actions on this matter even before Act 10/1998 was enacted (as for instance, the Autonomous Communities of Catalonia, the Basque Country and Madrid). The Basque Country in the early 1990s proceeded to the identification of uncontrolled landfills for planning purposes. As for Catalonia, the administrative body dealing with waste has for several years been implementing programmes on the detection of polluted soils by means of regional campaigns. In Madrid, the Combined Action Plan of the Environmental Service includes among its objectives the study of polluted soils that need restoring actions, as well as the establishment of a polluted soils control system.

204. Regarding the cleaning-up and restoration of these soils, the polluter appears to be the person responsible to carry out such operations (once he has been required to do so by the Autonomous Community's competent authority). Subsidiarily, the holders of polluted soils and the non-holder owners of polluted soils (in this specific order) must undertake these actions (Article 36 of the Act 22/2011). These operations can be carried out by means of voluntary agreements between the aforementioned persons, or by means of collaboration agreements concluded between them and the public administration.

The owners of lands where polluted soils had been identified should state this fact in any transfer deed of the land (Article 33.2 of the Act 22/2011). Article 8 of RD 9/2005 sets the manner in which proof will be introduced in the Property Registry of administrative resolutions on the declaration of contaminated soil and of those carried out by land owners who carry on potentially contaminating activities on their lands. That puts into effect the legal provision which requires the formal title in whose name the side note has been issued, its content, effects, and duration and cancellation requirements. However, these provisions do not apply to creditors who as a result of a process of execution have become owners of polluted soils, on condition that they transfer the ownership of the land within a one-year period from the date on which they became owners. The assessment of damages caused to the human health or the environment is made by the administration after hearing the interested persons' allegations. If the estimation presents difficulties and the applicable legislation does not provide for specific criteria Annex III of RD 9/2005 establishes the following criteria:

(1) When the protection of human health is the priority:
   (a) that the concentration in the soil of any of the substances listed in Annex V exceeds 100 or more times the generic reference levels established in the Annex for the protection of human health, according to its use;
   (b) that the concentration in the soil of any chemical contaminant no listed in Annex V for that soil exceeds 100 or more times the generic reference level calculated in accordance with the criteria established in Annex VII.
(2) When the protection of ecosystems is the priority:
   (a) that the lethal or median effective concentration for soil organisms obtained in toxicity testing is inferior to 10 mg of contaminated soil per gram of soil;
   (b) that the lethal or median effective concentration carried out with leachates obtained by the regulated procedure DIN-38414, is inferior to 10 ml of leachates per litre of water.

In any case, according to RD 9/2005, the extent of recovery operations will be such that they ensure that the remaining contamination, if there is any, is left at acceptable risk levels for the current and forecasted use of the land. On the other hand, pursuant to Article 7 of RD 9/2005, the recovery of contaminated soil will be carried using the best available techniques according to the characteristics of each case. The recovery operations must ensure that permanent solutions are brought forth, prioritizing, as much as possible the treatment techniques in place that avoid the generation, transfer and elimination of wastes. When complete recovery of contaminated soil is not possible, recovery solutions whose purpose is to reduce exposure may be accepted when they include means of confinement or containment of the affected soils. In any case, a soil will no longer be considered contaminated for a particular use once an administrative resolution declaring it new status is accepted based on inspection of the affectivity of the recovery operations carried out.

Chapter 6. Noise Pollution

205. Noise pollution caused by traffic, industry and recreational activities appears to be one of the most serious environmental problems in Spanish towns, whose population is quite frequently exposed to noise emissions exceeding 65 dB(A). Despite this situation, Spain had not adopted any basic act on noise pollution until 2003, when Act 37/2003 of 17 November on Noise adopted Directive 2002/49/CE on the evaluation and management of environmental noise into Spanish law.

206. The Act provides a somewhat broader definition of noise pollution than the Directive, and includes the presence of noises or vibrations in the environment, no matter what their origin is, which may cause irritation, risk or harm to people, to their activities, or to goods of any nature, including when they disturb the enjoyment of sounds of natural origin, or when they cause significant effects to the environment. According to Article 2, the Act is applied to 'all acoustic emitters, whether private or public, as well as structures in terms of their role as acoustic receptors'. Noise pollution stemming from domestic activities and from neighbours, if it does not exceed tolerable limits in accordance with local use, are not included under the Act's scope of application. Noise pollution produced in the workplace will continue to be governed by the applicable sectorial regulation and is not regulated in the Act.

The Act legislates on a variety of acoustic areas, according to the predominant use of the land. The defining of types of acoustic areas has been left to the Autonomous Communities (Article 7). However, the Act establishes three specific types of acoustic area: 'noise abatement areas' (areas containing railways, ports, airports, etc.) (Article 10); 'special acoustic protection areas' (Article 25), and 'natural sound reserves' (Article 21), which can be delimited by the Autonomous Communities. The Government must set the acoustic quality objectives for every type of acoustic area, all over Spain, in such a way that it ensures a certain level of protection against noise pollution. The Government will also establish the quality objectives to be applied to habitable interior spaces of buildings.

Chapter III of the Act clarifies the instruments to be used in order to best fulfil the established acoustic quality objectives. In terms of preventive measures, the Act refers to land use and urban planning, administrative intervention of acoustic emitters, the self-monitoring of acoustic emissions by their producers, and the prohibition of granting construction licenses. In terms of corrective measures, the law stipulates the declaration of 'special acoustic protection zones' and 'special acoustic situation zones', and the adoption of regional improvement plans. The Act stipulates as well some intermediary instruments which could be either preventative or corrective: the creation of noise maps (which must be presented between 30 June 2007 and 30 June 2012) and action plans on the issue of noise pollution (which must be presented between 18 July 2008 and 18 July 2013).

Finally, Chapter IV of the Act introduces the general system of penalties and sanctions. These sanctions range from EUR 600 to EUR 300,000, and imply the possibility of the suspension or withdrawal of authorization and the temporary cessation of business activity.

207. RD 1513/2005, of 16 December, implements that part of Act 37/2003 that covers the evaluation and management of environmental noise, and RD 1367/2007, of 19 October, implements the part of the Act that refers to noise zoning, quality targets and noise emissions. Together, both texts fully implement Directive 2002/49/CE into Spanish law.

RD 1513/2005 specified the concepts of environmental noise and its effects on the population, together with a series of measures to achieve the RD's objectives, such as the creation of strategic noise maps and action plans, and the provision of information regarding these issues. The RD understands 'noise pollution' to be 'undesired or harmful external noise generated by human activities, including noise emitted by transport, road, rail and air traffic and industrial sites such as those described in Annex I of Act 16/2002, 1 July, on the integrated prevention and control of pollution'. It also incorporates other definitions such as the noise map (which presents data on an existing or foreseen acoustic situation in terms of a noise index that shows to what extent any relevant and binding noise limit is being exceeded, the number of people affected in a specific zone or the number of residences exposed to certain noise levels in a specific areas'), the strategic noise map (which is a 'noise map designed to evaluate overall noise exposure in a given zone resulting from different sources of noise, or used to make overall predictions for the zone') and noise disturbance ('the level of disturbance that noise causes to a population, determined by surveys taken in the zone').

RD 1367/2007 defines the indices of noise and vibrations (the LAmax for evaluating maximum noise levels), and how these indices are to be applied (according to the Annexes of RD 1513/2005 and the Annexes of RD 1367/2007). It also defines the effects and disturbance the noise has on the population and the environment. Likewise, the RD defines the different types of acoustic area, these definitions being adopted by the Autonomous Communities when classifying areas according to noise levels. These acoustic areas must include: (a) predominantly residential zones, (b) predominantly industrial zones, (c) zones predominantly used for performances and recreational purposes, (d) zones used for purposes not defined in the previous section, (e) zones predominantly used for health, educational or cultural purposes that require special protection from noise pollution, (f) zones affected by general transport infrastructures or other public machinery, and (g) natural spaces the require special protection from noise pollution. Likewise, the RD defines noise abatement areas as those:

> that are designed to make the functioning or development of road, rail, air or port infrastructures compatible with land use, activities, installations or buildings, or that can be applied to zones that are affected by noise originating from such infrastructures.

Table A of Annex II of the RD also establishes the noise quality targets for every existing urban area (between 50 and 75 Ln according to the area), Table B of the same Annex includes the noise level targets for the internal space of certain buildings (between 35 and 45 Ln according to use).

208. Likewise, some Autonomous Communities (as for instance Catalonia and the Balearic Islands) have approved a municipal standard ordinance on noise pollution that can be totally or partially adopted by the local authorities depending on their own needs. Such standard ordinances establish recommended outdoor and indoor guide values on the basis of the different moments of the day and noise sensitive areas. Levels from 50 dB(A) (during the night) to 70 dB(A) (diurnal) are established for outdoor areas, and values from 25 dB(A) (during the night) to 40 dB(A) (diurnal) are fixed for indoor environments. In addition, some municipalities (e.g., Madrid and Barcelona) have already undertaken actions to face the problems related to noise pollution, mainly from traffic sources.

209. RD 1367/2007 regulates noise emitters by fixing emission and reception levels and the procedures and methods for evaluation noise and vibrations.

210. Accordingly, motor vehicles must comply with previously approved noise levels. The maximum noise level for a motor vehicle is obtained by adding 4 dB(A) to the vehicle's stationary noise level as specified in the vehicle's technical specification document, this level being evaluated in accordance with the procedure applicable to the vehicle. Motor vehicles to be used by the emergency services must be equipped with a mechanism that reduces their noise levels to between 70 and 90 dB(A) when measured from a distance of 3 m and in the direction of maximum noise so that they can circulate through residential areas at night.

211. Recreational craft with inboard motors or mixed motors without an integrated exhaust, jetboats, outboard motors and mixed motors with an integrated exhaust must be designed, constructed and assembled in such a way that their noise levels do not exceed those established in Royal Decree 2127/2004, of 29 October, which regulated the safety requirements of recreational craft and jetboats and the components and noise levels of their motors.

212. Civil subsonic aircraft whose maximum mass on take-off is equal to or greater than 34,000 kg, or whose certified internal capacity is greater than nineteen passengers require a noise certificate in compliance with the regulations of the International Civil Aviation Convention. RD 1422/1992 of 27 November on Limitation of the Use of Civil Subsonic Aeroplanes (which transposes Directive 92/14/EC) and RD 1257/2003, of 3 October, on Procedures for the Introduction of Restrictions related to Airports (which transposes Directive 2002/30/EC), restricts the access of civil subsonic airplanes and similar aircraft to civil airports which have more than 50,000 movements from such aircraft per natural year.

213. Machinery used in outdoor activities, public works and construction in particular must comply with the current legislation regarding noise levels from machinery used outdoors. Such machinery therefore needs to satisfy legal requirements regarding noise emissions before they can be sold. Appliances should first be submitted for type approval and certification, which is carried out by the AENOR. RD 212/2002, of 22 February, which regulates noise emission from outdoor machinery, adopts Directive 2000/14/CE, of 8 May, regarding the convergence of EU Member

States' legislation on noise emissions from outdoor machinery, which aims to harmonize permitted noise emissions from outdoor machinery in order to eliminate obstacles to the free circulation of this machinery throughout the EU.

214. New road, rail and airport infrastructures must adopt the necessary measures so that their noise emissions to the corresponding noise areas do not exceed the levels established in the RD. All new industrial, port, commercial, storage, sports or leisure installations, establishments or activities must take the necessary measures so that their noise emissions to the corresponding noise areas do not exceed the levels established in the RD.

215. Workplace environment. Legislation on occupational safety and hygiene aims to ensure the highest possible level of protection for workers, in order to prevent health damage caused by certain continuous or punctual activities. Besides the applicable international legislation – particularly the ILO Convention No. 148, ratified by Spain on 24 November 1980 – Act 31/1995, of 8 November, on prevention of labour risks and RD 1316/1990 of 27 October on the Protection of the Workers against Risks Deriving from Exposure to Noise during the Work Time may be mentioned.

Chapter 7. Radiation

§1. PREVENTION OF MAJOR ACCIDENTS

216. RD 886/1988 of 15 July on Prevention of Major Accidents in Certain Activities, as modified by RD 952/1990, of 29 July, transposed the Directive 82/501/EEC (Seveso I). RD 1254/1999 of 16 July on the Control of Major Accident Hazards Involving Dangerous Substances, abolished the former regulation and transposed Directive 96/82/EEC (Seveso II).

RD 1254/1999 is applied to those establishments in which hazardous substances are present in equal or superior quantities to those specified in Annex 1. However, the system of exceptions in its scope of application is very important and has been extended by RD 119/2005, of 4 February, and RD 948/2005, of 29 July. The RD is not applicable to military establishments, installations or storage areas; risks or accidents caused by ionizing radiation; the transport of hazardous substances via roads, train lines, interior, maritime or aerial navigable routes including temporary in-route storage, loading and unloading activities and transport to or from docks, quays, or qualified train stations; the transport of hazardous substances by pipeline, including pump stations; mining and mineral exploitation activities in mines and quarries or through drilling, except for thermal and chemical treatment activities and storage related to those operations in which hazardous substances are used such as those in Annex I; off-shore exploration and extraction of minerals, including hydrocarbons; waste dumps with the exception of facilities dealing with mine waste disposal, including waste ponds and embankments which contain harmful substances such as those listed in Annex I, and in particular when they are used in relation with the thermal and chemical treatment of minerals; and the establishments regulated by the Regulations of Explosives, passed by RD 230/1998 of 16 February.

RD 1254/1999 was developed by RD 1196/2003 of 19 September. That RD approved the basic civil protection guidelines for planning and monitoring to combat the risk of serious accidents involving hazardous substances. Those guidelines constitute the technical regulatory instrument for the execution of the obligations, responsibilities and jurisdiction that RD 1254/1999 assigns to both the holders of establishments as well as the official administrations responsible for risk prevention and control activities. The extent to which RD 1196/2003 repealed the basic guidelines made it necessary to adopt the new RD 119/2005 of 4 February and RD 948/2005, of 29 July in order to adapt RD 1254/1999 to the new situation.

217. The Ministry of Internal Affairs is the competent authority for gathering the necessary data to elaborate the catalogue of activities that are likely to cause emergency situations. This ministry is also the competent authority to assess the information on accidents that took place within the national territory and to notify them to the EC; to examine the external emergency plans elaborated by the Autonomous Communities; to propose to the National Commission of Civil Protection the approval of these plans; and to conduct the execution of these plans in those cases in which the accident has consequences beyond the national territory.

218. The Autonomous Communities receive and evaluate the compulsory notifications from the industrial operators, assess, approve and apply the external emergency plans (in collaboration with the State and local administrations), promote self-protection, and ensure the elaboration of the internal emergency plans. In general terms, the municipalities elaborate the municipal action plan, as well as coordinate and conduct the implementation of the measures foreseen in the external emergency plan.

219. Likewise, the industrial installations must comply with certain requirements specified by Act 2/1985 on Civil Protection. Basically, they should elaborate an internal emergency plan for the installation, which constitutes a basic element for the elaboration of the external emergency plan by the Autonomous Community. In this respect, it is also necessary to mention the Civil Protection Basic Standard (approved by RD 407/1992 of 24 July). This standard aims to establish the criteria to be followed by the diverse planning actions, as well as the criteria for the homologation of the different emergency plans. This regulation is complemented by RD 1468/2008, which modifies RD 393/2007, regarding self-protection in centres, establishments and buildings dedicated to activities that can lead to emergency situations, RD 2267/2004, of 3 December, which approves the safety regulations against fires in industrial establishments, and RD 903/2010, of 9 July, regarding the evaluation and management of flood risk.

220. Finally, the provisions on industrial safety established by Act 21/1992 of 16 July – particularly those contained in its Title III – must also be taken into account. According to this Act, industries are considered activities dedicated to the acquisition, repair, maintenance, transformation or reuse of industrial products, containers or packaging, as well as the use, recovery and disposal of wastes or bi-products, no matter what the nature of the resources or technical processes used. Furthermore, engineering, design, technological consulting and technical assistance directly related to industrial activities are also included under its scope of application. The Act considers as hazards related to the industrial activity those activities that can cause damage to the population, flora, fauna, goods or environment. In particular, it mentions fires, explosions and other events capable of causing fire-burns, intoxication, poisoning, asphyxia, electrocution, risk of pollution from industrial plants, electromagnetic disturbances and radiation, as well as any other event that could be considered a hazard in the international legislation applying to industrial safety. Basically, the Act requires the industrial installations to adopt the necessary measures to prevent and limit industrial hazards, specifically by means of safety plans covering the overall industrial undertaking, installations, production processes and safety regulations.

§2. Energy

221. There are currently eleven nuclear plants in Spain (Almaraz I and II, Ascó I and II, Cofrentes, José Cabrera, Sta. María de Garoña, Trillo I and Vandellós II, plus two plants related to atomic energy production: Juzbado and El Cabril). In this respect, Act 25/1964 of 29 April on Nuclear Energy – partially amended by Act 40/1994 of 30 December – regulates the peaceful use of nuclear energy throughout the national territory. For this purpose, the Act defines the competent authorities, specifies the protection and safety precautions to be taken against ionizing radiation, establishes the civil liability from nuclear damages, as well as defines the nuclear hazard which is covered by it, the role of the State in the restoring of nuclear damages. A new penalties scheme was introduced by Act 54/1997. Pursuant to Act 15/1980 of 22 April creating the Council of Nuclear Safety, radioactive installations were still sub-divided in installations of the First, Second and Third Categories. Plants for manufacturing uranium and industrial irradiators are installations of the First Category. Installations authorized to use radionuclides without limiting their activity, accelerators and X-ray generators whose maximum voltage is higher than 200 kV are included in the Second Category. Finally, the Third Category covers installations that can use radionuclides in a limited quantity and X-ray installations not included in the Second Category.

222. RD 1836/1999 of 3 December on Nuclear and Radioactive Installations distinguishes between nuclear and radioactive installations. Both types of installations must be recorded in the Radioactive Installations Registry within the General Directorate of Energy. The following establishments are deemed to be 'nuclear installations': nuclear plants, nuclear reactors, and establishments manufacturing, treating, using or storing nuclear substances. Installations where ionizing radiation sources are situated, apparatus with a voltage higher than 5 kV emitting ionizing radiation, and sites, laboratories or plants manufacturing, processing or storing radioactive substances are deemed to be 'radioactive installations'. The liberalization of the electric market has meant the update of RD 1836/1999 by RD 35/2008 of 18 January 2008, in particular to ensure that it covered safety at nuclear power stations. For this reason, the new RD now requires nuclear power station authorities to ensure that they continually adopt the new techniques that will allow them to manage the power station in accordance with the latest safety requirements. Likewise, the RD establishes mechanisms for working in conjunction with the competent Administrations to authorize installations and activities whose location and nature may affect first category nuclear or radioactive installations. The RD requires the authorities to adopt procedures to ensure that companies contracted to by installation, external companies that work at the installation and the staff of the installation comply with the requirement to make the installation's authorities aware of any incident that affects or may affect the safe functioning of the installation and that they comply with the current regulations regarding nuclear safety and radiation protection.

223. The Nuclear Safety Council, created by Act 15/1980, is the competent body for nuclear safety in Spain. The Act's contents have been modified on several occasions, and have been brought up to date and in line with the requirements of Aarhus Convention by Act 33/2007, of 7 November. In accordance with the Act, the Nuclear Safety Council was created as 'a Public Law entity that is independent of the General State Administration, with legal personality and its own assets independent of those of the State, and is the sole competent body on questions of nuclear security and radiation protection' (Article 1 Act 15/1980, modified by Act 33/2007).

Its general functions consist of proposing to the Government the necessary regulations on questions of nuclear safety and radiation protection, along with any revisions it believes to be necessary; presenting reports to the Ministry of Industry, Tourism and Commerce on nuclear safety, radiation protection and physical protection prior to the concession of authorizations; carrying out all necessary inspections of nuclear and radioactive installations and transport; inspecting and monitoring nuclear and radioactive installations throughout their active lives and during their closure; setting in motion any disciplinary proceedings that it considers necessary; collaborating with the competent authorities in radiation protection programmes; awarding and revoking the authorizations given to entities and companies that provide services in the field of radiation protection; and reporting on and assessing the public authorities regarding the issues for which it is responsible (Article 2 of Act 15/1980, modified by Act 33/2007). Act 33/2007 also strengthens the role of the Nuclear Safety Council in the ambit of physical protection from materials and nuclear and radioactive installations and, in order to guarantee the necessary independence, it specifies the requirements that must be fulfilled when external services are contracted. In addition, to protect themselves from future disciplinary action, the Act requires workers at nuclear installations to report any incident that may affect the safe functioning of the installations. Finally, the Act establishes an Evaluation Committee to act as an assessment and consultative body. This committee will be open to participation by representatives of the institutional, territorial, scientific, technical, business, union and environmental ambits, whose mission will be to pass on recommendations to the Nuclear Safety Council in order to improve transparency, access to information and public participation in the areas that fall within its remit.

It should be noted that the Council for Nuclear Safety has concluded agreements with several Autonomous Communities under which the Council partially transferred its competencies on radiological protection of radioactive installations and granting licenses for the operating staff.

224. The authorizations required for nuclear and radioactive installations vary, depending on the category in which the specific establishment is classified. A summary of the legal provisions on this matter follows:

- Nuclear installations: authorization of sitting, construction, exploitation, modification, execution of modifications, temporary storage, change of the operator, and dismantlement. To close a nuclear installation it is also necessary to obtain a closure declaration (introduced by RD 1836/1999).
- Radioactive installations of the First Category (following the classification laid down by Act 15/1980), and radioactive installations intended for scientific, medical, agricultural, commercial or industrial purposes: authorization of placement, construction, exploitation, dismantlement and closure declaration (and authorization of modification and change of the operator where relevant).

- Radioactive installations of the Second and Third Categories (following the classification laid down by Act 15/1980): authorization for putting into service, closure declaration (and authorization of modification and change of the operator where relevant).

Management of radioactive wastes was regulated by RD 2088/1994 of 20 October, which transposed Directive 92/3/EURATOM, on the Monitoring of Transport of Radioactive Wastes among Member States or originating in or going to destinations outside the European Community, and Order of 21 May 2003, on Management of Solid Waste with Radioactive Content generated in radioactive facilities of the second and third category in which unsealed radioactive isotopes are manipulated or stored. The revision of this Directive by Directive 2006/117/EURATOM, of 20 November 2006, regarding the monitoring and control of the movement of radioactive waste and spent nuclear fuel meant that Spanish law had to be brought up to date by RD 243/2009, of 27 February, which regulates the monitoring and control of the movement of radioactive waste and spent nuclear fuel between EU Member States and to and from destinations outside the EU.

Directive 96/29/EURATOM establishes the basic regulations for protecting the health of workers and the general population against risks resulting from ionizing radiation, and is applied to, among other activities, the transport to, from and within the EU of radioactive substances. This Directive has been incorporated into Spanish Law by means of the aforementioned RD 1836/1999 (modified by RD 35/2008), and by RD 783/2001, which contains the Regulations on the protection of health from ionizing radiation.

225. In addition, the Council for Nuclear Safety monitors every activity carried out in nuclear plants that could affect the nuclear safety and radiological protection. In this sense, the Council can give the technical instructions to ensure the adoption of the necessary safety requirements and conditions. The Council can even suspend or stop the activities of any installation for nuclear safety or radiological protection reasons. Nuclear installations should periodically inform the Council on their operations. In case of incidents, they should immediately contact the Council through an automatic data transfer system. Likewise, for monitoring purposes, the Council has set up its own measurement stations network throughout the territory, as well as programmes on collection of samples, measurements and analysis of data.

226. Finally, the Council for Nuclear Safety approves the internal emergency plans. By contrast, external emergency plans fall within the competence of Civil Protection. These plans should comply with the Nuclear Emergency Basic Plan. It should be noted that nuclear and radioactive installations were excluded from the scope of RD 886/1986 of 15 July on the Prevention of Major Accidents in Certain Activities, modified by RD 952/199, of 29 July (in that they are covered by specific legislation applying to nuclear and radioactive matters). This RD adopts both the Directive 82/501/CEE regarding the risk of serious accidents in certain industrial activities, and the modifications made by Directives 87/216/CEE and 88/610/CEE. The approval of Directive 96/82/CE meant that both RDs had to be adapted by RD

1254/1999, of 16 July, which approves the measures for monitoring the risks inherent in serious accidents involving hazardous substances. This RD lists those activities that can cause emergencies and creates an inventory of centres, establishments and buildings where these take place. It also requires nuclear authorities to have a self-protection organization and an internal emergency plan for preventing risks and controlling any accidents that may occur. The RD also states that the competent bodies and authorities can demand information and establishes the capacity of the Public Administrations to develop an emergency plan to form, along with the previously mentioned internal emergency plan, a single and integrated plan of action.

227. In Spain, while the production of electric energy from nuclear sources has decreased considerably, the production of classic thermoelectric energy has been emerging as the main supplier of electricity. Electric energy consumption has been increasing uninterruptedly and in the year 2000, it reached 200,000 million kWh. Act 54/1997 of 27 November on the Electric Sector constitutes the main piece of legislation on this matter. RD 2017/1997 of 26 December, RD 20/1997, RD 277/2000 and RD 1955/2000, of 1 December develop the Act. The Act has also been amended by several regulations: Act 66/1997 of 30 December, Act 34/1998 of 7 October, Act 50/1998 of 30 December, Act 13/2003 of 23 May, Act 36/2003 of 11 November, Act 62/2003 of 30 December, RLD 5/2005 of 11 March, and Act 17/2007 of 4 July. The Act works toward a triple objective: to ensure the supply of electricity, to guarantee the quality of that supply, and to ensure that it is done at minimal cost, all of that without forgetting the protection of the environment. The Act abandons the classic concept of unified use of the national electricity system as a public service held by the State, and entrusts these duties to private enterprises. Furthermore, it liberalizes transport and distribution through the allowance of third parties access to the networks.

228. RD 2818/1998 of 23 December develops the content of Act 54/1997, on the Electricity Sector, whose Chapter II provides for a special system for cogeneration and energy production activities from renewable sources (solar, wind, minihydraulic, biomass, and others). This RD covers the generation of electric energy by installations using renewable resources, waste or cogeneration. It aims to make the installations using renewable energy sources viable, through a dual system that facilitates the marketing of the generated electricity and that fixes a certain bonus over the market price. RD 436/2004, of 12 March establishes the methodology for the updating and systemization of the legal and economic structure of electric energy production in a special scheme. In this way, the electricity generated from renewable sources will enjoy regulated retribution which is laid out in detail in Articles 32–39 of the RD. The RD was modified by RD 1370/2006, of 24 November, which approves the National Greenhouse Gas Emissions Allocation Plan; RD 61/2006, of 31 January, which regulates certain technical specifications of petrol, diesel, fuel oils and petroleum liquid gases and the use of certain biofuels; RD 47/2007, of 19 January, which approves the basic procedure for certifying the energy efficiency of new buildings and, more recently, RD 661/2007, of 25 May; and RD 1578/2008, of 28 September, on photovoltaic energy. Mention should also be made of Act 17/2009, of 23 November, on free access to the activities and execution of services and Act 25/2009, of 22 December, which adapts various Acts to Act 17/2009, of 23 November. The system consists of regulatory intervention in the price of the electricity produced. This is done by establishing a system of tariffs or benefits for the production of renewable electricity for periods of ten or twenty years, with the incentive that producers of electricity from renewable energies or technologies have the right to sell all their electricity on the grid and to obtain a legally fixed price or a price fixed in accordance with the market.

For their part, the Autonomous Communities have competencies to promote renewable energies and energy efficiency within the limits of their territory. Several Autonomous Communities have passed acts to regulate the renewable energy sector without precluding the subsequent development of sectorial regulations regarding certain aspects of the law. For example, there is Act 2/2007, of 27 March, on the promotion of renewable energy and energy saving and efficiency of Andalusia, Act 1/2007, of 15 February, on the promotion of renewable energy and energy saving and efficiency Castile-La Mancha, and Act 10/2006, of 21 December, on Renewable Energies and Energy Efficiency and Saving of Murcia.

Currently, Spain generates 20,000 MW of wind energy and 500 MW of thermoelectric energy. The Spanish Government is providing important support for the renewable energy and services sector by means of the 2000 AQUEST Plan, which aims to improve the energy efficiency of 2000 public buildings and thus reduce energy consumption by 20% for the 2012 horizon.

Chapter 8. Other Sectors

§1. Noxious Substances

229. RD 363/1995 of 10 May on Notification of New Substances and Classification, Packaging and Labelling of Hazardous Substances, still constitutes the applicable legislation for hazardous and noxious substances. It has been first amended by RD 700/1998, of 24 April, RD 507/2001 of 11 May, RD 99/2003 of 24 January and RD 119/2005 of 4 February. It has been lastly modified by RD 1802/2008 of 3 November which adapts it to EU's Regulation (EC) nª 1907/2006 (REACH: Registration, Evaluation, Authorization and Restriction of Chemical substances) by RD 717/2010 of 28 May, which approves the Regulation on classification, packaging and labelling of hazardous substances and by RD 255/2003, of 28 February, which approves the Regulation on classification, packaging and labelling of dangerous preparations.

230. REACH as established by Regulation (EC) 1907/2006 is the European regulation concerning the Registration, Evaluation, Authorization and Restriction of Chemicals. This regulation updates the legislative framework on chemicals in the EU. Its main objective is to ensure a high level of protection of human health and the environment and to do this, it establishes the obligation of recording all chemicals that are marketed within the territory of the EU.

231. On the other hand, Regulation (EC) No. 1272/2008 of 16 December 2008 on classification, labelling and packaging (CLP) of substances and mixtures, amending and repealing Directives 67/548/EEC and 1999/45/EC, and amending Regulation (EC) No. 1907/2006 establishes the new European regulation on classification, labelling and packaging of substances and chemical mixtures.

This is the new legal framework which settles a European system for classifying and labelling chemicals based on the Globally Harmonized System of the United Nations (UN GHS). Since its entry into force, the industry should establish the hazards of substances and mixtures before marketing and classify them according to the hazards identified. The CLP focuses on the harmonization of the provisions and criteria for the classification and labelling of substances, mixtures and certain specific articles within the EU, taking into account the classification criteria and labelling rules of the GHS.

232. Directive 2008/112/EC amends several Directives to adapt them to Regulation (EC) No. 1272/2008. In Spain, RD 1436/2010, of 5 November amends several RD for implementing this Directive. The main changes that the transposition of Directive 2008/112/EC involves are the replacement of the term 'preparation' or 'prepared' by 'mixing' or 'mixtures', the redefinition of 'hazardous substance', and 'coating'. In relation to emissions of volatile organic compounds it has also been introduced a gradual replacement up to 1 June 2015 of the risk phrases for signs of danger.

Part II. Nature Conservation and Management

§1. Background

233. The concern for nature, and specifically for the preservation of specific natural areas and species, is not new in the Spanish legal system. There are some precedents that go back to 1916, when the first Act of National Parks was approved. This Act followed the American model and allowed the constitution, in 1918, of the first National Park, the Covadonga National Park. The protection of natural areas was fragmented and sporadic for a long period of time. It was basically a State undertaking, given that their protection was declared through an Act or national decree. The general norm on this matter was for almost twenty years Act 15/1975 on Natural Spaces, even though through the use of urban legislation (the so-called Special Plans) the local entities could also protect specific areas of great value that could not have been protected otherwise. There also existed a hunting and forest legislation that, although intended for other purposes, contained specific tools that could be applied to the protection of species.

It should be acknowledged that until the late 1970s Spain was a mere spectator to the new globally advised approaches regarding nature protection and the new tools that could be more effectively used to defend the natural resources against continuous degradation. In the world forum, the new ideas, promoted by the World Strategy for the Preservation of the Nature of the United Nations, were already deeply rooted, and the bets were on a much more global treatment.

The renewal of the Spanish legislation took place after the approval of the Constitution and especially after the creation of the Autonomous Communities, which have been particularly creative on this subject. Practically all of them have approved general laws on nature protection and have constituted and managed their own natural spaces. The new legislation has changed the traditional focus and is more globally minded. We should also mention here that the State profoundly modified Act 15/1975 by means of Act 4/1989 of 27 March on Natural Protected Areas and Wild Flora and Fauna Preservation (in turn modified by several acts such as 40/1997, of 5 November; 41/1997, of 5 November; 53/2002, of 30 December; 43/2003, of 21 November; and 62/2003, of 30 December), and more recently by means of Act 5/2007, of 3 April, on the National Parks Network and Act 42/2007, of 13 December, on Natural Heritage and Biodiversity, which repeal and substitute Act 4/1989 of 27 March. Act 4/1989 introduced internationally ratified nature conservation law to Spain. This consolidated the process started at the beginning of the 1980s which saw the ratification of multilateral agreements regarding, among many other issues, wetlands, the international trade in endangered, migratory and regional species, and European natural heritage. These developments came about at the request of the Council of Europe and due to Spain's entry into the EU on 1 January 1986.

Currently, Act 42/2007, of 13 December, establishes the basic legal system for the conservation, sustainable use, improvement and restoration of the natural heritage and Spanish biodiversity, thus bringing Spanish law into line with new European and universal regulations that have appeared in recent years. Nevertheless, it should be taken into account that on 15 April 2008 the Constitutional Court heard an appeal lodged by the Governing Council of Castile and León regarding Articles 25, 45.1, 53, 58, 62.3 a), 62.3 g), 62.3 j) and 66.2 of Act 42/2007, of 13 December, on Natural Heritage and Biodiversity, which relate, among other aspects, to how Autonomous Communities are affected by the inclusion of habitats in the Spanish Catalogue of Threatened Habitats, the conservation measures used in the Natura 2000 Network, the List of Specially Protected Wild Species, the prohibitions and limitations related to hunting and fishing, and the make-up of the Spanish Committee charged with assessing biosphere reserves.

§2. State Organization for the Protection of Nature

234. Every Autonomous Community has a specific internal organization for nature preservation, although not all of them have taken on the relevant competencies for protecting natural spaces. Those Communities that have taken on exclusive responsibility for this matter through their statutes of autonomy have the necessary competencies to draw up and execute legislation and the possibility creating additional protection regulations. The State Administration has the power to create basic legislation. On a national level, the General Directorate for Natural Environment and Forestry Policy (under the Secretary General for the Rural Environment) exercises the powers that, according to RD 1130/2008, of 4 July, fall within the competence of the Ministry of Environment. Specifically, these functions are:

(a) The formulation of the Spanish strategy for Natural Heritage and Biodiversity and its sectorial plans.
(b) The drafting of the reports prior to the Declaration of environment impact, which are submitted by the General Directorate of Quality and Environmental Evaluation.
(c) The drafting of common criteria for the development, conservation, management and financing of Nature Network 2000 and of protected natural spaces, its integration into sectorial policies, especially in rural and regional development, and its consideration in the planning and construction of infrastructures.
(d) Action as a scientific authority on the Convention on CITES.
(e) The formulation of strategies, plans, programmes and directives for regulating and conserving the natural heritage and biodiversity and for promoting the conservation and restoration of natural resources and of basic criteria and preventative measures to promote the preservation of genetic resources, flora,

fauna, habitats, countryside, ecosystems and natural spaces, especially those that are fragile or degraded, complementing national and international biodiversity preservation programmes.

(f) The functions attributed to the General Administration of the State by Act 42/2007, 13 December, on Natural Heritage and Biodiversity, without prejudice to the competencies that correspond to other bodies and departments.

(g) The formulation of a national action plan against desertification.

(h) The creation, application and monitoring of the National Plan for priority hydrological-forest restoration in collaboration with the autonomous communities.

(i) Participation in the elaboration of forest protection plans and especially, forest fire defence and forest health plans.

(j) The duties that Acts 3/1995 of 23 March, on Livestock Systems, and 43/2003, of 21 November, on Forests, modified by Act 10/2006 of 28 April, attribute to the General Administration of the State.

(k) The creation of the Spanish Inventory for Natural Heritage and Biodiversity in accordance with Article 9 of Act 42/2007, of 13 December, on Natural Heritage and Biodiversity, natural heritage accounting, the development of the EIONETNaturaleza Network and the national centre of the European Environment Agency.

(l) Programming of projects financed by European funds, and the drafting of the necessary documentation, as well as the monitoring and evaluation of those projects.

(m) Participation in representing the ministry to international organizations, monitoring international agreements and promoting international cooperation on issues within its area of competence.

The following bodies are subdirectorates within the General Directorate for the Natural Environment and Forestry Policy:

- The General Subdirectorate for Biodiversity, which has the competencies indicated in paragraphs a) to f) of the previous section, and those indicated in paragraph m).
- The General Subdirectorate for Natural Heritage and Biodiversity, which has the competencies indicated in paragraph k) of the previous section, and those indicated in paragraph m.

235. Act 42/2007, of 13 December, on Natural Heritage and Biodiversity created two important bodies:

The first of these is the *State Council for Natural Heritage and Biodiversity,* (Art. 8) whose aim is to promote participation in activities that help achieve the objectives of the Act. This body was created by RD 948/2009, of 5 June, which determines the composition, functions and operating rules of the State Council for Natural Heritage and Biodiversity.

The second created by the Act is the *State Commission for Natural Heritage and Biodiversity* (Article 7). This is a consultative body to encourage cooperation in questions of Heritage protection between the State and the Autonomous Communities. Its reports and proposals are submitted for approval and dissemination to the Sectorial Conference on the Environment, and it has also taken on some of the functions of the now defunct *National Commission for the Protection of Nature*. This second body was created by RD 1424/2008, of 14 August, which determines the composition, functions, operating regulations and committees attached to the *State Commission for Natural Heritage and Biodiversity* (this being modified slightly by the aforementioned RD 948/2009, 5 June.

§3. General Regime of Protection

236. Making use of its exclusive powers for enacting basic environmental legislation, the Spanish Parliament approved Act 42/2007, 13 December, on Natural Heritage and Biodiversity. This Act, together with Act 5/2007, 3 April, on the National Parks Network, constitutes the nucleus of this matter at present. But we should not forget that the Autonomous Communities have assumed the most important role in this matter, both from the legislative and management perspectives.

237. Act 42/2007 establishes protection, preservation, restoration and improvement measures regarding natural resources. They constitute general rules, but the Act also focuses specifically on the protected natural areas (distinguishing different categories) and on the protection of the wild flora and fauna. The legislation on natural spaces is of great importance, because it addresses a great variety of climates in Spain, which result in a rich diversity of landscapes and ecosystems, going from high mountains with snow most of the year and even some glaciers, to the semi-desert areas of the peninsular south-east, with scarce rainfall and acute summer droughts. Between these two climatological extremes we also find canyons, humid zones, large rivers, immense beaches, enormous meadows and centennial forests of fir, beech and holm oak.

Act 42/2007 declares that protected natural areas are those areas of the national territory, inland waters included, and the marine spaces within the national jurisdiction, including the exclusive economic zone and the continental platform, that contain systems or elements that are natural, representative, singular, fragile or threatened, or that are of special environmental, scientific, geological or educational interest, or that are especially set aside for the protection and maintenance of biodiversity, geodiversity and the associated cultural and natural resources, and that are declared protected natural spaces.

238. Among the main administrative tools covered by the Act are: The Spanish Natural Heritage and Biodiversity Inventory (Article 9), which includes, among other things, information regarding:

(1) The Spanish Catalogue of Threatened Habitats.
(2) The List of Specially Protected Wild Species, including the Spanish Catalogue of Threatened Species.

(3) The Spanish Catalogue of Invasive Exotic Species.
(4) The Spanish Inventory of Protected Natural Spaces, the Natura 2000 Network and Internationally Protected Areas.
(5) The Inventory and Forestry Statistics of Spain.
(6) The Spanish Inventory of Wild Species Gene Banks.
(7) The Spanish Hunting and Fishing Inventory.
(8) The Spanish Inventory of Zoological Parks.
(9) The Spanish Inventory of Traditional Knowledge regarding Natural Heritage and Biodiversity.
(10) An Inventory of Sites of Geological Interest that includes at least the geological features listed in Annex VIII.
(11) A Spanish Inventory of Marine Species and Habitats.
(12) A Spanish Inventory of Wetland Areas.

The Strategic Natural Heritage and Biodiversity Plan (Articles 12–14) for the protection of the most important habitats and species. This plan has to define the objectives, criteria and actions that promote conservation, sustainable use and the restoration of natural heritage, land and marine based natural resources and biodiversity. It incorporates a diagnosis of the state and progress of Spanish natural heritage and biodiversity, the objectives to be reached during the period in which it is active and the actions to be taken by General State Administration, together with the budgetary estimates needed for its execution.

The act maintains the existing instruments for planning the resources used in the Natural Resource Management Plans ('Plan de Ordenación de los Recursos Naturales'; PORN) and the Directives for the Regulation of Natural Resources, created by Act 4/1989, of 27 March (Articles 15–23).

PORNs have the following fundamental objectives:

(a) To identify and georeference the significant spaces and elements of the Natural Heritage of a territory and, in particular, those included in the Natural Heritage and Biodiversity Inventory, and to identify the values that characterize them and their relationship with the rest of the territory.
(b) To identify the level of conservation of the elements that make-up the natural heritage, biodiversity, geodiversity and environmental and geological processes of a given territory.
(c) To identify the capacity and intensity of the way in which natural heritage, biodiversity and geodiversity are used, to determine alternative management methods and to identify the limitations that need to be put in place in view of the general conservation levels.
(d) To formulate the guiding criteria of the policies behind economic and social activity (both public and private) so that they are compatible with the requirements of the present Act.
(e) To establish the protection regimes for the different spaces, ecosystems and natural resources present in the PORNs' area of application in order to maintain, improve and restore the functionality and connectivity of the ecosystems.
(f) To specify and promote measures for conserving and restoring natural resources and the elements of biodiversity and geodiverstiy which need them.

(g) To help establish and consolidate ecological networks composed of spaces of high natural value that allow the movement and dispersion of plant and animal species and the natural flows which guarantee the functionality of ecosystems.

As part of the Strategic State Plan for Natural Heritage and Biodiversity, the Ministry of the Environment and the Autonomous Communities will together draft some directives to regulate natural resources. The Autonomous Communities' PORNs should comply with these directives, which will establish and define the general criteria and regulations that govern the management and use of natural resources. This provision (Article 16.2) has been challenged as unconstitutional by the Government of the Canary Islands in the Constitutional Court.

An important new development is the incorporation of eco-corridors in environmental planning. Article 20 of the Act states that:

> In their environmental planning or their Natural Resources Regulation Plans, the Public Administrations will provide the mechanisms needed to achieve environmental connectivity in the territory by establishing or re-establishing eco-corridors, in particular between the protected spaces of the Natura 2000 Network and between those natural spaces that are particularly important for biodiversity. For this reason, priority will be given to the role of water courses, fishing routes, mountain areas and other elements of the territory that are linear or continual or that act as links, regardless of the condition they are in, between protected natural spaces.

The Natural Heritage and Biodiversity Fund (Article 74) Acts as a co-funding tool which aims to ensure that the objectives and territorial cohesion of the act are achieved. It also seeks to apply measures designed to support sustainable forest management, the strategic prevention of forest fires, territorial custody and the protection of natural and forest spaces that are partly funded by the General State Administration.

Chapter 1. Protected Natural Areas

§1. General Categorization

239. The Act 47/2007 includes a general categorization of protected natural areas, which adds the new category of 'Protected Marine Areas' to existing ones. Those categories can be enlarged by the sectorial legislation passed by the Autonomous Communities.

According to the resources and values to be protected and the management objectives to be fulfilled, the natural areas will be classified according to the wording of Act 47/2007 in, at least, one of the following categories:

- Parks: Natural areas which, due to the beauty of their landscapes, the importance of their ecosystems, or the singularity of their flora, fauna or geomorphologic formations possess ecological, aesthetic, educative or scientific values whose preservation deserve preferential attention. Exploitation of natural resources can be limited and uses opposed to the values that have justified the creation of the park in the first place are prohibited. Certain natural spaces of high cultural and ecological value which are liable to be declared as parks, can be declared National Parks if their preservation is deemed to be in the nation's general interest. These are governed by Act 5/2007, of 3 April, of the National Parks Network.
- Natural reserves: Natural areas, created in order to preserve ecosystems, communities, or biological elements, which for reasons of their rarity, fragility, importance or singularity deserve a special attention. Resource exploitation will be limited, except when compatible with the preservation of the protected values. Generally, the collection of biological or geological objects is prohibited except when permitted by a prior administrative authorization for research or educative reasons.
- Protected Marine Areas: Natural spaces designated for the protection of ecosystems, communities and biological or geological elements of the marine environment, including intertidal and subtidal zones that because of their rarity, fragility, importance or singularity deserve special protection. These natural spaces can adopt this specific category or be protected by any other form of protection provided for by this Act, in which case, their legal jurisdiction will be that which is applied to these other figures, without affecting their inclusion in the Network of Protected Marine Areas. At the proposal of the coastal Autonomous communities and the General State Administration, the Sectorial Conference will establish the basic common management criteria to be applied to the Marine Areas included in the Network. – Natural monuments: Natural areas constituted by formations of notorious singularity, rarity or beauty, deserving a special protection. Natural monuments also include singular and monumental trees, geological formations, paleontological and mineral deposits, stratotypes and other elements that may have a special interest due to the singularity or importance of their scientific, cultural or landscape values. At general monuments, it will be prohibited to exploit resources, except in those cases where the Administration permits this for research or conservation reasons. – Protected landscapes: These are parts of the territory of particular aesthetic or cultural value that the relevant Administration

believes should receive special protection in accordance with the Landscape Agreement of the European Council.

The principal objectives of Protected Landscape Management are to conserve the singular values that make them special and to preserve the harmonious interaction between nature and culture in a specific area. Special efforts will be made in Protected Landscapes to maintain the traditional practices that help preserve its values and natural resources.

240. The designation and management of protected natural spaces will be the responsibility of the Autonomous Communities in whose territory they are located. The designation of parks and reserves will require the prior drafting and subsequent approval of a 'Natural Resources Regulation Plan'. It should also be noted that in the protected natural areas declared by law, Peripheral Areas of Protection can be established in order to avoid ecological or landscape impacts coming from the exterior. Also, to contribute to the maintenance of the protected natural areas and to compensate the affected population economically and socially, so-called Areas of Socio-economic Influence can be established, specifying the economic regime and the corresponding compensations for the imposed limitations. The municipalities in which the protected natural area or peripheral area of protection are located will constitute these areas. These elements have already appeared in previous legislation.

241. The Act also incorporates the regulation of other protection mechanisms. One of these is the European Ecological Network, Natura 2000, which is made up of Places of Community Interest, Social Conservation Zones and Special Bird Areas. These spaces will be regarded as protected spaces under the specific name Natura 2000 Network protected spaces and their range and limits will be established by the Autonomous Communities in their legislation and in the corresponding planning tools. The Autonomous Communities will define these spaces and will inform the Ministry for the Environment about them, who will in turn communicate them to the European Commission. The Autonomous Communities will also specify the conservation measures to be adopted. The Act includes eight updated annexes containing the contents of Directive 79/409/CEE of the Council, of 2 April 1979, regarding the conservation of wild birds, and of Directive 92/43/CEE of the Council, of 21 May 1992, regarding the conservation of natural habitats and wild plants and animals.

The Act refers likewise to areas protected by different international treaties (internationally important wetlands protected by the RAMSAR Convention; the natural sites in the World Heritage List, protected by the UNESCO Convention for the Protection of World, Cultural and Natural Heritage; the areas protected by the Convention for the Protection of the North-East Atlantic Marine Environment (OSPAR); the Specially Protected Zones of Importance to the Mediterranean (ZEPIM), protected by the Convention for the Protection of the Marine Environment and the Coastal Region of the Mediterranean; the Geoparks designated by UNESCO, the Biosphere Reserves designated by UNESCO, and the Biogenetic Reserves of the European Council). The Act states that within the framework of the Strategic State Plan for

Natural Heritage and Biodiversity the Ministry of Environment in conjunction with the Autonomous Communities will create a series of conservation directives that will be approved by the Sectorial Conference on the Environment, in parallel with the directives of the Natura 2000 Network, to provide a guiding framework for the planning and management of these spaces.

The Act creates the Spanish Inventory of Protected Natural Spaces, Natura 2000 Network, and Areas protected by international agreements. This will be included in the Spanish Inventory for Natural Heritage and Biodiversity and will be dependent on the Ministry of the Environment. To comply with international commitments, the natural spaces listed in the Spanish Inventory of Protected Natural Spaces will be assigned, along with their original title, to the relevant internationally established categories, in particular those established by the International Union for the Conservation of Nature.

242. In the ambit of biodiversity protection, the Act creates the List of Specially Protected Species. Any taxa or populations included in this list will be periodically monitored to assess their conservation status and will be protected from negative human activities. At the heart of the List of Specially Protected Species will be the Spanish Catalogue of Threatened Species which will include any taxa or populations that the relevant technical and scientific information indicates are threatened. These species will be listed as either 'endangered' or 'vulnerable' according to the risk of extinction that they face. The inclusion of a taxon or population in the 'endangered' category may lead to the designation of critical areas that will be included in the Spanish Catalogue of Endangered Habitats. Such a designation will in turn require the drafting of a recovery plan to ensure conservation, in accordance with Act 4/1989, of 27 March. As is generally the case with all the plans and management tools envisaged by the Act, this plan will last a maximum of three years and is to be funded by the Government through the Natural Heritage and Biodiversity Fund. Recovery plans for the 'vulnerable' category will follow a similar procedure, although these will last a maximum of five years. At the proposal of the State Commission for Natural Heritage and Biodiversity, the Sectorial Conference on the Environment will approve the Strategies for the Conservation of Threatened Species, which will constitute the guiding framework for the recovery and conservation plans that are drafted and approved by the Autonomous Communities.

Likewise, with the aim of preserving the genetic and biological heritage of wild species, the Act states that the Public Administrations will promote the creation of a network of biological and genetic material banks and a Spanish Inventory of Wild Species' Biological and Genetic Material Banks, which will contain all the available data regarding this matter. The Act also envisages the creation of the Spanish Catalogue of Invasive Species, which will include all the exotic species and subspecies that are or that may become a serious threat to native species, habitats, ecosystems, agriculture or economic resources associated with the use of natural heritage. Hunting and fishing will be monitored by the Spanish Hunting and Fishing Inventory, which will record all the information regarding the population, capture and the health of the gene pool of those species that can legally be hunted, in particular, migratory species.

Section IV is centred on promoting the sustainable use of natural heritage and biodiversity, with the first chapter focussing on the Spanish Biosphere reserves that form part of the World Biosphere Reserves Network of the MaB (Man and Biosphere Reserve) Programme of UNESCO. The regulation, characterization and promotion of these Biosphere Reserves is based on the fact that they constitute an integrated, participatory and sustainable management model of natural heritage and resources with the aim of combining the preservation of biological diversity and ecosystems with sustainable environmental development that improves the welfare of the population, strengthens the roles of public participation, of research and of education in integrating development and the environment, and provides training in new methods for improving this integration.

243. The second chapter of section IV regulates access to genetic resources derived from wild species and the distribution of the benefits resulting from their use, in accordance with the Biological Diversity Agreement and the International Treaty on Phytogenetic Resources for Food and Agriculture of the United Nations Food and Agriculture Organization.

244. The third chapter covers the international trade in wild species in terms of the principles of sustainability and, in accordance with international law, in particular the Agreement on Biological Diversity, the International Treaty on Phytogenetic Resources for Food and Agriculture of the United Nations Food and Agriculture Organization and the European regulations regarding the protection of threatened species through trade restrictions.

245. Finally, the fourth chapter of this section focuses on applying the aspects of the Agreement on Biological Diversity and the World Intellectual Property Organization regarding the promotion of traditional knowledge in order to conserve Natural Heritage and Biodiversity.

246. Protected Marine Areas. In Spain, the first marine wetland area to be protected by environmental law by means of Act 91/1978, of 28 December, which extended the zone's external protected area to a nautical mile. Likewise, Royal Decree 1115/1982 created the National Hunting Refuge on the Chafarinas Islands, which includes a marine area around the islands. However, during the 1980s and 1990s when responsibility for protecting the environment was transferred to the Autonomous Communities, these spaces began to be declared protected natural spaces that cover both land and maritime zones. The Cabo de Gata-Níjar Natural Park is considered the most important Protected Marine Areas in Spain, both in terms of its size and conservation objectives. It was established by Decree 314, of 23 December 1987 of the Governing Council of Andalusia. There is no specific legislation in Spain regarding the protection of marine species or areas, although Act 4/1989, of 27 March, on the conservation of natural species and wild plants and animals envisaged the possibility of creating protected marine or marine wetland zones.

The new Act 42/2007 on Natural Heritage and Biodiversity, which substitutes the previous Act, specifically provides for marine biodiversity and establishes certain basic regulations regarding the issue. The Act establishes Protected Marine Areas as a new marine classification status for protected natural spaces, to be used alongside the other classifications of Parks, Reserves, Natural Monuments and Protected Landscapes. In accordance with Article 32 of Act 47/2007, a Protected Marine Area is a designated natural space for the protection of ecosystems and biological or geological communities or elements in the marine environment, including the intertidal and subtidal areas, which because of their rarity, fragility, importance or singularity require special protection. These elements can adopt the specific character of Protected Marine Area or protect themselves under any other classification status envisaged by the Act, in which case they will be governed by the legal system applicable to these other classifications. The Act also establishes the creation of a Network of Protected Marine Areas.

The Act 42/2007 will approve plans or management mechanisms that will establish the necessary conservation measures and the limits to be applied to the exploitation of natural resources in each case and in each group of areas that are incorporated into the Network of Protected Marine Areas. The exploitation of fishing resources will be restricted in accordance with Article 18 Act 3/2001, of 26 March, on Marine Fishing by the State because this responsibility is exclusive to the State. At the proposal of the coastal Autonomous Communities and the General State Administration, the Sectorial Conference will establish the minimum common management criteria to be applied to the Marine Areas included in the Network.

Furthermore, the Act establishes that the General State Administration is responsible for the carrying out the administrative functions referred to by the Law, whilst also respecting the Statutes of Autonomy of the coastal Autonomous Communities, in the following instances:

- When concerning those spaces, habitats or critical areas located in sovereign or nationally governed marine areas, provided that there is no ecological continuity between the marine ecosystem and the natural land area that is to be protected, this being ascertained by the best existing scientific evidence.
- When these functions affect either species whose habitats are located in the spaces referred to in the previous paragraph or highly migratory marine species.
- When, in accordance with international law, Spain has to administer spaces located in areas subject to international law or on the high sea.

Recently, section III of the Act 41/2010, of 29 December 2010, on Protection of Marine Environment, has developed the regulations concerning Protected Marine Areas and their Network.

247. To date, the Autonomous Communities have declared several spaces that cover the marine zone nearest to the coast, as well as two national marine wetland parks: the Cabrera Archipelago (Act 14/1991, 29 Abril) and the Atlantic Islands of Galicia (Act 15/2002, of 1 July).

In particular, various spaces that include land and marine areas have been declared as Specially Protected Zones of Importance for the Mediterranean (ZEPIM), within the framework of the 1995 Protocol on specially protected zones and biodiversity in the Mediterranean.

By 2010 there were nine ZEPIM covering a total surface area of 148,358,885 ha. They are distributed as follows:

Andalusia

- Island of Alborán (2001).
- Cabo de Gata-Níjar (2001).
- Eastern Almerian sea beds (2001).
- The Maro-Cerro Gordo Cliffs (2003).

Catalonia

- Cap de Creus (2001).
- Medes Islands (2001).

Valencia

- Columbretes Islands (2001) Balearic Islands.
- Cabrera Archipelago (2003) Murcia.
- Mar Menor and the Eastern Mediterranean Zone of the coast of Murcia (2001).

§2. Parks and Reserves

248. Of particular importance in the Parks category are the National Parks. Act 5/2007, 3 April, on National Parks Network aims to establish the basic legal system for the National Parks Network, whose objectives are declared to be of general interest to the State. The first section sets out the General Provisions that affect the definition of the act's objectives and the definitions associated with the law and, in particular, the definition of the area of socio-economic influence, whose precise demarcation is referred to in the declarative laws of each Park. Article 2 states that public bodies and in particular the Public Administrations have the general obligation in their respective areas of competence to ensure the protection of the National Parks Network.

249. The National Parks are defined as:

> natural spaces of high ecological and cultural value that have been little affected by human exploitation or activity and that because of their beauty, their diverse ecosystems or their singular flora, fauna or geology possess outstanding ecological, aesthetic, cultural, educational and scientific values that need to be conserved and that are of general interest to the State (Artícle 3, a).

The National Parks Network is defined as a 'system made up of those spaces declared as National Parks, which constitute the most singular and valuable collection of characteristic spaces of Spanish natural heritage, and the basic regulatory framework and system of relations needed for their functioning' (Article 3, d). The Network thus provides the best possible legacy for future generations. In this regard the Act includes an Annex that catalogues the natural systems of Spain that should be represented in the National Parks Network.

250. The second section of Act 5/2007 regulates the National Parks Network, the functions of the General State Administration for achieving its objectives, the structure, composition and objectives of the Network Council and the functions and characteristics of the Administrative Plan for the National Parks Network. Article 5 list the functions of the General State Administration, which include creating and reviewing the Administrative Plan for the National Parks Network, monitoring and evaluating the Network, developing and funding the specific programme of common actions of the Network, including the aforementioned Plan, proposing cooperation mechanisms to achieve the objectives of each of the National Parks and of the Network as a whole, increasing and consolidating, preferably on the basis of voluntary agreements, the public heritage of the National Parks Network, promoting improved scientific knowledge of issues relating to the Network, adequately disseminating the available information and representing Spain, within its competencies, in the equivalent international networks. The Act establishes the need to monitor and generally assess the degree to which the Network's objectives are complied with. To this end, the Act establishes that every three years the competent Ministry will draft a report on the current state of the National Parks Network which will be presented to the Senate and made available to the public. This report will be accompanied by an annex containing information written by each Park's administrative body and that details the situation in each of the National Parks.

251. According to the current legislation, in order to be declared a National Park, an area should meet a series of requirements. These requirements are listed in Act 5/2007, 3 April (Article 9), which replaces the previous system, and are as follows:

- The Park will be highly representative, in terms of its species and natural characteristics, of one or some of the natural systems included in the Annex of the Act.
- It will have an important proportion of those species and communities found in natural systems or of those that are threatened in Spain, as well as the territorial and ecological capacity and ecologically significant populations to guarantee that these species and communities maintain or obtain a favourable level of conservation. – It will have a sufficient continuous and unbroken surface area to allow these biological and physical characteristics to be maintained and to ensure that the natural processes present can continue with little or no human intervention. To this end, the surface area of the National Park, except for in duly justified cases, will be at least: 15,000 ha for inland or marine wetland National Parks in mainland Spain; at least 5,000 ha for inland or marine wetland National Parks on islands; and at least 20,000 ha for marine National Parks. This requisite is not applicable to those National Parks that were created before the current act.
- The surface area of the National Park is continuous and unfragmented, except in cases where this is duly justified.

– It will have an adequate surface area containing natural formations that are not subject to agriculture, mining, forestry or water extraction, or that contain artificial elements that significantly alter the aesthetics of the landscape or the functioning of the ecosystems.

Furthermore, the proposed National Park will contain no land that is or that can be developed.

Declaring an area a National Park is the responsibility of the Autonomous Communities or of the National Government once the decision has been approved by the legislative bodies of those Autonomous Communities in which the National Park is to be located. State law will be used to incorporate a declared National Park into the National Parks Network. A proposal for a new National Park must include the necessary submissions and be made available for public scrutiny for a minimum period of two months. It must be submitted for consideration to the Network Council before it can be submitted by the Ministry of the Environment to the Council of Ministers.

For National Parks in the marine environment, Act 5/2007 makes certain stipulations in addition to the aforementioned minimum size of the park. On the one hand, the Act states that the General State Administration is responsible for managing National Parks located 'in sovereign or nationally regulated marine areas when the protected ecosystem is not contiguous with the terrestrial part or the marine terrestrial zone located in the Autonomous Community'. On the other hand, according to the fourth additional provision regarding the designation and loss of National Park status for those parks governed by the General State Administration, the initial approval of the proposal will be made by the National Government and the requirement for approval by the legislative bodies of the Autonomous Communities will be substituted by a mandatory report from those Autonomous Communities whose activities may affect the protection of the natural space. This provision has been the object of an appeal on the grounds of unconstitutionality (pending ruling) by the Autonomous Community of the Canary Islands.

252. The principal legal purposes of a declaration designating a National Park, which takes precedence over other sectorial regulations, are as follows (Article 13):

- To establish that the activities that the Public Administrations must undertake will be of public utility or social interest so that they achieve the objectives of the Network.
- To establish that the competent Administration has the power to exercise the rights of first refusal and repurchase regarding onerous legal acts or transactions inter vivos which lead to the creation, transmission, modification or extinction of real rights regarding rustic goods within the National Park, including any operations or negotiations by virtue of which it acquires the majority of the capital stock of those associations who enjoy the aforementioned real rights.
- To prohibit various activities such as:
  - Recreational and competitive fishing, recreational and commercial hunting and commercial logging.

– Mining, hydroelectric generation and the installation of infrastructures for communications, energy and other purposes, except for in duly justified reasons of environmental protection or social interest, and provided that there is no other satisfactory solution. Should these activities or installations (with the exception of mining) be present when the National Park is created and cannot be prevented or removed, the competent Administrations will adopt the necessary measures to redress their effects, within the period established by the Act designating the National Park.
– Other forms of exploiting natural or agricultural resources, except for those that are compatible with achieving the aims of the Park, that are enshrined as recognized rights and make a recognized contribution to the Park's cultural and ecological values and that do not interfere with natural processes. Should any of these activities occur when the National Park is created, the competent Administrations will adopt the necessary measures to eliminate them within the period established by the Act designating the National Park.
– Flights over the Park at less than 3,000 m, unless expressly authorized or in cases of force majeure.

• To establish that the land set aside for the National Park cannot be used for development or construction, although this does not include the installations established in the Park's Use and Management Master Plan, which are needed to ensure that the Park is properly managed and that its objectives are met.
• To establish that the area's Water Plans and the Administrations responsible for managing water supplies must ensure that they provide water resources of sufficient quantity and quality to maintain the values and achieve the objectives of the National Parks Network.

253. The declaration of a National Park will require the previous elaboration and subsequent approval of a 'Natural Resources Regulation Plan' (PORN),which must at least cover the area protected by the park. As has been indicated, the PORNs are governed by Act 42/2007, of 13 December, on Natural Heritage and Biodiversity, in particular Article 16 thereof.

254. The National Park management bodies will also make use of the following management and planning technical tools:

– Article 7 of Act 5/2007, of 3 April, on the National Parks Network maintains the Master Plan as the basic instrument for coordinating and achieving the objectives of the National Parks Network. The National Parks Network Master Plan is partially in force and was approved by RD 1803/1999 of 26 November. The National Parks Network Master Plan has been challenged in the Constitutional Court by the Andalusian Government, due to a conflict about jurisdiction raised by the Andalusian Government against some of its sections. In its ruling 101/2005 of 19 April, the Constitutional Court declared certain sections of the Plan unconstitutional for infringing on the jurisdiction of Autonomous Regions. A new Master Plan is in the process of being drafted. This Plan constitutes the basic planning tool for the National Parks Network and must include, among other things, the necessary actions to be taken in order to preserve the image and internal coherence of the network and the guidelines that must be followed by the Management and Use Master Plans of the National Parks. This Plan will set up the objectives to be achieved during its ten-year term as regards preservation, research, public use, education and awareness. It will specify the goals to be achieved in collaboration and cooperation with other administrations or national and international bodies.

It will also regulate its financial resources and fix the distribution criteria for the economic resources. Finally, it will incorporate provisions regarding its follow-up and evaluation, execution, validity and revision. As is the case with all other processes covered by the Act, an open and participatory procedure must be followed when drafting and revising the Master Plan, and the plan must be submitted to environmental evaluation to further guarantee the availability of information and public participation. The Ministry for the Environment and Marine and Rural Affairs is responsible for drafting the revision and adapting the Plan to the rulings of the Constitutional Court. During the transitional period between the old and new Plans, the Act states that the previous Master Plan is to remain in force in all areas that have not been declared unconstitutional by the Constitutional Court.

- The Management and Use Master Plans of the National Parks (PRUG), which constitute the technical tools to articulate the guidelines for the Park management and preservation, as they define, among other things, the planning and general provisions for the preservation, public use and research activities.

255. The current Management and Use Master Plans of the National Parks are the following:

- RD 1410/1986 of 30 May, approving the Management and Use Plan of the Caldera de Taburiente National Park (BOE, 8 July 1986).
- RD 1531/1986 of 30 May, approving the Management and Use Plan of the Garajonay National Park, BOE, 28 July 1986).
- RD 1621/1990 of 14 December, approving the Management and Use Plan of the Timanfaya National Park (BOE, 19 December 1990).
- Decree 242/1991 of 3 December, which approved the Management and Use Plan for the Cabañeros Natural Park (DOCM, 11 December 1991). Correction of errors in Decree 242/1991 (DOCM, 20 December 1991).
- Decree 64/1994 of 15 March, which approves the Management and Use Master Plan for the Sierra Nevada National Park (BOJA, 21 April 1994).
- Decree 153/2002 of 24 October, which approves the Management and Use Plan of the Teide National Park (BOC, 11 December 2002).
- Royal Decree 384/2002 of 26 April, which approves the Management and Use Master Plan for the Picos de Europa National Park (BOE de 18 May 2002) (annulled by the Supreme Court in May 2005).
- Decree 39/2003 of 4 February, approving the Management and Use Plan of the Aigües Tortes and Sant Maurici Lake National Park. (DOGC, 19 February 2003).

- Decree 48/2004 of 10 February, which approves the Management and Use Plan of the Doñana National Park (BOJA, 4 March 2004).
- Decree 117/2005, of 24 May, of the Government of Aragon, which regulates the organization and functioning of the Ordesa and Monte Perdido National Park (BOA, 15 June 2005).
- Decree 58/2006 of 1 July, which approves the Management and Use Plan of the Land and Marine National Park of the Cabrera Archipelago, for the 2006–2012 period (BO. Illes Balears, 11 July 2006).
- Decree 106/2007, of 22 May, which regulated the organization and functioning of the Monfragüe National Park (DOE, 29 May 2007).

256. The management of a National Park requires the delimitation of its different areas. The organization of the territory will depend on the activities that can be carried out in it, taking into account the ecological characteristics, preservation level and fragility of its different areas.

Zoning will establish the permitted and prohibited uses for each area and create the following classification from major to minor levels of protection:

- Reserve zone: Zone closed to public use. Access will be only permitted after previous authorization and only for scientific purposes or environmental management.
- Restricted use zone: Public access will be regulated through permits. The marked paths will not be abandoned in any case, except when the Park administration expressly permits it.
- Moderate use zone: Access by vehicles is admitted.
- Special use zone: Accommodates constructions and essential services for the Park administration and visitors.
- Traditional settlements zones: Pursuant to the existence of an urban area within the Park boundaries, and with the aim of rendering the Park's objectives compatible with the need for a rational and controlled urban development, a zone of traditional settlement can be established, including urban areas and places inhabited by a non-disperse population.

257. All the natural areas declared to be Parks are included in an integrated system of protection and management of the Spanish natural patrimony called the National Parks Network. This network is constituted by the National Parks, which are themselves a selection of the best and most representative natural systems of the country; its legal framework; the material means and human resources needed for its management; and finally, the institutions involved in its correct operation. Nowadays, the Spanish National Parks Network is made up of fourteen National Parks, nine of them located in the Iberian Peninsula and five of them in the islands, with a total cover of 325.897 ha, that is, 0.6% of the Spanish national territory. The biggest is the Sierra Nevada (Nature Network 2000, Biosphere Preserve and European Charter), followed, in this order, by Picos de Europa (Nature Network 2000 and Biosphere Preserve), Doñana (Nature Network 2000, Biosphere Preserve, European Diploma, World Heritage Site and RAMSAR), Cabañeros (Nature Network 2000), Teide (Nature Network 2000 and European Diploma), Monfragüe (ZEPA Nature

Network 2000, Biosphere Preserve), Ordesa and El Monte Perdido (ZEPA Nature Network 2000, Biosphere Preserve, European Diploma and World Heritage Site), Aigües Tortes and l'Estany de Sant Maurici (Nature Network 2000 and RAMSAR), Archipélago de Cabrera (Nature Network 2000 y Special Protection Zone of the Mediterranian – ZEPIM), Atlantic Islands of Galicia (Nature Network 2000), Timanfaya (Nature Network 2000 and Biosphere Preserve), Caldera de Taburiente (ZEPA Nature Network 2000), Garajonay (Nature Network 2000 and World Heritage Site), and, finally Tablas de Daimiel (Nature Network 2000, Biosphere Preserve and RAMSAR).

258. National Park management in Spain has caused a major conflict in terms of jurisdiction. Initially, Act 4/1989, entrusted the management of these spaces exclusively to the State, which caused some Autonomous Communities to challenge this law. After Constitutional Court Sentence 102/1995, of 26 June, a new model was established which set up a co-management system between the State and the Autonomous Communities. Spanish National Parks were co-managed by the national administration and the administration of the Autonomous Community in which the National Park is located through a joint management commission, in which both administrations are equally represented. The only exception was Aigües Tortes and Sant Maurici, which was exclusively coordinated by the Autonomous Community of Catalonia through a coordination commission.

259. This new National Parks management model was designed in the second semester of 1996, in order to take account of the conclusions of Constitutional Court Decision 102/95 on Act 4/1989 regarding National Parks management. Act 41/1997 of 5 November defined the new management model at all levels, and foresees the constitution of management and participation bodies (the joint commissions and the Network Council). RD 1760/1998, which developed Act 41/1997, specified the composition and operation of the Natural Parks Network Council, of the joint commissions of the aforementioned Parks, and their patronage. The Network Council acts as the State tutorial body of the National Parks Network and ensures management homogeneity. The joint commissions, on which both State and Autonomous Communities representatives sit, elaborate the management and use of natural resources plans. Finally, the patronages, with State, Autonomous Communities, local entities and citizen representation, look for the correct observance of the legislation established regarding the National Parks.

260. The Constitutional Court, in several Sentences (194/2004, of 10 November; 35/2005 and 36/2005, of 17 February), has declared this collaborative management system between the State and the Autonomous Communities unconstitutional for inter-community National Parks. Similarly, in the case of inter-regional National Parks, the Constitutional Court considered the granting of management of these spaces to the State unconstitutional, even though it is a co-management system, because it violates the Autonomous Region's jurisdiction on protected natural spaces and the self-organization of their services. According to the Constitutional Court, the State had to limit its participation, as corresponds to its role as a coordinator, to implementing methods by which the affected Autonomous Communities could manage the part of the park in their respective territories, integrating its activities in a suitable manner.

261. Act 5/2007, of 3 April, on the National Parks Network establishes that the National Parks are to be managed by those Autonomous Communities within whose boundaries they are located, except for National Parks in sovereign or nationally regulated marine areas, which will be managed by the General State Administration if the protected ecosystem is not physically linked to the land or marine and land areas situated in the Autonomous Community. In those cases where a National Park extends over the territory of two or more Autonomous Communities, the Communities in question will reach a common agreement to establish how they will collaborate and manage the Park together. This last aspect has been challenged in the Courts by the Autonomous Community of the Canary Islands on the grounds of unconstitutionality (ruling pending).

Nevertheless, the Act establishes the basic contents of the Management and Use Master Plans, which have to be approved by each and everyone of the National Parks (Article 17), and the basic contents of the Boards, which are to participate socially in the National Parks (Article 18). These Boards must issue reports on all aspects linked to the management of the Parks, and must include representatives from the three Administrations, the institutions and associations whose activities are linked to the National Park, and environmental organizations.

262. Article 6 of the Act regulates the Network Council, a consultory body that was first set up by Act de la Ley regula el Consejo de la Red, como órgano colegiado de carácter consultivo, que ya existía desde la Ley 4/1989, but which has now been expanded and given increased powers. The Council is made up of the:

> Autonomous Communities in which the National Parks are located, representatives of the municipalities included in the National Parks' areas of socioeconomic influence, the presidents of the Boards, representatives of those associations whose activities are linked to the protection of the environment, representatives of unions and agricultural, fishing and business organizations and representatives of the owners of land within the boundaries of the National Parks.

The Council is responsible for, among other things, providing information on: proposals for new National Parks or proposals to modify existing parks; proposals to revoke the National Park status of a Park; the Master Plan of the National Parks Network and any revisions thereof; any State provisions that directly affect the National Parks; the annual report of the National Parks Network; the triennial reports on the state of the National Parks Network which the Ministry for the Environment will present to the Senate; and the Management and Use Master Plans of the different National Parks before these are approved. The specific composition and functioning of the Council was specified in RD 12/2008, of 11 January.

263. National Parks is an autonomous administrative public body, dependent on the Ministry of Environment, responsible for developing and coordinating the planning and management of the National Parks Network. This body is also in charge of the management of forests, lands and real estate within the national property previously dependent on the Institute of Nature Preservation (ICONA) and the Institute for Agricultural Development and Reform (IRYDA), and whose management parameters are getting progressively closer to its general preservation objectives. The autonomous National Parks body was created on 23 June of 1995 by RD 1055/1995, declaring the merger between the ICONA and the IRYDA Institutes, dependent of the Ministry of Agriculture, Fishery and Food, through the General Secretariat of Rural Development and Nature Preservation. A year later, it was incorporated to the just created Ministry of Environment, practically keeping the same powers declared by RD 1055/1995, as stated in Article 2 of RD 1538/1996 of 21 June. Through the approval of Royal Decree 1477/2004, of 18 June (modified by Royal Decrees 2182/2004, of 12 November and 236/2005, of 4 March), the autonomous National Parks body was attached to the Ministry of the Environment, through the Secretary General for Land and Biodiversity. Currently, RD 1130/2008, of 4 July, which sets out the basic organic structure of the Ministry of the Environment and Rural and Marine Affairs, establishes that the autonomous National Parks body is to be the responsibility of the Secretary of State for the Rural Environment and Water of the Ministry of the Environment and Rural and Marine Affairs.

Nevertheless, the secondary additional Provision of Act 5/2007, 3 April, on the National Parks Network authorizes the Government to create a 'State National Parks Network Agency' under the auspices of the Ministry of the Environment, the aim of which is to execute the competencies which the Act attributes to the General State Administration and, in particular, to coordinate the National Parks Network. These competencies will be temporarily executed in their present form by the autonomous National Parks body.

264. Order MAM/1742/2006, of 29 May, created the National Parks Network Scientific Committee. This Order modified the previous one from 12 July 2001, which created the 'National Parks Specialized Scientific Committee' in order to support the research programme specified in RD 1803/1999, of 26 November, which in turn approved the National Parks Network Master Plan. The aim was to comply with the Ruling 101/2005 of the Constitutional Court, of 19 April 2005, which redistributed competencies between the Central Administration and the Autonomous Communities regarding the National Parks and the Master Plan.

Chapter 2. Monuments and Landscapes

§1. LANDSCAPES

265. The main difficulties in the consideration of the landscape as a protected resource arise when trying to define which characteristics or elements make a specific landscape worthy of protection and which specific elements should therefore be protected. One of the main characteristics of the Spanish peninsula is its polymorphism, that is, the multiplicity of landscapes that can be found throughout its territory. There is no landscape uniformity to be found in Spain, except on the northern and southern sub-plateaus, and the presence of mountain ranges of different magnitudes fragmenting its territory is continuous.

266. Perhaps for this reason, the Spanish landscape regulation is fragmentary, dispersed and very flexible, setting up a limitations regime that permits the coexistence of activities of an economic nature with criteria such as on landscape preservation. Normally the regulations contain basic guidelines and do not establish binding legal tools for the use, protection, preservation and restoration of the landscape.

267. In Spain, landscape protection can be found in several special Acts, but the most general one is again Act 47/2007 (Article 34). This Act maintains the regulations specified in Act 4/1989, which represented a significant step forward in the protection and preservation of the landscape, creating the concept of 'protected landscape' as a specifically protected natural space. Protected landscapes are those places which, due to their aesthetic or cultural value, require a special protection. This protection takes place independently of whether the landscape is considered to be an integral element of another specific protected natural space, the Natural Parks. Sometimes both the architectonic and landscape patrimony are considered to be a 'natural estate of cultural interest'. References to landscape protection can also be found in the text and forewords of several Acts which declare specific areas to be protected natural spaces.

268. Act 4/1989 establishes several limitations on the activities carried out in protected areas when they could cause a significant effect on the landscape:

– A prior EIA will be required for those activities that could cause a transformation in land use involving deforestation when they affect areas of more than 100 ha.
– During the elaboration of a Natural Resources Plan for a specific protected area, any activity that could result in a significant transformation of its environment is prohibited.
– The exercise of any activity should respect the surrounding ecosystems.
– The use of the natural resources inside National Parks will be limited when incompatible with the beauty of the landscape.
– If the use of the natural resources inside reserves is incompatible with their fragility, it will be limited.

- The limitations created for the peripheral protection zones (created in order to avoid ecological or landscape impacts from the exterior) are to be observed.
- The discharging or dumping of wastes capable of altering landscape conditions is prohibited.
- The altering of landscape conditions of a protected natural area through the ploughing or cutting of trees is prohibited.
- Storage of junk that could alter in any way the perspective or harmony of the landscape is prohibited.

269. Spain has no State law concerning landscapes. At Autonomous community level, Catalonia has Act 8/2005, of 8 June, on the protection, management and regulation of landscapes, and Decree 343/2006, of 19 September, which implements the aforementioned act; Valencia has Act 4/2004, of 30 June, on land regulation and landscape protection, and Decree 120/2006, of 11 August, which approves the landscape regulations; and Galicia has Act 7/2008, 7 July, on landscape protection. The following Special Acts also include some dispositions on landscape protection.

270. Act 22/1988 of 28 July on Coasts includes, among its objectives, landscape protection. The Act prescribes the rational use of coasts according to their specific nature and respecting the landscape, environment and historic patrimony. The foreword of the Act considers the environment as a common patrimony that should be preserved for the use and benefit of the citizens.

271. Royal Decree 2/2008, of 20 June contains the redrafted text of the new Land Act and, as we will see in Part III, considers that rational land use can be ensured through planning tools which allow for the coexistence of different possible uses, as well as the coordination of the different managers of the resource. Royal Decree 2/2008, together with the Municipality Urban Plans, created landscape protection measures in order to avoid the degradation of the territory. Article 2 states that, in keeping with the principal of sustainable development, public policies regarding the regulation, occupation, transformation and use of land should ensure, among other things, the efficacy of the measures adopted to conserve flora and fauna and to improve the natural environment and the protection of the natural heritage and the landscape. Likewise, Articles 4 and 5 establish the right of the citizen to be able to enjoy an appropriate landscape and the citizen's corresponding duty to respect that landscape. Article 10.2 states that:

> installations, constructions and buildings must be adapted to the environment in which they are located; to this purpose the location, size and height of buildings, walls, fences or other installations will not be permitted to obstruct, interrupt or disfigure the harmony and appearance of landscapes in open and natural rural and marine spaces or of urban settlements of historical, artistic or traditional value.

The land-use legislation provides another interesting figure: the so-called 'Special Plans'. Specific sites or perspectives are subject to a Special Plan, such as natural areas with a significant landscape interest; historic, singular or picturesque enclaves;

singular buildings characterized by their architectural values or location or by their historical relevance, beauty, design or the botanical variety of their gardens or parks; built-up areas of traditional or aesthetic value, etc.

From the Spanish legal perspective, there has traditionally been a partial disconnection between urban planning and environmental protection. We will analyse in Part III how this is progressively changing. Urban planning should ensure the correct integration of environmental planning and environmental legislation. In addition, new buildings and infrastructural works should be adapted to the landscape, including watercourses and lakes as well as those measures whose main concern is to produce natural land restoration. Urban planning should also address landscape preservation by creating special protected areas through the delimitation of specific spaces to be protected and preserved from urbanization.

272. Forest Acts (specifically, Act 43/2003, of 21 November, on Forests, which revokes the former Act of 8 June 1957, on Forests) are the third instrument for landscape protection (plus measures focused on agricultural aspects such as Autonomous Communities agriculture Acts, and those with a more environmental character such as the Autonomous Communities high mountain Acts). As mountain landscape preservation and nature preservation in general is not possible without the help of the local population, the depopulation of some Spanish areas has resulted in the degradation of their landscapes, and what is even worse, a desertification trend involving a great risk of total abandonment and a degradation of the natural environment. To avoid this, the legislation establishes the possibility to carry out specific economic activities in these mountain areas, preserving at the same time the natural values. An environmental impact study of the area in question, with a special consideration of its landscape values, would be very useful before an economic project is authorized.

§2. Monuments

273. The preservation of the historical patrimony of Spain is regulated by Act 16/1985 of 25 June on the Spanish Historical Patrimony and by RD 111/1986 of 10 January which partially develops Act 16/1985.

There also exist, on this matter, specific dispositions approved by the Autonomous Communities.

274. Act 16/1985 defines the concept of historical patrimony as the real estate and movable goods with an artistic, historical, paleontological, archaeological, ethnographic, scientific or technical value. This wide concept also includes natural sites, gardens and parks with a specific artistic, historical, or anthropological value, that can be declared as 'goods of cultural value'.

275. For the purposes of this monograph we will concentrate specifically on the so-called 'monuments' and 'historical gardens'. Monuments are those works which constitute architectonic or engineering accomplishments, as well as sculptures of colossal dimensions as long as they have an historic, artistic, scientific or social interest. Historical gardens are limited areas which are a product of human intervention in natural elements, sometimes including artificial works, and considered as having a significant interest due to their historical origin or aesthetic, botanical or sensorial values. Any work affecting monuments or historical gardens declared to be of cultural value or their surroundings, as well as the placement of any kind of signal or symbol on them, will require the express authorization of the bodies competent to enforce the Act.

276. The Act establishes two main prohibitions regarding these protected goods: first, the prohibition of placing any kind of commercial advertising, wiring, antennas or visible conducts on historical gardens or facades of monuments declared of cultural value; second, the prohibition of any construction work that could result in the transformation of the monument's or historical garden's character or that could disturb its contemplation by the public.

277. Act 42/2007, of 13 December, on Natural Heritage and Biodiversity, also refers to the concept of 'natural monument'. According to this Act, natural monuments are those areas or natural elements constituted, basically, by formations notorious for their singularity, rarity or beauty, therefore deserving to be specially protected. Also included in this definition are singular and monumental trees, geological formations, paleontological and mineral deposits, stratotypes and other elements of interest because of their singularity or their scientific, cultural or landscape value.

Chapter 3. Wildlife Protection

278. The Iberian Peninsula enjoys the most important biotic and abiotic diversity of Western Europe, which represents more than 50% of the existent fauna of the EU, and more than 80% of the EU flora. It could be said that Spain is responsible for the preservation of approximately 85,000 species, that is, the greatest part of the existing biodiversity in the European continent. Nevertheless, the preservation status of these biological diversity elements is worrisome. According to data from the Spanish Sustainable Development Strategy, Madrid, 2007:

> in Spain together with the great habitat diversity, there is a high specific diversity, of around 85,000 known species with more than 8,000 species of vascular plants and between 50,000 and 60,000 animal species, with a significant percentage of endemism. In the European context, our biological heritage has special relevance, since approximately 54% of the total number of species known in Europe is located in Spain, and nearly 50% of the unique species in Europe are present in our country. In addition to being the country with the highest number of species of birds, mammals and reptiles, Spain has a great wealth of domesticated biodiversity, with at least 500 species of cultivated plants and 174 cattle species, being the local varieties and native cattle species one of the main components of biodiversity, and the foundation of farming systems with low environmental impact. In spite of this wealth, the consequences of climate change and man's action are diminishing the biological diversity in Spain at a faster rate than during any other period in history. In this sense, it is important to point out the extinction of numerous native species of cattle and wild species of interest for agriculture and food. In the last one hundred years, at least 17 species of animals and 24 species of plants have become extinct, and the number of species declared in danger of extinction has increased from 75 in 1990, to 156 in 2004. Among the species of threatened emblematic vertebrates, we can mention the Iberian lynx, the imperial eagle, the brown bear of the Pyrenees and the Cantabrian Mountains the European mink, the Lammergeier and the Capercaillie of the Cantabrian Mountains and the Pyrenees.

279. Act 42/2007, of 13 December, on Natural Heritage and Biodiversity reversed Act 4/1989 of 27 May, on the Preservation of Natural Spaces and Wild Flora and Fauna. Section III of the Act focuses on the conservation of wild biodiversity and establishes that the Autonomous Communities have the obligation to adopt the necessary measures to guarantee the conservation of biodiversity that lives in the wild, preferably by preserving habitats and establishing specific regimes to protect those species that are particularly in need. The introduction of non-native species is prohibited if these are likely to, kill, harm, intentionally disturb, compete or interbreed with the native species, or upset the ecological balance. Likewise, section III prohibits the possession, transport, trafficking and trade in live or dead specimens.

280. Act 42/2007 created the List of Specially Protected Species. Any taxon or population included in this list is to be periodically evaluated to determine its conservation status. Also, it is prohibited to negatively affect any such species. The list of Specially Protected Species incorporates the already existing Spanish Catalogue of Threatened Species, which on the basis scientific recommendations includes species that have been classified as 'in danger of extinction' and 'vulnerable'. The inclusion of a taxon or population in the 'in danger of extinction' category may lead to the designation of critical areas that will be included in the Spanish Catalogue of Threatened Habitats. The Act also maintains the obligation set out in Law 4/1989, of 27 March, regarding the drafting of a recovery plan to ensure their conservation.

At the proposal of the State Commission for Natural Heritage and Biodiversity, the Sectorial Conference on the Environment will approve the Conservation Strategies for Threatened Species, which will provide the guiding framework for the recovery and conservation plans drafted and approved by the Autonomous Communities.

To complement these 'in situ' conservation measures, the Act establishes the obligation to develop breeding programmes for species included in the Spanish Catalogue of Threatened Species outside the species' natural habitat, especially when such programmes form part of the aforementioned conservation strategies or recovery and conservation plans. Likewise, in order to conserve the genetic and biological heritage of wild species and to integrate 'ex-situ' and 'in situ' operations into the conservation programmes, the law establishes that the Public Administrations must promote the creation of a network of banks containing biological and genetic material and a Spanish Inventory of Wild Species' Biological and Genetic Material Banks, which contain all the available data regarding this issue.

281. Act 42/2007 also deals with the spread of invasive species as a result of globalization and exchanges of all kinds. Hence the creation of the Spanish Catalogue of Invasive Exotic Species, which will include any species or subspecies that seriously threatens or may seriously threaten native species, habitats, ecosystems, agriculture or economic resources associated with the use of the natural heritage.

282. The Act also regulates the protection of species in relation to hunting and fishing. Given that these activities exploit natural resources, their practitioners must guarantee to respect the spaces, dates, methods of capture and species specified by the Autonomous Communities and to ensure that under no circumstances will they hunt or fish any of the species included on the List of Species of Special Interest, nor any species protected by the EU or use any methods prohibited by the EU. The Spanish Hunting and Fishing Inventory will provide information on the population levels, capture rates and status of the gene pool of those species that can be legally hunted or fished, with particular attention given to migratory species.

283. The national authorities have established the following action programmes addressed to the preservation of the most paradigmatic Spanish species, which will also be the common ground for the different Autonomous Communities' plans:

- National Strategy for the preservation of the Iberian lynx of February 1999, breeding plan for the Iberian lynx and ex-situ conservation plan.
- National Strategy for the preservation of the Cantabric brown bear of 19 October 1999.
- National Strategy Project for the preservation of the Iberian wolf of June 1999.
- National Strategy Project for the preservation of the bearded vulture of 4 July 2000.
- National Strategy Project for the preservation of the imperial Iberian eagle of 9 July 2001.
- National Strategy Project for the preservation of the Pyrenees capercaillie in January 2005.
- National Strategy Project for the preservation of the white-headed duck, of January 2005.
- Project for the 'Diagnosis of the preservation status of the Cantabric capercaillie' of June 1999.

Currently, several strategies are being developed for the preservation of other species (European mink, Balearic shearwater, Bonelli's eagle, Audouin's gull, giant river clam, marbled teal, crested coot), as well as a strategy to combat the environmental impact of pesticides on wild fauna. 9. Furthermore, in October 2004 a strategy against the use of bait in the natural environment was adopted.

284. The National Catalogue of Threatened Species, established by RD 439/1990 of 30 March was revised by different orders of the Ministry of the Environment which included new species and excluded or changed the category of others (Orders of 9 July 1998, 9 June 1999, 10 March 2000, 28 May 2001, 21 October 2002, 10 June 2003, 28 May 2004, 27 June 2005 and 26 April 2006). The National Red Books of Threatened Species, elaborated by different expert groups and of great scientific relevance, co-exist with the catalogue.

285. Together with the general legislation on species preservation, we should also mention other legislation regarding this matter:

- RD 1095/1989 of 8 September, which defines the species that can be fished or hunted, and establishes provisions on protection.
- RD 1118/1989 of 15 September, which defines the marketable fishing and hunting species, and establishes provisions in this respect.
- RD 1997/1995 of 7 December, which establishes measures for protecting biodiversity by means of habitats, flora and fauna preservation (amended by RD 1193/1998 of 12 June), modified by RD 1421/2006 of 1 December.
- RD 1739/1997 of 20 November, which establishes the implementation measures for the CITES Convention of 1973, and Regulation (EC) No. 338/97, on the Protection of Species of Wild Fauna and Flora by Regulating Trade Therein.

286. Concerning wetlands and within the context of the biodiversity strategy, the National Commission for the Protection of Nature approved the Strategic Plan for the Preservation and Rational Use of Wetlands (October 1999). This integral plan aims to address the great problems caused by coal pollution in those areas; update the existing inventory; implement a series of preservation measures for these natural enclaves and increase their importance within the hydrological resource, land use and biodiversity preservation.

Chapter 4. Agricultural Resources

287. The industrial development experienced by Spain during the 1960s, as well as the progressive evolution from an agricultural to a service economy, has left the country with an agricultural population index and agricultural contribution to the GDP similar to those of the most developed nations. In the last twenty years, the Spanish countryside has lost more than 2.5 million jobs and its percentage of total employment has dropped from 27% to 8%. The EU average is 6%.

288. Technology has significantly improved, as can be seen from the use of fertilizers, phyto-sanitary products and machinery. In the last twenty years, more than 1 million hectares have been left uncultivated. Today only 75% of the total national territory is being cultivated (20 million ha). The creation of new irrigation lands, cultivation on slopes and manure accumulation have had a very great environmental impact and have led to a significant loss of landscape quality. The consequences of the industrialization of agriculture are, among others, erosion (30% of the national territory presents a maximum level risk of desertification by erosion, and 45% present a medium-high risk level), the exhaustion of aquifers (almost 60% of the Spanish wetlands have already disappeared), the use of fertilizers and pesticides, and the production of agricultural wastes. Environmental concern has become a key element in the agricultural policy of the EU after the amendment, in 1992, of the Common Agricultural Policy (CAP). We should mention here that there are three dispositions which play a very important role in the implementation of this new policy: (EEC) Regulation No. 2078/92 on Agro-environmental Measures (EEC) Regulation No. 2079/92 on Advanced Retirement and (EEC) Regulation No. 2080/92 on Reforestation of Agricultural Lands.

289. The Spanish agricultural policy, according to (EEC) Regulation No. 2078/92 on Agricultural Production Methods Compatible with the Requirements of Environmental Protection and Natural Preservation, should focus on the following objectives:

- to promote those agricultural production practices that can diminish the polluting effects of agriculture and which, together with the reduction of the production, should result in a better market balance;
- to promote a more environmentally friendly extensive agriculture, including the transformation of herbaceous land into extensive pastures;
- to promote an exploitation of agricultural lands compatible with the protection and improvement of the environment, the natural space, landscape, natural soil resources and genetic diversity;
- to promote the preservation of abandoned agricultural and forest lands when their upkeep might be necessary for ecological reasons, such as the risk of fire or natural dangers, in order to mitigate the consequences of abandonment of rural areas;
- to promote, in the long-term, the abandonment of agricultural production on some lands for environmental reasons;
- to promote land management with recreational purposes, based on free public access;

– to promote farmers' awareness of the need of rendering agricultural production compatible with the requirements of environmental protection and preservation of natural spaces.

Act 45/2007, of 13 December, on the sustainable development of the rural environment regulates and establishes measures to encourage the General State Administration and the other Public Administrations to adopt measures for the sustainable development of the rural environment. The Act creates two consultory bodies to govern the agrifood sector and rural affairs; the State Agrifood Council and the Farming Assessment Committee. Both bodies have been created within the framework of Act 10/2009, of 20 October, regarding the creation of State consultory bodies in the agrifood sector and the conditions of representation for professional agrarian organizations. Articles 38, 39 and 40 of Act 45/2007 establish the creation of the Inter-Ministry Commission for the Rural Environment, the Council for the Environment and the Committee of Rural Development Associations. Both instruments have been created within the framework of Royal Decree 865/2008, 23 May. Finally, Royal Decree 752/2010, of 4 June approved the first sustainable rural development for the 2010–2014 period in application of Act 45/2007.

290. The following legislation aims to achieve the aforementioned objectives: Royal Decree 4/2001, which establishes an aid system for the use of environmentally compatible agrarian production methods and updated by Royal Decree 1203/2006, of 20 October. This Decree has been implemented by means of Royal Decree 585/2006, of 12 May, which establishes criteria for reducing agro-environmental grants and for providing compensation to disadvantaged areas in accordance with their compliance with good agricultural practices.

291. The State aids system foreseen by the (EEC) Regulation No. 2078/92 is implemented in Spain through a national programme divided into two parts: first, a programme consisting of four horizontal measures applying to the whole national territory (aids to extensive agriculture, to agro-environmental education, to the protection of species in danger of extinction and to the promotion of ecological agriculture); second, a national frame programme which incorporates the zone programmes proposed by the Autonomous Communities. The Spanish State legislation incorporates, basically, the objectives of the aforementioned EU Regulations, changing their formulation in some cases or adding some other generic principles regarding the improvement of the quality of life in rural areas in others (among others, to be in tune with the foreseen market changes; to improve in the long-term the forest, agricultural and livestock breeding resources; to contribute to a natural space management compatible with the environmental balance; to compensate the loss or decrease of agricultural income).

292. The implementation in Spain of (EEC) Regulation No. 2080/92 has been carried out through a national programme on 'Aids to forest investments in agricultural exploitations'. This programme is sub-divided, as regards its implementation, into two sub-programmes: first, the reforestation and improvement of already forested zones; second, forest development and planning actions in rural areas. The national programme includes criteria on: areas of possible reforestation; most suitable species; and aids and premium scales and control procedures. It also establishes the following measures: reforestation aids; annual premium per forested hectare; annual compensation per hectare for the loss of income caused by the reforestation; aids for the investment in improvement of the already reforested areas and the improvement of cork oak groves.

The regional and zone programmes are carried out through the legislations of the Autonomous Communities, which differ starkly in environmental, social and administrative aspects, and through the Collaboration Agreement between the State and the Autonomous Community, which sets the Autonomous Community's quota in the national contribution. It also establishes systems of coordination, follow-up and revision of the Agreement.

293. The results of these measures have not been as satisfactory as was expected, due to the excessive number of programmes adopted (three of a national character and sixty-three of a regional character) and the difficulty to orderly implement them. Furthermore, they followed different criteria and did not provide for a real follow-up.

As a consequence of the initiatives established, generically, by the CAP and specifically, by the European Commission Communication on 'Guidelines for sustainable agriculture', of January 1999, Spain has modified the structure of the former Ministry of Agriculture, Fishery and Food in several ways since the old RD 1490/1998 of 10 July (currently revoked). This disposition constituted a clear progress as it recognized the need to direct part of the new rural development policy contents toward environmental goals. Agriculture is now considered as an intersectorial policy regarding the environment. This tendency was maintained in Royal Decree 1417/2004, 11 June, which set down the basic structure of the Ministry of Agriculture, Fish, and Food. This Decree was modified by Royal Decree 1371/2006, of 24 November, and then partially repealed by Royal Decree 1130/2008, of 4 July, which implemented the basic organic structure of the new Ministry of the Environment and Rural and Marine Affairs.

294. The most relevant legislation on agricultural matters is:

- Act 45/2007, of 13 December, on the sustainable development of the rural environment.
- RD 1852/1993, on ecological agricultural production and its indication on agrarian and food products (modified by Royal Decree 506/2001, of 11 May), modified by RD 1614/2005, of 30 December.
- RD 261/1996 of 16 February on the protection of water resources against nitrate pollution from agricultural sources, which incorporates Directive 91/676/EEC.
- RD 145/1999 of 29 February, promoting native breeds of cattle in an extensive production regime (modified by Royal Decree 1567/1999, of 8 October).
- RD 1366/2007 of 19 October, which establishes the regulatory bases of the subsidies aimed at promoting native breeds of livestock which are specially protected because of a danger of extinction.

- RD 4/2001, 12 January, about an aid system for the use of environmentally compatible agrarian production methods.
- RD 5/2001 of 12 January, on an aid system to promote the anticipated cessation of agrarian activity.
- RD 6/2001 of 12 January, on the promotion of forestation of agricultural lands, modified by RD 1203/2006, of 20 October.
- RD 117/2001 of 9 February, which establishes the basic regulations for the promotion of investments for the improvement of transformation and marketing conditions for agrarian, forestry and food products (modified by Royal Decree 326/2003, of 14 March).
- RD 1201/2002, of 20 November, which regulates integrated agricultural production, and which was modified by RD 108/2010, of 5 February.
- RD 824/2005, of 8 July, on fertilizers, modified by RD 108/2010, of 5 February.
- RD 108/2010, of 5 February, which modifies various royal decrees regarding agriculture and agrarian industries to adapt them to Act 17/2009, 23 November, on the free access to the activities and execution of services, which incorporates Directive 2006/123/CE of the European Parliament and Council, of 12 December 2006, regarding services in the internal market.

295. We should add to this list the legislation on disadvantaged areas, constituted by:

- Royal Decree 3482/2000 of 29 December, which regulates the official compensation in certain disadvantaged areas, modified by RD 1203/2006, of 20 October and developed by RD 585/2006, of 12 May, which establishes the criteria for reducing agro-environmental grants and for providing compensation to disadvantaged areas in accordance with their compliance with good agricultural practices.
- Royal Decree 613/2001 of 8 June, for the improvement and modernization of the production structures of agrarian exploits (modified by Royal Decrees 499/2003, of 2 May and 1650/2004, of 9 July).

These dispositions are targeted at those regional areas where the preservation of the environment is most needed for three fundamental reasons: low birth rates, a low quality of life level, and a scarce population. In other disadvantaged areas specific conditions will be established in order to render the preservation of agricultural production compatible with environmental protection, as well as with the preservation of the tourist potential of the area and of the seaside, where relevant.

296. This subject has a transectorial character, because in the Spanish environmental legislation there are several references to the agricultural sector. As a consequence, it is sometimes necessary to take environmental dispositions which do not specifically concern agricultural matters into account in order to achieve a global view:

- Legislation regarding zoning and land use, as will be analysed in Part III, grants special protection to specific areas due to their exceptional agricultural, forestry or stockbreeding value, their natural resources exploitation possibilities, their landscape, historic or cultural values, or either for the defence of their fauna or flora or for ecological balance purposes. It also establishes that the improvement of the rural areas can be subject to Special Plans which prohibit construction and uses which may harm the environment and which permit or allow the modification of specific vegetal elements, gardens and trees. This special land-use planning can affect vegetable gardens, crops and forests, by imposing use restrictions intended to avoid their disappearance or modification.

- Legislation regarding water and coastal management regulates the use of water for agricultural purposes and specifies which cultivation or crops are permitted in the coastal areas.

Chapter 5. Forests

297. The importance of forestry in Spain is evident, given that according to the Third National Forest Inventory 1997–2007 the forests and other open areas cover more than 26 million ha, or more than half of the national territory. The forested areas take up nearly 15 million ha. Of them, 45% have a coniferous tree cover, 44% broad-leaf species and the remaining 11% are mixed forest. The other 12.1 million ha include bush-like vegetation and open spaces, with scarce or no vegetation at all. 'Forests' include all territory not intended for residential, industrial or commercial agriculture purposes. The concept, then, is very wide, including not only thick forest but also desert areas and pastures.

298. The Spanish forest policy has experienced significant changes in recent years which have emerged in the approval of new regulations which work toward sustainable forest management. These are the main premises of this issue that can be inferred: multi-functionality, integration of forest planning in land-use planning, territorial and subsidiarial cohesion, integration of forest policy with international environmental objectives, inter-administrative cooperation and the obligatory participation by all interested social and economic agents in the making of decisions concerning the forest environment.

299. The specific legislation on this matter is currently contained in Act 10/2006, 28 April, which modifies Act 43/2003, of 21 November, on Forests, the object of which is to ensure the conservation and protection of Spanish forests and to repeal the former Forest Act of 8 June 1957, which was valid for almost a half a century. The Act of 1957 did not include any specific dispositions regarding protection, preservation and improvement of the forests, both public and private. Its objectives were to discipline the forest property regime, the easements and in rem rights over it, and the legal regime of its uses and forest industries. It also established economic planning projects, including the possibility of administrative intervention for the protection of private forests, which represent two-thirds of the total surface of Spanish forests. It also contained dispositions for the defence of forests against plagues and fires, as well as for the National Parks.

300. The Act of 8 June 1957 did not consider the forest as a whole as a subject deserving of protection. The legislation only protected specific forests that, due to their location or their characteristics, played a relevant role in some natural processes, especially the hydrological processes. Due to its limited scope, the Forest Act was more a forest property Act than an environmental Act.

301. Because of this worrisome deficiency in forestry legislation, the Spanish Ministry of Environment has opted for the elaboration of a Spanish Forest Strategy, approved on 17 March 1999 by the Environment Sectorial Conference.

302. A series of basic instruments was needed to implement the Spanish Forest Strategy. The first of these was administrative reorganization, for which purpose the

Sectorial Conference on the Environment, which includes all public administrations, was made responsible for forestry matters. Another instrument was the former National Forest Council, created by RD 203/2000 of 11 February, which was recently repealed by Royal Decree 948/2009, of 5 June, which determines the composition, functions and operating regulations of the new State Council for Natural Heritage and Biodiversity. From this organizational point of view, the existence of the Forest Protection Service against Noxious Agents must be noted, having as its basic priority the preservation of the forest ecosystems and the upkeep of the natural balance. Second, the elaboration of a basic State Act on forests and forest uses, in compliance with Article 149(1.23) of the Spanish Constitution. This new Act was Act 43/2003, of 21 November, on Forests. Third, the establishment of incentives and financial backups in order to contribute to the sustainable maintenance of private forests. And finally, the enlargement of the list of cases where EIA is compulsory, for a better protection and preservation of forest ecosystems.

Within the framework of the Spanish Forest Strategy, national forest planning is a fundamental factor. The Spanish Forest Plan is currently the main instrument for planning policy related to the forests in our country on a general level. This Plan, approved by the Council of Ministers on 5 July 2002, proposes the reforestation of 3.8 million ha and the resulting storage of up to 60 million tonnes of carbon during the stipulated thirty years of application. The costs calculated by the Ministry of the Environment add up to EUR 2,200 million in the next seven years. This plan consists of actions related to the land (the restoration of the vegetation cover and repopulation efforts, sustainable forest management ...), socio-economic and cultural actions (the promotion of forest product industries, forest culture and the social value of the forest ...) and institutional actions (coordination instruments and exterior forest policy).

The other great factor, as previously stated, is the basic regulation on forest issues: Act 43/2003. This Act aimed to set up an effective instrument to ensure the preservation of Spanish forests, as well as to promote their restoration, improvement and rational use, using collective solidarity for support. Among its most notable aspects is a new planning instrument for use by the Autonomous Communities known as the forestry resources regulation plan (FRRP) These are used for forestry planning within the framework of territorial regulation.

303. Act 43/2003, of 21 November, was modified by Act 10/2006, 28 April. This modification was significant because it introduced new management principals, such as caution and the adaptation of woodlands to climate change, as well as new protective measures (e.g., protective woodlands), regulations relating to forest fires and many other issues. The Act was also modified by Act 25/2009, of 22 December, which adapted various laws to the Act regarding free access to the activities and execution of services.

Act 10/2006 also introduces a general regulatory modification because it states that the Government is responsible for approving the basic common directives regarding the regulation and exploitation of forests, whereas the Autonomous Communities will be responsible for approving the instructions for regulating and exploiting forests.

304. On the other hand, the Autonomous Communities have produced a forest legislation adapted to the environmental evolution, with a new and more open concept of forest, which includes its great social relevance. Some of these Acts are: Autonomous Regulation 13/1986, of 4 July, which regulates the Montes de Álava; Act 6/1988, of 30 March, on the Forests of Catalunya; Act 13/1990 of 31 December on the Protection and Development of the Forest Patrimony of Navarra; Act 2/1992 of 15 June on the Forests of Andalusia; Act 3/1993 of 9 December on the Forests of Valencia; Act 2/1995 of 10 February on the Protection and Development of the Forest Heritage of the Rioja; Autonomous Regulation 3/1994, of 2 June, on Forests and the Administration of Protected Natural Spaces in Biscay, modified by Autonomous Regulation 3/2007, of 20 March; Act 16/1995 of 4 May on Forests and the Protection of Nature in the Autonomous Community of Madrid; Act 3/2004, of 23 November, on the Protection of Forests and Forestry Regulation in the Principality of Asturias; Autonomous Regulation 7/2006, of 20 October, on the Forests of Gipuzkoa; Act 15/2006, of 28 December; the Forests Act of Aragon; Act 3/2008, of 12 June; the Forests and Sustainable Forests Management Act of Castile-La Mancha, Act 3/2009, of 6 April; and the Forests Act of Castile and Leon.

305. Regarding nature legislation related to forests, Act 4/1989 of 27 March on Preservation of Natural Areas and Wild Flora and Fauna was a point of reference for forest matters from its approval until its modification, Act 43/2003 is intended to be an effective instrument for guaranteeing the conservation of Spanish forests, and for promoting their restoration, improvement and reasonable exploitation. The Act is based on certain principals of sustainable forest management. From these are derived other principals such as the integration of forestry planning into territorial regulation, the promotion of forest products and rural development, the conservation of woodland diversity and the integration of forestry policies into international environmental objectives.

306. Act 10/2006, of 28 April includes a new Chapter on the 'legal system for protective forests and forests with other levels of protection'. The importance of these woodlands, whether private or public, is gauged according to their particular characteristics, such as being situated at the headwaters of a drainage basin, helping to regulate the hydrological system, preventing or reducing avalanches or floods, protecting settlements, crops or infrastructures, being located in priority areas for erosion prevention measures, preventing or reducing landslides or the silting up of reservoirs, protecting crops and infrastructures from the wind or being located on the edges of areas for capturing surface or underground water, among others. These characteristics mean that these forests should be regulated and placed on a register so that the Administrations can ensure that they are properly safeguarded. The Autonomous Communities are responsible for giving protective forest status to areas of woodland. Likewise, the Autonomous Communities can establish other special protective measures for privately or publicly owned forests that help preserve biodiversity by maintaining the ecological systems, the flora, the fauna and the genetic diversity that form part of the protected natural spaces, the Natura 2000 Network, the biosphere reserves or other legally protective entities, by being located in areas of influence, by constituting important elements of the landscape, or by being included in areas at high risk of fire, among other characteristics. When the Autonomous Communities designate woodlands as protective forests or forests with other levels of protection, they also have to create the corresponding administrative public registers.

307. Act 10/2006 introduces another instrument for protecting forests by adding Article 35*bis* to Act 43/2003, which establishes that:

> in public contracting procedures, the Public Administrations will adopt the necessary measures to prevent the acquisition of wood and other products derived from illegal logging in other countries and to encourage the acquisition of products from certified forests. The Public Administrations will disseminate information to the public to encourage the responsible consumption of these products.

308. Land-use legislation and planning constitutes another relevant tool for forest protection. One of the objectives of RLD 2/2008, of 20 June, which approves the redrafted text of the current Land Act, is to reconcile land use with the concept of sustainable development. In its preamble, it states that:

> without doubt, urban growth continues to be necessary, but today at the same time it is clear that urban growth must be carried out in a manner that is consistent with the requirements of sustainable development in order to minimize its impact by, for example, regenerating existing urban areas. The EU is clear on this point in its European Territorial Strategy or in the more recent European Commission Communique regarding a Thematic Strategy on the Urban Environment, which favours the idea of the compact city and warns of the dangers of scattered and uncontrolled urban growth, such as impact on the environment, social segregation, and economic inefficiency due to the increased cost of supplying energy, constructing and maintaining infrastructure and providing public services. In addition to being an economic resource, land is also a scarce and non-renewable natural resource. From this perspective, the environmental value of all rural land should be carefully weighed up [,,,] Likewise, urban land, land that is already developed, has an environmental value as a collective cultural creation that is permanently recreated, which means that its characteristics should be an expression of nature and its regulation should encourage its renovation and use.

In accordance with this, Article 2 of the Act states that public policies relating to the regulation, occupation, transformation and use of land have the common aim of using this resource for the common good and according to the principal of sustainable development, which means that these policies:

> should encourage a rational use of natural resources which harmonizes the requirements of the economy, employment, social cohesion, equal treatment and opportunities for women and men, health and safety and environmental

protection and which helps prevent and reduce pollution. The following are particularly important objectives:

(a) Adopting effective measures for conserving and improving the environment, the flora and fauna populations, the cultural heritage and the landscape.

(b) Protecting the rural environment and preserving the idea that land does not necessarily have to be developed or that it is unsuitable for urban development.

(c) Creating an urban environment which uses land efficiently, which has sufficient infrastructures and services, which implements and functionally combines the uses of such infrastructures and services for general society.

309. Concerning erosion and desertification, the powers regarding the basins' hydrologic forest restoration are shared between the State and the Autonomous Communities. The Collaboration Agreements subscribed to with this purpose in mind between both of them have included reforestation with species of the maximum ecological value for the climate, topography and soil conditions; correction works of torrents and gullies, such as active defence actions aiming to diminish the dragging of solids; and forest mass treatment to preserve and improve the condition of the protective vegetal cover.

The purpose of these actions is to generate integrated effects on the area to be protected, intended to stop and control the erosion process and to promote the recovery of the biologic capacity of degraded areas; to increase and improve the vegetal cover, to increase its biodiversity and soil resources; to protect and improve the hydrological resources' quality and to diminish the flood and inundation risks; to render the development of rural areas compatible with environment preservation and the protection of current ecosystems; and other induced effects, such as the generation and protection of the biodiversity and increase of aesthetic or recreational values.

The absence of an instrument for national planning on this matter has provoked the Ministry of the Environment to come up with a plan which constitutes the general framework for the development of projects for the restoration, preservation and improvement of the protective vegetation cover: the National Priority Action Plan on the issue of hydrological-forest restoration, erosion control and defence against desertification, which provides for the participation of the Autonomous Communities in the making of decisions in coordination with the General Directorate on Biodiversity (Ministry of the Environment). Among its objectives are the maintenance and improvement of the protective function of the forests for soil and water resources; erosion control, the improvement of the water system and the regulation of river flows; the restoration, preservation and improvement of the protective vegetation groundcover; the identification and ranking of priority action areas.

On the subject of desertification, it should also be mentioned, that the PAND can be found in the provisions of the Spanish Forest Strategy. Between 2005 and 2008, the Ministry of the Environment invested more than EUR 82.5 million to fight against the effects of desertification in Spain through agreements with thirteen Autonomous Communities. Finally, Order ARM/2444/2008, of 12 August, approved the aforementioned National Action Programme against Desertification in compliance with the United Nations Convention to fight against desertification.

310. Finally, in relation to forest fires, which is one of the greatest problems in the Spanish territory, the Order of 17 June 1982 approving the Basic Plan Against Forest Fires recognizes in its foreword the great serious social and economic problems caused by forest fires and their impact on climatology and the environment. This Order was substituted by an Order on 2 April 1993 which published the resolution by the Council of Ministers to approve the Basic Directive regarding Emergency Civil Protection during Forest Fires.

311. The regulations on forest fires can be found in Act 43/2003, of 21 November, on Forests (Chapter III of section IV – Articles 43–50), which revokes, on this point, the former Act 81/1968, of 5 December, on forest fires, modified by Act 10/2006. This Act grants jurisdiction for the responsibility of organizing forest fire defence to the public administrations, which, working together must adopt means conducive to the prevention, detection, and extinction of forest fires no matter who the forested land belongs to.

312. The following, among others, are the means of forest fire prevention included in the Act: the coordinated organization between the State administration and the administration of the Autonomous Regions to create specific programmes on forest fire prevention based on investigations into the causes of such fires; the development by the public administrations of awareness and sensitivity programmes on the prevention of forest fires, promoting public participation and encouraging a sense of co-responsibility in the general population for the protection of forests; the regulation by the Autonomous Communities of all activities that are fire risks, and the establishment of safety norms applicable to housing developments, buildings, construction sites, electrical facilities, and transport infrastructure in forested land and its surrounding area, that may contain fire hazards or be affected by them; fire watches and specific investigation into forest fire causes, mobilization of personnel and methods of extinction.

Act 42/2003 also echoes the importance of the role of civilians in the prevention of forest fires. According to that document, any person who is aware of the existence of a forest fire is obligated to report it, or if possible, to help extinguish it. Furthermore, the Act puts special emphasis on the need for coordination among the different administrations, not only in the prevention of forest fires, but also in their extinction. The Act also provides for the possibility of the establishment of high fire risk zones by the Autonomous Communities. These zones would appear in the forest fire defence plans which are approved by each Community's own administration. Finally, the Act establishes the obligation to restore land burned in forest fires, and prohibits changing the use of the land due to a fire.

Additionally, the Action Plan for the Prevention and Fight against Forest Fires, which was approved by the Council of Ministers on 10 June 2005, should also be mentioned. This Plan stipulates the creation of an Inter-ministerial Commission on the Prevention and Fight against Forest Fires, which is to be developed from thirteen ministerial departments with the aim of coordinating from the Ministry of the Presidency the monitoring of execution of the proposed measures. Furthermore, the magnitude of personal and material damage caused by a very large fire in the province of Guadalajara on 16 July 2005 motivated the adoption of Royal Decree Act 11/2005 of 22 July, which approves urgent measures on the issue of forest fires. In order to facilitate the application of these measures, which are intended to alleviate, compensate and repair, when possible, material and personal damage caused by either this fire or by those in Extremadura on 21 July 2005, Royal Decree 949/2005 was approved on 29 July.

313. One of the most important modifications that Act 10/2006 makes to Act 43/2003 is regarding the fight against forest fires. Many forest lands are deliberately set on fire so they can be used for agriculture, grazing, industrial activities or development. To impede these changes in the use of forest lands, the Act follows the example set by the regulations passed in other Mediterranean countries and in some Autonomous Communities and prohibits the use of burnt forest lands for any other purpose for at least thirty years, and prohibits any activity on these lands that may be incompatible with the regeneration of the forest. Thirty years is regarded as the minimum time needed for most forests to regenerate themselves and, by extension, prohibits the re-designation of forest land for development or other purposes, which would be detrimental to forest regeneration aims that are at the heart of sustainable forestry management. Nevertheless, the Autonomous Communities can approve exceptions to these prohibitions if they show that the change in the use of forest land had been approved before the fire took place.

314. Likewise, as has been indicated, forest fires are one of the areas assigned by Act 10/2006 to the new special environment sections of the public prosecutor's offices of the Supreme Court and the Provincial Courts.

315. The compensation fund established by Act 81/1968, which has since been abolished, has not yet been applied effectively. This circumstance is acknowledged by RD 875/1988 of 29 July on Compensation of Costs Resulting from Forest Fire Extinction, which regulates the full operation of the fund, and RD 3769/1972 on the Compensation of the Costs Caused by Forest Fire Extinction when located in areas either managed by the State or the Autonomous Communities. In accordance with Act 43/2003, the General State Administration, through the Insurance Compensation Consortium, will guarantee to cover accident claims exclusively for people who participate in extinguishing forest fires. Over time, regulations have been approved to alleviate the effects of forest fires. Examples of these are Royal Decree Act 12/2009, 13 August and Act 3/2010, 10 March, both of which approved urgent measures to alleviate the damage caused by forest fires and other natural disasters that occur in the various Autonomous Communities.

316. On a more general level, another important innovation of Act 10/2006 was to create a natural heritage fund. However, this fund has been absorbed by the new

Fund for Natural Heritage and Biodiversity, created by Article 74 of Act 42/2007,of 13 December, on Natural Heritage and Biodiversity. Its objectives are to implement measures that will support the objectives of the Act, such as sustainable forest management, strategic prevention of forest fires and the protecting of forest and natural spaces that are funded by the General State Administration.

Chapter 6. Fish Resources

317. Fishing constitutes a key economic activity for several Spanish regions, in spite of the ever expanding limitations regarding the international fishing banks. Spain has more than 140 zones which were declared of fishing interest by Council Directive 2006/44/CE of 6 September 2006, regarding the quality of continental waters that require protection or improvement to be suitable for sustaining fish (which substitutes and codifies Directive 78/659/CEE, modified by Directive 91/692/CEE and Regulation (CE) No. 807/20039. Geographically speaking, the best quality fishing waters can be found in the upper reaches of rivers in northern Spain.

318. Concerning general legislation, the Spanish law regarding fishing is based on a general reference Act and other specific dispositions of a regional or sectorial character. It differentiates between marine and freshwater fishing. The basic Act regarding this matter is Act 42/2007, 13 December, on Natural Heritage and Biodiversity, which states that fishing will only be permitted for those species specified by the Autonomous Communities, although this declaration cannot under any circumstances affect those species included in the List of Specially Protected Species or those protected by the EU. Continental fishing will be regulated to guarantee the conservation and promotion of the species that are authorized for this practice. The Autonomous Communities will determine the land and waters where these activities can be practiced, as well as the dates when each species can be fished. In addition, the Act establishes a list of prohibited or restricted fishing methods.

319. The fishing sector continues to be economically important in Spain. At the end of 2008, Spain had 11,394 maritime fishing vessels. These vessels caught more than 800,000 tonnes of fish worth more than EUR 1,600,000,000. Article 149.1.19 of the Spanish Constitution gives the State exclusive competence in fishing matters.

Marine fishing is partially regulated by Act 22/1998 of 28 July on Coasts. This Act, when referring to the public use of the marine public domain (specifically the sea and its seaside), provides that this use will be public and free for the common uses which because of its nature, such as fishing, does not require works or facilities of any kind and which is carried out according to the Act and its implementing regulations. Moreover, as indicated, Act 42/2007 also creates Protected Marine Areas as natural spaces designated for the protection of ecosystems, communities and biological and geological elements of the marine environment, including intertidal and subtidal areas, which require special protection because of their rarity, fragility, importance or singularity.

320. Section 1 of Act 3/2001, of 26 March, on State Marine Fishing regulates marine fishing and establishes the ambit of application and the measures for conserving, protecting and regenerating fishing resources, the legal administration of fishing activities, the regulation of non-professional fishing, the measures for controlling and inspecting marine fishing and the regulation of the fishing sector. Section II concerns the regulation of the fishing sector in terms of the size of the fishing fleet and its competitive capacity, as well as training for professionals dedicated to fishing activities and other people working in the fishing sector. Section III establishes the conditions for the marketing and transformation of fishing products throughout the national territory, from their initial sale to their final consumption, guaranteeing that these products have been captured in accordance with the regulations regarding the conservation and protection of fishing resources. Section IV of the Act also covers the research into fishing and oceanography carried out by the Spanish Oceanography Institute, and section V covers the protection of fishing resources. In August 2010, the Government approved a project for a Sustainable Fishing Act, which is currently going through Parliament and which incorporates the principals of sustainability and responsible fishing, as well as the more recent changes in the fishing policy regulations of the EU and, in particular, those changes that refer to the fight against illegal, undeclared and unregulated fishing.

321. Another important legislation on this matter is RD 345/1993 of 5 March, establishing provisions on the production of shellfish and the quality required of shellfish waters, and Annex IV of the Regulation on the Public Water Administration and Hydrological Planning of 29 July 1988.

322. Through its Order of 1 September 1997, the Ministry of Agriculture, Fishery and Food (which now forms part of the Ministry for the Environment and Rural and Marine Affairs) forbad the practice of submarine fishing in certain areas, in order to permit the regeneration of fish resources, specifically shellfish and their ecosystem. This was also the objective of the construction of artificial reefs.

323. Finally, we also should mention here the Order of 9 June 1999, which includes in the National Catalogue of Threatened Species some cetaceans, marine invertebrates and flora species, while simultaneously excluding others or changing the category in which they were included.

324. The legislation on inland fishing basically has two provisions, one of them specifically addressed to the subject – Act of 20 February 1942 on Freshwater Fishing (and its RD of 6 April 1943) and the well-known Act 42/2007, which applies to the subject in a general way.

325. The Act of 20 February 1942 regulating the promotion and preservation of freshwater fishing, defines the object of the fishing law to be the preservation, promotion and use of the fish and other useful species that inhabit all inland waters, whether public or private, in a permanent or transitional way. This Act also establishes several absolute prohibitions, such as the use of dynamite and other materials or chemical substances that explode on water contact; the use of any substance to poison fish or to deoxygenate the water; to smash the water, throw stones into it or scare the fishes in any other way into the fishing nets; to fish by hand or with firearms and to hit the stones under which the fishes take refuge; to arbitrarily reduce the water flow, to alter the course or to destroy the aquatic vegetation; and the use of any other fishing procedure declared as noxious. Even an otherwise permitted procedure, when used in a specific river, may be prohibited if it might be harmful according to the competent administration.

Furthermore, RD of 6 April of 1943 implementing the Fresh Water Fishing Act, regulates matters related to the preservation and promotion of the species, establishing the minimum size of the caught fish, the establishment of closed seasons, the prohibition of fishing nets and procedures, the restocking of freshwater bodies, and the granting of fishing licenses.

326. We should also refer to Act 42/2007, which establishes that fishing in continental waters can only target those species specified by the Autonomous Communities, although under no circumstances may this declaration affect those species included in the List of Specially Protected Species or those protected by the EU. In all cases, inland fishing will be regulated in such a way to ensure the preservation and promotion of the authorized fishing species. The Autonomous Communities will determine the waters where fishing activities may be carried out, as well as the specific time periods for the fishing of each species. Act 42/2007 also establishes general prohibitions in fishing matters, such as the possession, use and marketing of all mass or non-selective procedures for the capture or death of the animals, as well as fishing during the reproductive and breeding period or when migratory species are migrating to breeding places. It also provides for the declaration of a temporary *moratorium* or special prohibitions when there are biological or health reasons to do so or when non-native species have been introduced.

327. RD 1095/1989 of 8 September (which develops Article 33(1) of Act 4/1989) listing the species which may be hunted or fished and the dispositions for their protection, should also be taken into account. In order to ensure the preservation of the genetic diversity and the preservation of autochthonous species, the introduction of new species or the strengthening of populations in the natural spaces, an administrative authorization from the competent bodies of the Autonomous Communities will be required, and this authorization can only be granted if the genetic diversity of the area is not affected and if compatible with the plans on natural resources and the conditions or requirements imposed by the Autonomous Communities. RD 1095/1989 declares that, in any case, any other chasing, death or capture of other species or in conditions different from those set out in the RD will require an exceptional and express authorization from the competent bodies of the Autonomous Communities.

328. Finally, the National Fishing and Hunting Census, dependent on the Ministry of the Environment and Rural and Marine Affairs is responsible for the updating and keeping of the most complete possible information on populations, captures and genetic evolution of the authorized species, including the data compiled by the competent bodies of the Autonomous Communities. The entitled users of the fishing resources will be compelled to give the necessary information to the aforementioned competent bodies of the Autonomous Communities.

Chapter 7. Subsoil and Minerals

329. This sector, partly related to other sectors such as transportation and industry, produces a direct effect on the environment, through phenomena of global and regional scope like climatic change or the acidification of waters and soils (that also affects the vegetation and causes the degradation of forests), and other impacts, even more important on a local scale, such as atmospheric pollution. Most of these problems are caused by the excessive use of fossil combustibles, specifically petroleum derivatives.

Spain suffers from a shortage of primary energy sources. The forms of energy with a low environmental impact have a vital importance for the energy policy of the country. They also present a great potential, due to geographical reasons. In consequence, the Renewable Energies Plan in Spain 2005–2010 was approved 21 July 2005. The Plan assumes a revision of the Plan to Promote Renewable Energies in Spain 2000–2010, which was in effect up to that time, and states the growing and excessive dependency on exterior energy, the necessity to preserve the environment and ensure sustainable development. Therefore, it promotes effective formulas for efficient energy use and the use of clean energy sources. The substantial growth in renewable sources, along with a major improvement in energy efficiency corresponds to reasons of economic, social and environmental strategy, in addition to being fundamental in order to comply with international commitments on environmental issues.

A draft plan is being studied to succeed the 2005–2010 Plan. This draft is known under the provisional title of the National Action Plan for Renewable Energies (PANER) 2011–2020 (in accordance with Directive 2009/28/CE of the European Parliament and Council, of 23 April 2009, regarding the promotion of energy from renewable sources).

330. The Spanish national mining policy is based on the following legislation

- Act 22/1973 of 21 July on Mining, amended by Act 54/1980 of 5 November, with a special consideration of the energetic mineral resources.
- RD 2857/1978 of 25 August on General Mining Regulation.
- RD 975/2009, of 12 June, on the management of waste from extraction activities and the protection and rehabilitation of spaces affected by mining activities.

331. Act 22/1973 of 21 July on Mining, amended by Act 54/1980 of 5 November, provides for the elaboration of studies, data collection and environmental protection in this sector. The Ministry of Industry will carry out, in collaboration with the Superior Council for Scientific Research, the necessary studies to adequate the National Programme on Mining Research to the estimations included in the Social and Economic Development Plans, in order to achieve its continuous updating and permitting the adjustment of government actions to resource management programmes. The Ministry of Industry should also carry out the appropriate studies to fix the conditions for environmental protection, which will be compulsory applied in the use of the resources.

332. RD 2857/1978 of 25 August establishing the General Mining Regulation defines the scope of the regulation and includes a classification of the mineral resources mentioned in the Mining Act. The scope is limited to: exploration activities, research, uses and benefits of minerals extracted from all mineral beds and other geological resources that, whatever their origin and physical condition, exist on the national territory, territorial sea, continental platform and seabed under Spanish jurisdiction or sovereignty.

The environment receives particular protection from RD 975/2009, of 12 June, on the management of waste from extraction activities and the protection and rehabilitation of spaces affected by mining activities. This RD implements the European Parliament and Council Directive 2006/21/CE of, 15 March 2006, on the management of waste from extractive industries. This Directive aims to achieve the objectives of the EU's policy on the environment, which states the minimum requisites needed to be established to prevent or reduce as far as is possible any adverse effects on the environment or human health resulting from the management of waste from extractive industries. The RD regulates the management of waste from extractive industries on dry land, that is, the waste resulting from the activities of research and exploitation regulated by Act 22/1973, 21 June, on Mines. Therefore, the Act is not applied to waste generated by activities of research and exploitation that are not directly related to mining, such as food waste, used oils, scrapped vehicles, spent batteries and accumulators, etc. Waste resulting from submarine research and exploitation of mineral resources are also exempt from the Act.

The RD regulates the procedures, the objectives and the contents of the restoration plan, paying particular attention to the management of mining waste, the environmental responsibility of the person or body in charge of the research and exploitation of mineral resources (including the financial guarantees or their equivalent which they must take on), the inspection system or control measures regarding research and exploitation of mineral resources and, in particular, the mining waste facilities.

The RD establishes the obligation for all those carrying out mineral resource exploitation to undertake restoration works of the natural spaces affected by the mining activities. The open-cast mining exploitations and the underground exploitations, whose facilities or open-air works could seriously damage the natural space where they are located, will be subjected to restoration works. In any case, before the granting of the authorization or exploitation concession, the promoter must present to the Provincial Directorate of the Ministry of Industry and Energy or the competent body of the Autonomous Communities, a restoration plan of the natural area affected by his activities. This plan, which must be presented together with the authorization or concession request, will contain thorough information on the site of the mining activities, the mining waste management plan, the measures foreseen for the preservation of the affected natural area, and the implementation timetable and estimated cost of the restoration works. No authorizations, permits or concessions regulated by the Mining Act can be awarded unless the promoter also presents a restoration plan and, once awarded, work may not start until the corresponding financial guarantees or their equivalent have been constituted. There are two guarantees: the first ensures compliance with the plan for restoring the land affected by the exploitation, preparation, concentration and profiting from mineral resources, and the second ensures compliance with the conditions imposed by the plan for restoring the natural space affected by mining waste installations. The competent body may require the Plan to be extended or modified.

The disciplinary regime applicable to the protection and rehabilitation of spaces affected by extraction activities is that of the Mining Act, modified by the first additional provision of Act 12/2007, of 2 July, including, when appropriate, the expiry of the research permit, authorization or exploitation concession; Act 10/98, of 21 April, on waste, particularly the part concerning the management of mining waste; and Act of 23 October, concerning environmental responsibility. Irregardless of this, the RD states that in accordance with Article 116.2 of the Act on Mines when the holder of the permit, authorization or concession fails to comply either fully or partially with the restoration plan, then the research and exploitation work can be provisionally or fully suspended.

Part III. Zoning and Land-Use Planning

§1. Introduction

333. Land-use planning and urban zoning law, which define the right of property, constitute some of the most important tools in environmental law. The increase in the environmental awareness during these last decades has caused planning law to assume a greater role in this matter. In any case, and given that land-use legislation and zoning define the legal status of real estate property, it can be said that there has never been a clear separation between urban planning and environmental protection. Through urban planning, environmental values can be saved and preventive actions can be implemented that will benefit nature and the environment. But to achieve this objective, urban planning must be sensitive to the environmental issues, problems should be reasonably anticipated and correct coordination between plans and competent bodies must exist. This objective has been expanded by the most recent environmental legislation which has introduced such planning as a new requirement to be taken into account in urban planning. Specifically, this refers to the application of SEA in the process of drafting and modifying new plans that affect the environment. This has already been analysed in Chapter 5.I. General and Administrative Legislation, which mentions the European Parliament and Council Directive 2001/42/EC of 27 June 2001 on the assessment of the effects of certain plans and programmes on the environment, and its complementary transposition into Spanish law by Act 9/2006, of 28 April, on the assessment of the effects of certain plans and programmes on the environment, presently substituted by Act 21/2013 on environmental assessment.

In this Part, we will try to consider this issue from a general perspective. First, we will analyse the distribution of powers between the administrations – the State, the Autonomous Communities and the local entities. We will then highlight the important role played by the local entities in planning matters, since they are responsible for using the urban planning tools in the defence of the environment. Substantive environmental legislation (on coasts, water, natural protected areas, etc.) also has a great impact on this sector, because within its framework specific plans with environmental content are elaborated and precise limits are established, that will have to co-exist with the other planning tools and therefore will necessarily condition their traditional content.

We will also mention the general regime applicable to this sector. Even though we will basically concentrate on the State legislation, due to the specificities of the Autonomous Communities' legislation in this matter, we should remember here that the Autonomous Communities have been the administrations that have shown the greatest creativity and have played the most significant role in planning. Any detailed study on this subject will thus require special attention to the specific legislation which each of these Autonomous Communities has been producing in the exercise of their powers. Finally, we will pay attention to land classification and the general regime of land use for environmental protection purposes.

§2. Powers on Urban Planning

I. The State and the Autonomous Communities

334. Before the passing of the Land Act of 1956, the urban planning powers were essentially local. After the approval of the Act, the State was given an important role in giving guidance, approving plans and surveillance, for the most part at the local entities' expense. The amendment of the Act of 1976 did not alter the status quo as far as the local entities were concerned. Their powers were still recognized, but the final approval of the so-called Urban Plans and the control over land-use planning remained within the State's power. Two new entities were created in order to resolve the internal discrepancies existing between ministries on this subject: the Central Urban Planning Commission, which had consultative powers and included representatives of the interested ministries and of the Ministry of Public Works and Urbanism, which was the most directly involved on these matters; and the Director Plans of Coordination, the most general plans on zoning and land-use. The Act of 1976 tried to complete this scheme by giving special attention to the Great Metropolitan Areas (Madrid, Barcelona, Bilbao and Valencia) in order to give to each of them and their respective area of influence a unitary approach.

335. The Constitution of 1978, which brought about a definitive internal transformation of the State, deeply altered this situation, since the decentralization principles on which it was inspired obviously had a direct impact in this matter. In the Statutes of Autonomy of the Autonomous Communities it is declared that they hold the exclusive powers in zoning, urban planning and housing matters. That means that they have the legislative, management and implementation powers as regards this subject. It also means that the administrative bodies of the Autonomous Communities substitute the administrative bodies of the State administration in exercising the powers previously given to the State by the Land Act of 1976 and its developing legislation. Therefore, the above-mentioned State legislation was in force only in so far as their prescriptions were not altered by subsequent Autonomous Communities' laws. In any case State laws were considered as substitute law (in force only if no similar provision existed at the Autonomous Community level).

This exclusive power held by the Autonomous Communities to enact legislation in this matter did not and does not operate automatically. In fact, urban planning regulation is shared with the State. This is due to different reasons, such as the fact that urban planning affects the right of property and that the Constitution declares in its Article 139(1) that all Spanish citizens have the same rights and the same duties in any part of the national territory. The Constitution also states, in its Article 149(1.1), that this guarantee falls within the State's power. Moreover, the State also holds exclusive power over the basic guidelines and coordination of economic planning (Article 149(1.2)). But this is not all. Given its global character, urban planning requires the acknowledgment of several sectorial aspects (forests, waters, industry, mining, energy, defence, roads, public works, harbours and coasts, etc.) in which the State has powers of greater or lesser importance. Finally, the Constitution, as we have already pointed out, declares that the State has the exclusive power to enact the basic legislation in environmental matters. This will necessarily affect the whole regulation on this issue.

From what has already been said we can deduce that the Autonomous Communities' legislative powers on land-use and zoning matters cannot be exercised single-handedly. The relations existing between the different administrations involved in this issue must be intensified and the interests and general or sectorial powers held by the Autonomous Communities should be balanced with the ones held by the State. But this objective is not easy to achieve in practice. The exact distribution of the urban planning powers between the State and the Autonomous Communities has proved to be a very delicate matter, and the legislation approved on this subject either by the State or by the Autonomous Communities has been brought to the Constitutional Court several times. We should mention here the Constitutional Court Decision STC 61/1997 of 20 March, annulling approximately 80% of the provisions of an important State law: the consolidated text of the Act on Zoning and Urban Planning approved by RDL 1/1992 of 26 June. Later, other Constitutional Court Decisions (STC 159/2001, of 5 July, 164/2001, of 11 July, STC 54/2002, of 27 February) have also been relevant. The vague and un-certain boundaries existing between the powers of the State and the powers of the Autonomous Communities have constituted an important source of conflicts. Bearing in mind that even today several questions still arise concerning the legality and scope of the different laws, we will not be giving to this question the in-depth approach that it deserves.

II. Local Entities

336. Urban planning matters have been traditionally located at the local level, subject to greater or lesser control by the superior levels of administration. According to the Constitution, the local entities can manage their own interests autonomously (Article 137), and urban matters are obviously within their interest. In this sense, the affirmation and determination of urban planning powers is common both in the general legislation regarding the local regime and in the substantial urban planning legislation. That is also the case for Act 7/1985 of 2 April on the Basics of the Local Regime. In this sense, it is the common practice for the municipalities to elaborate territorial urban plans applying within their jurisdiction (municipal general urban plans, at least) and at the same time, to intervene in the elaboration of the supra-municipal plans that may affect them.

Nevertheless, it should be remembered that the municipalities do not act alone in these matters, given the concurrence of interests of different levels on the decisions on territorial and urban planning. The urban plans produced by the local entities should also respect the legislation and urban planning of the administrations of a higher territorial jurisdiction.

§3. Basic Urban Planning Legislation

I. State Legislation

337. As already mentioned, the Spanish Constitutional Court has been called to elucidate whether the State had appropriately exercised its legislative powers on urban planning matters. Nowadays, after various failed attempts, basic State legislation binding all administrations (regional and local ones included) has been created, in particular RLD 2/2008, of 20 June, which approves the Rewritten Text of the Land Act. This State legislation is fairly generic and only focuses on the most important aspects, leaving many lesser aspects to be legislated for by the Autonomous Communities. For their part, the Autonomous Communities should respect the provisions of this Act, although they have plenty of room to design and implement their own planning models.

The Act basically regulates the following aspects: the basic conditions that guarantee that constitutional rights and duties regarding land throughout the State are equally executed and fulfilled; the economic and environmental guidelines of the Act's legal system; the guidelines by which it is evaluated; and the land responsibilities of the Public Administrations. The Act contains a list of citizens' rights and duties regarding land ownership, and regulates the urban planning legal system for property law, land guidelines, land use, the state of land, the transfer of estates, land valuation, land confiscation, legal sanctions, judicial reviews of decision, etc.

The Act makes the following specific references to the pairing of sustainability and planning:

- The Act establishes that, in the light of the principle of sustainable development, urban planning policies should favour the rational use of natural resources and the protection of the environment, help prevent and reduce pollution, and in particular promote effective measures for the preservation and improvement of flora, fauna and the natural world, the protection of cultural heritage and the landscape, the protection of the rural environment and the preservation of land that is not needed or appropriate for urban development.
- The basic criteria for land use that the Act imposes on the Public Administrations include the duty to adhere to the principles of energy efficiency, to guarantee the supply of water, to prevent natural risks and serious accidents, to prevent and protect against pollution and to limit the effects of pollution on health and the environment.
- The Act requires that the basic elements of installations, constructions and buildings should be adapted to the environment in which they are located. They must therefore be adapted to open and natural rural and maritime spaces. To strengthen respect for areas of natural beauty, the Act specifies that in the immediate environs of picturesque roads or paths, it is prohibited to construct buildings, walls, fences or any other element that restricts the view of the area of natural beauty or

that breaks the harmony or disfigures the appearance of the landscape. – Any administrative actions that infringe the regulations governing the greenbelt and open spaces will be declared null and void.
- In the rural ambit, any land that is legally protected because of its environmental, cultural, historical, archaeological, scientific or landscape value will remain under such protection and that only those changes to its natural state as are expressly authorized by law will be permitted.
- Land can only be removed or excluded from protected natural spaces and the spaces included in the Natura 2000 Network when the reason for such changes can be scientifically justified. Furthermore, in accordance with the 'Birds' and 'Habitats' Directives, the public must be informed of any proposed change. In the case of the Natura 2000 Network this will be carried out before the proposed change is presented to and accepted by the European Commission.

Finally, the Act expressly refers to SEA plans and programmes and to the existence of specific sectorial legislation (Act 9/2006, of 28 April, on the evaluation of the effect of specific plans and programmes on the environment). Plans or programmes regulating land use or zoning should be subject to an environmental assessment before they can be approved or modified in the manner prescribed by sectorial law. And although all this should be carried out in accordance with Act 9/2006 and the laws on urban development of the Autonomous Communities, the Redrafted Text of the Land Act refers to basic contents that need to be included regarding procedural phases and the importance of subsequently monitoring aspects of the plans that are directly related to sustainability.

II. Autonomous Communities' Legislation

338. The legislation of the Autonomous Communities that regulates zoning and land use is particularly thorough and wide-ranging. The following are the most important pieces of legislation. Note that after Constitutional Court Decision 11/1997, practically all of the Autonomous Communities' legislation on urban planning has been amended as follows:

- Andalusia, Act 7/2002 of 17 December on Urban Planning.
- Aragon, Act 3/2009, of 17 June, on Urban Development. (BOE. No. 170, of 15 July 2009).
- Asturias, LD 1/2004 of 22 April, which approves the Rewritten Text of valid legal resolutions related to Land and Urban Planning.
- Balearic Islands, Act 8/2003 of 25 November, on Urgent Measures related to Land and Urban Planning.
- Canary Islands, LD 1/2000 of 8 May, which approves the Rewritten Text of the Land Planning and Natural Spaces Acts.
- Cantabria, Act 2/2001, on 25 June, on Territorial Regulation and the Land Development Legal System.
- Castile-León, Act 5/1999 of 8 April on Urban Planning.

- Castile-La Mancha, LD 1/2004, of 28 December 2004, which approves the Redrafted Text of the Act on Territorial Regulation and Development.
- Catalonia, LD 1/2010, of 3 August, which approves the Redrafted Text of the Act on Land Development.
- Extremadura, Act 15/2001, of 14 December, on Land and Territorial Regulation.
- Galicia, Act 9/2002 of 30 December, on Urban Planning and Rural Environment Protection-Madrid, Act 9/1995 of 28 March, on Territorial, Land and Development Policy Measures.
- Murcia, LD 1/2005, of 10 June, which approves the Rewritten Text of the Land Act.
- Navarra, Act 35/2002, of 20 December, on Territorial and Land Development Regulation.
- Valencia, Act 16/2005, on 30 December, of the Valencian Government on Valencia Land Development.
- La Rioja, Act 5/2006, of 2 May, on Territorial Land Development Regulation.
- Basque Country, Act 4/1990 on 31 May, on Territorial Regulation.

None of the acts mentioned contains all the environmental requirements that must be followed when drafting and modifying plans or programmes that could have a significant environmental effect. Various Autonomous Communities have specific regulations in this area which complement the zoning and land-use regulations. For example, Catalonia has Act 9/2006, of 28 April, on the evaluation of the effect of certain plans on the environment.

§4. Land Classification and General Regime of Land Uses for Environmental Protection Purposes

339. Spanish urban planning law commonly classifies the different types of land. In accordance with the categories laid down by the State's basic legislation, land can be classified as (a) urban land, (b) rural land

340. In general terms, 'urban land' refers to the land which has already been effectively urbanized (with road access, water supply and collection infrastructures, electricity, etc.).

341. Land is classified as 'rural land' in the following cases:

> if it is subjected to any special regime of protection either by zoning or sectorial legislation on the basis of its ecological, landscape, historic, cultural, or scientific values or because of the need to protect against potential natural or technological risks, including flooding, serious accidents or any others covered by the territorial and land development legislation. Rural land is also that which, under the zoning or land use plan, can be developed. Such land remains rural until the process of development is concluded.

342. Any territorial or urban plan can delimit, within the zone that cannot be urbanized, special protection areas in which all activities that could, in any way, transform its nature or destiny, damage its specific value or infringe the established limitations, will be avoided.

343. The urban legislation also contains a specific administrative sanctioning regime, addressed to those who infringe its prescriptions. Criminal punishment is also established, as provided by the Criminal Code since 1995. New crimes have been typified regarding urban planning. Thus, it will be considered a crime when promoters or technical directors carry out unauthorized construction works on land destined for roads, green areas, goods of public domain or places that have a landscape, ecological, artistic or cultural value which is legally or administratively recognized. It also constitutes a crime to construct a non-authorized edification on land that cannot be urbanized.

§5. Urban Planning

344. It is difficult to give a clear overview of this subject, and it poses a significant risk, due, on one hand, to the visible differences among the laws applicable in the various Autonomous Communities and, on the other hand, the extent of the State government's legislative power in this area. As the typology and scope of the specific planning tools are usually established by the Autonomous Communities' rules mentioned above, it is practically impossible to generalize. It would be necessary to analyse all the legislation of seventeen Autonomous Communities separately, as they contain the diverse typologies of the existing plans, their scope and their environmental aspects. Nevertheless, we can point out the following general ideas.

345. The urban plans are ordered hierarchically: those of a lesser territorial scope must be adapted to the prescriptions of those with a higher territorial scope. Urban planning must also be coordinated with sectorial planning (natural spaces, coasts, etc.). Anyway, the main purpose is to include the environmental issues and concerns in the plans, in order to balance the different interests and to make more reflexive decisions.

Nowadays, consideration of the environment absolutely must be incorporated into urban planning. This justifies that the requirement that an SEA be sought during the development of plans or projects. This is a consequence, as has been mentioned, of implementing Directive 2001/42/EC of the European Parliament and of the Council, of 27 June 2001, on the Assessment of the Effects of Certain Plans and Programmes on the Environment. Currently, we have to apply the obligations contained in the Spanish Act that transposes the directive into national law: Act 21/2013 of 9 December on Environmental assessment. It should be remembered that some Autonomous Communities have already enacted specific acts on this matter. As has been mentioned, a few years ago the Autonomous Community of Catalonia passed an act that should be applicable when drafting o modifying plans and programmes that could affect the environment.

346. Coming back to topics that are strictly related to planning, it is worth mentioning the typology of urban plans and how environmental aspects are incorporated into them. Leaving aside the plans with a major territorial scope (State urban plans, general urban plans, territorial plans whether partial or sectorial, and territorial director plans of coordination), let us note that the general municipal plans, apart from creating the already mentioned figure of land that cannot be urbanized, usually include general measures in order to protect the environment, to preserve nature and to defend the landscape, natural elements and urban or historic complexes, respecting always and in each case the specific substantive legislation. These provisions will be more restrictive for land that cannot be urbanized, which constitutes the most protected areas in environmental terms.

Although some differences as regards their denomination and specifics exist between the Autonomous Communities, the general municipal plans are normally developed by the so-called Partial Plans, Special Plans, Urban Action Plans and detailed studies. We are especially interested in Special Plans because they have traditionally played a key role in environmental protection within the planning framework. This is so because the main objective pursued by these plans can be landscape protection in order to preserve specific areas. In those cases, the plan is usually addressed to natural areas with landscape interest, picturesque or topographically or historically singular plots, representative buildings, gardens and parks which stand out for their beauty or botanical species. The plan can also be addressed, with protection purposes, to vegetable gardens, forests and cultivated spaces, and it can include suitable restrictions on use intended to avoid its disappearance or transformation. Special Plans have also been used at the provincial level, such as in Barcelona and Girona, where this technical planning tool was used to protect important natural areas of Catalonia.

347. In the elaboration of the plan, the coordination of the different actions and the balance of the conflicting interests must always be pursued. Thus, the plan constitutes a way to achieve the objectives that their creator wants to implement. A phase of public information in order to ensure debate and the participation of the authorities with sectorial powers, in order to ensure that those powers are correctly specified, are commonly foreseen in the planning elaboration procedure.

SEA already mentioned is today a mandatory tool which requires many plans and programmes to be evaluated before they can be approved in accordance with Directive 2001/42/EC of the European Parliament and of the Council of 27 June 2001. Chapter 5.I. General and Administrative Legislation should be referred to in order to see how this process should function under the Spanish legal system.

348. We cannot finish this Part without making a last mention of the close relationship that exists between urban planning and protected natural areas. The State Act 42/2007, of 13 December, on Natural Heritage and Biodiversity, has set guidelines for environmental protection. We have already mentioned the existence of the Natural Resources Plans (PORN) and the Management and Use Rector Plans

(PRUG), regarding some specific natural spaces that deserve to be specially protected. The contents of these plans as well as the contents of the plans made under the Autonomous Communities' substantive environmental legislation, are directly binding for urban planning purposes, in such a way that, if their contents were contradictory, the urban plans would have to be adapted to them, because their prescriptions are always prevalent.

Part IV. Liability Questions

§1. Introduction

349. The Spanish Constitution establishes certain provisions on liability with regard to environmental matters. Article 45(3) states that penal or administrative sanctions shall be established for violations of the environmental legislation, and that wrongdoers shall be obliged to repair the damage caused. The legislator is thus committed to undertake legislative actions addressed to punish breaches of the environmental legislation. Having this in mind and pursuant to Article 53.3 of the Constitution, it is necessary to turn to general legislation to identify the cases of environmental liability established in the Spanish legal system and the precise scope of each type of liability. It should be noted that the express mention of environmental liability in the Constitution enhances the major importance of these questions in the Spanish system of environmental law.

§2. Criminal Liability

350. Following Article 45 of the Constitution, the environmental crime was included in the Criminal Code for the first time in 1983. Article 347*bis* of the Criminal Code as introduced in 1983 had certain deficiencies, as a result of which it was rarely applied by the courts. In fact, only four guilty verdicts were rendered by the Supreme Court, although some of them were especially relevant – for example, the Supreme Court decision of 30 September of 1990, Cercs Thermal Plant case. Later, the new Criminal Code, approved by Organic Act 10/1995 of 23 November, brought significantly progress by clarifying environmental criminal liability in Spanish law. There are currently sixteen articles devoted to environmental crimes.

351. Individuals breaching criminal norms, whether with criminal intent or negligence, may be prosecuted and convicted for criminal offences. At this point it should be noted that, following the general principle *societas delinquere non potest*, companies cannot usually be convicted for criminal offences. This results in the need to determine which individual inside the company has the power to take decisions regarding the prosecuted activities. In other words, it has to be proved who knew or who should have known of the infringement and who had the power to prevent or stop it. Article 31 of the Criminal Code may help in this difficult task, since it establishes that managers of a company (whether de iure or de facto) and individuals representing the company or acting on behalf of it are deemed to be liable for criminal offences. Nevertheless, the last reform of the Criminal Code, which entered into force on 23 December 2010, significantly modified this aspect of Spanish law. Currently, for the first time since the law of ancient Rome, the new Article 319 allows for legal persons (e.g., a company) to be held criminally responsible for environmental crimes committed on behalf of or by these legal persons, or by their de facto or de jure legal and administrative representatives. This opens up new possibilities in environmental law and also raises important questions about how it should be applied.

352. Criminal sanctions apply where the following conditions are met: (a) there is a breach of the administrative environmental legislation, and (b) this breach constitutes an especially serious infringement. In the absence of precise provisions in the applicable legislation, it is up to the courts to determine the cases where a serious breach is deemed to occur in such a way that an administrative sanction (usually a fine) is not enough to punish the infringement. In this sense, Article 325 of the Criminal Code specifies that it is a criminal offence to carry out a polluting action in breach of administrative legislation which is likely to seriously harm certain legally protected interests (public or individuals' health, flora, fauna, etc.).

This concept of environmental crime has brought about multiple problems in practice. There is a particularly interesting academic debate on the acceptability and limits of this kind of structure for a criminal offence (even though the Constitutional Court had already accepted it in Decisions 127/1990 and 62/1994). In any case, matching and perfectly delimiting both criminal and administrative liabilities constitutes an objective that is far from being achieved nowadays.

353. Article 325 of the Criminal Code defines the basic environmental crime as any breach of the Acts or general legislation protecting the environment that directly or indirectly involves emissions, discharges, radiation, extractions, excavations, dumps, noises, vibrations, injections or landfills, in the atmosphere, soil, subsoil, marine, inland or underground waters (even if affecting cross-boundary spaces). Underground water abstractions that could seriously damage the natural balance are also deemed to be environmental crimes. There are also express legislative offences covering the dumping of solid, liquid, toxic and dangerous waste. Certain acts of authorities or public employees that officially support the granting of notoriously illegal license or hushing-up infringements are also deemed to be criminal offences. Finally, there is a Chapter specifically devoted to the protection of the flora and fauna (Articles 332–337). This chapter deals with the cutting, burning, uprooting, harvesting, illegal traffic of threatened species, the hunting or fishing of threatened fauna, etc.

354. Any person subject to a criminal proceeding shall enjoy the right to be presumed not guilty, as well as to not plead guilty; the right to be informed about the facts and nature of the accusation; the right to defence and legal counsel; the right to a public trial without delays and with the observance of all the necessary safeguards; and the right to use any pertinent and lawful means of evidence and defence.

355. The criminal proceeding may lead to punishment by imprisonment. The court can however suspend the execution of such a penalty if it is minor, if it is the first time that the individual is convicted and if civil liability is insured. Other complementary penalties are also foreseen in the legislation (dismissal from public office or employment, prohibition to be a candidate in elections, prohibition to exercise a professional activity, etc.).

356. Most crimes are punishable by fines. It is worth noting that administrative fines are in several cases higher than criminal fines. Courts fix the amount of the fine, the term and the way of the payment in accordance with the criteria established by the Criminal Code. They have, however, some deal of discretion which allows them to take into consideration certain traits such as the particular economic situation, family expenses, etc., of the sentenced person. If the latter fails to pay the fine, it can be substituted by weekend arrests or community work.

The Criminal Code also contains other kinds of criminal penalties such as demolition of the illegal building, total or partial closure of the enterprise, etc. As criminal actions can cause damages to individuals or goods, criminal liability can be supplemented with civil liability. Civil liability questions are usually included in the action brought before the criminal court, although they can be separately decided during a subsequent civil proceeding.

357. In Spanish Law, criminal law is usually considered as the *ultima ratio* and applied in accordance with minimum intervention criteria. That is to say that criminal law would constitute the legal instrument applicable to extreme situations where the seriousness of the infringement deserves an imprisonment punishment. But, as a matter of fact, it has been used quite often since 1995. The public administration sometimes understands that many cases that have been subject to criminal proceedings should have been subject to the administrative punishing regime. The concept of environmental crime – as explained – can certainly lead to such situations, since it is quite difficult to determine at the earliest stages whether a specific offence constitutes a criminal or an administrative infringement.

358. Lastly, it is worth noting the new points that have been incorporated into criminal environmental law in the past ten years. After Organic Act 15/2003 of 25 November was approved and took effect, several different articles of the Penal Code were modified. Consequently, new punishable offences have appeared whose only objective is to criminalize conduct related to animal abuse. It also should be mentioned that other articles of the Penal Code have been recently modified in Spain in accordance with a new legal instrument taken from EU law. We refer to European Parliament and Council Directive 2008/99/EC, of 19 November 2008, on the protection of the environment through criminal law. Its objective is to protect the environment through criminal law. This Directive obliges Member States to adopt criminal penalties in their national legislation regarding serious infringements of EU law. It obliges the Member States to adopt the necessary measures to categorize wilful infringements stemming from serious neglect as well as other measures concerning the issue of the responsibility of legal persons, their punishment, etc. According to Article 8 of this Directive, Member States had to adopt the measures necessary to comply with the provisions of this Directive before 26 December 2010. In line with these criteria, the Spanish State passed Organic Act 5/2010, of 22 June, which modifies Organic Act 10/1995, of 23 November, of the Criminal Code. This Act came into force on 23 December 2010. In addition to the aspects already mentioned, the modification of the articles has led to a new criminal code for certain crimes relating to the dumping of waste and animal cruelty and to more severe sentencing.

§3. Administrative Liability

359. This section deals with two different questions, which will be separately analysed:

- First, the administrative punishing regime. That is to say the power of the public administration to impose sanctions for breaches of the environmental legislation (citizens' liability in front of the public administration).
- Second, the liability of the public administration. Public administration can be liable for damages caused by the administration's action or lack of action. Administrative actions or non-actions can lead to injury to persons and goods, and the specific damage can be an environmental damage.

In the coming pages the system of responsibility in Spain will be commented on in relation to both aspects. However, the reader should take into account that some interesting changes have arisen as a consequence of the Directive 2004/35/CE of 21 April 2004 on Environmental Liability with regard to the Prevention and Remedying of Environmental Damage and its consequent transposition into Spanish law. The requirements of this Directive had to be implemented by the Member States by April 2007. The Directive affects §3 concerning 'Administrative Liability' but it also influences §4, concerning 'Private Law Liability'. The law transposing the Directive into Spanish law, will be treated specifically in §5.

I. Citizens' Liability before the Public Administration

360. The Spanish public administration holds broad monitoring and enforcement powers. It can impose administrative sanctions without judicial assistance at all. These administrative sanctions cannot, obviously, involve imprisonment penalties (Article 25(3) of the Constitution). In case of infringements, environmental legislation enables the public administration to impose fines, close establishments and installations, etc.

361. It is necessary that environmental legislation expressly confers such a power on the public administration (State, Autonomous Community or local). Following constitutional principles, it is also necessary that both the offence (act) and the punishment (sanction) are expressly established by a formal Act. Regulations can subsequently shape the contents of the Act in a more precise way, but they cannot establish new offences by themselves. The possibility of establishing offences and sanctions by municipal ordinances has become a particularly disputed question. It is quite a common technique in environmental matters and has sometimes been justified by the democratic legitimization of municipal authorities or by administrative decentralization. Non-retroactivity and proportionality principles also apply to the administrative punishing power. A statute of limitations also exists, and it is necessary to turn to the specific environmental norm in question to determine the concrete period of time established for the specific case. In the absence of specific provisions, the general rule established by Act 30/1992 of 26 November on the Legal Regime of the Public Administrations and Common Administrative Procedure, as amended by Act 4/1999 of 13 January, will apply.

362. Administrative infringements are classified as trivial, serious and very serious infringements. Penalties usually consist of fines. Public administrations appear to be especially concerned with keeping the amounts of the fines 'updated' – particularly during the last decade – likely for the purpose of ensuring the deterrent effect of the administrative sanctions. This constitutes quite an important aspect, since under the previous legislation polluters usually preferred to pay a fine rather than adopt the necessary measures to comply with the requirements established by the environmental legislation. Article 131(2) of Act 30/1992 expressly refers to this aspect. Finally, it must be noted that environmental legislation usually foresees sanctions such as the temporary or definitive closure of activities, publicity of the infringement and the punished person and the prohibition to exercise his professional activity. Administrative sanctions can be accompanied by the obligation to repair the damage caused (i.e., restoration of the environment and compensation for damages caused).

363. Administrative punishing powers can be exercised against both individuals and companies. This constitutes a relevant difference with respect to criminal liability. If several participants have caused the damage, they will be jointly liable. It must be pointed out that it is usually difficult to precisely determine the liable person in those cases where several polluting activities are simultaneously affecting the environment.

364. Public bodies must necessarily follow a specific administrative proceeding for imposing administrative sanctions. Articles 134–138 of Act 30/1992 lay down the general basic principles governing such proceeding, while RD 1398/1993 constitutes the detailed regulation of the administrative proceeding for the exercise of the administration's punishing power. However, it should be noted that it is always necessary to turn to the particular substantive environmental Act or regulation in question and to apply their provisions on the specific punishing regime for each matter (water, waste, coasts, etc.). Two phases can be distinguished in this proceeding: the investigation and decision phases. Competence over each phase is attributed to different administrative bodies. It is worth noting at this stage that administrative authorities have the power to grant injunctions within this proceeding (before the final decision is taken). Injunctive relief is usually given both to prevent further environmental impacts and to ensure the effectiveness of the final decision. Any person subject to such an administrative proceeding shall enjoy the right to be presumed not guilty, as well as the right to be informed about the facts and nature of the accusation; to be informed of the sanctions that could be imposed; to be informed of the authorities competent to investigate and to decide; to allege whatever treats in his favour, and to use any pertinent and lawful means of evidence and defence. The competent administrative authority can consider at any moment that the facts could constitute a criminal infringement. In this case, the administrative authority must stop the ongoing administrative proceeding and inform the Public Prosecutor. The administrative proceeding will remain suspended until a judicial decision is finally rendered. The same act cannot be punished twice, as both a criminal and an administrative infringement. This aspect is analysed below in a more detailed way. The final decision must be reasoned and should solve every question in dispute. This can be challenged by means of administrative remedies (whether before the same authority or a superior one – *reposición and alzada* remedies). Finally, it must be noted that administrative decisions can be subject to judicial review.

365. The Spanish environmental law system is often characterized by the outstanding difference between legal provisions and the real world. It could give the idea of administrative authorities exercising their enforcement and punishing powers to a great extent. But, in fact, the opposite is true, even though this is progressively changing. Many reasons could explain this situation: the insufficiency of both economic and human resources, heavy workloads, lack of political will, concern for the viability of industrial and economic activities, etc. This has likely resulted in criminal proceedings being more often used than expected to enforce environmental liability.

II. The Liability of the Public Administration

366. Act 30/1992, as amended by Act 4/1999, establishes the basic legal regime applying to this matter. RD 429/1993 deals with the procedural aspects of claims for damages brought against the public administration in a more detailed way.

The public administration's activity (or lack of it) can cause damage to persons and goods. The following rules characterize this specific liability regime:

- Damages that the injured person is not obliged to bear must be effectively caused.
- Damages caused by unpredictable and inevitable facts according to current state of-the-art standards do not imply liability.
- A person or a group of persons injured must be identified. Damages should be quantifiable.

- A causal link needs to be established between the damage and the action of the administration that caused it. Both the existence of the damage, and the causation link, has to be proven.
- An Act of God is an affirmative defence.
- Act 30/1992 establishes a form of strict liability. Actions may not be brought against a particular public employee but directly against the public administration.

If a particular responsible person is later internally identified, the public administration shall claim the cost of the compensation against him, as well as shall exercise disciplinary powers.

Claims against the public administration for damages should follow the administrative proceeding established for this precise purpose by Act 30/1992 and RD 429/1993. This constitutes the only administrative way to force the public administration to repair the damage caused. In general terms, this proceeding begins ex officio or by a claim of an interested party. The public administration gathers the necessary information and evidence and allegations of the interested party. Compensation agreements between parties are also allowed. The administrative decision can subsequently be subject to judicial review.

§4. Private Law Liability

367. Private law liability has a twofold character: contractual and non-contractual liability. Non-contractual liability constitutes the most usual type of civil liability related to environmental matters.

368. The legal regime ruling this question is established by the Civil Code, although some provisions regarding this matter can also be found in sectorial legislation (nuclear energy, waste, etc.). The Civil Code (Article 1.902) contains a form of classical civil liability according to which, if a person causes damage to another with some degree of fault – usually negligence –, that damage should be compensated. The most relevant aspects of Article 1.902 to be taken into consideration in environmental matters are the following.

369. First of all, environmental damage to individuals or goods has to be effectively and certainly caused. Future damages must be determined and economically quantified. Even though sectorial legislation usually contains more favourable rules for the plaintiff, in the absence of these the Civil Code establishes a one-year statute of limitation for the plaintiff to bring actions against the person who caused the damage. This time period counts from the moment at which the plaintiff took knowledge of the environmental damage, not from the moment when this damage was caused.

370. The plaintiff must be personally injured or have suffered property loss. An Act of God is an affirmative defence. However, the defence that the action which caused the damage was authorized by an administrative regulation or decision, is not accepted (i.e., such decisions do not prevent civil liability). The plaintiff must bring the legal action against the person who caused the damage. That is to say the person who will pay for Rectification the damage caused. Certain sectorial legislation (e.g., legislation on dangerous waste) foresees some alleviation of the plaintiff's burden of proof concerning the imputation of the damage. If several participants have caused the damage, they will be jointly liable. If the person suffering the damage has by his own actions contributed to the result, the compensation will be reduced or disallowed according to the specific situation.

371. A causation link needs to be established between the damage and the action that caused it. The burden of proof regarding causation rests upon the plaintiff – although certain provisions alleviating this burden exist in sectorial legislation. As a matter of fact, the proof of causation raises the most significant obstacles in environmental liability cases, since these issues are frequently complex and high levels of technical and expert evidence are required (e.g., to prove pollution from sources temporally or geographically remote).

372. Even though Article 1.902 contains a form of a fault-based liability regime (culpa-rule), Spanish civil courts have notoriously tended to interpret and apply it in accordance with strict liability criteria. They have applied strict liability standards if damages have been caused by activities that commonly involve any kind of risk. The standard of care applicable to the operators carrying out these activities is therefore different from that applicable to a reasonable person with ordinary prudence (i.e., they should behave in a more careful way).

373. Sectorial legislation – whether by the State or the Autonomous Communities – imposes strict liability standards in civil cases (as for instance, legislation regarding nuclear energy, hunting, mining or waste). The legislation that includes a strict liability regime commonly contains additional clauses tending to alleviate the plaintiff's burden of proof. The burden of proof may be switched and it may be the polluter who has to produce evidence to demonstrate that all the necessary care was taken.

374. There are multiple specificities regarding this matter in sectorial legislation (as for instance, the legislation of the Autonomous Community of Catalonia regarding IPPC, which requires the covered activities to contract a civil liability insurance).

375. The judgment of the civil court deciding the existence of civil liability will impose the obligation to restore the damaged environment. Personal and economic loss should be also complementary compensated, and appropriate corrective measures aimed to prevent new damages can be imposed. It is worth noting that some judgments have ordered the enterprises causing environmental damages to stop carrying out their activities.

376. The previous paragraphs capture the current situation regarding this matter in Spain: a civil legislation originally intended for other purposes that is progressively being adapted to environmental cases, and the existence of peculiarities in sectorial legislation. However, it must be taken into account that some legislative efforts have been undertaken in Spain to fulfil the requirements which are expressly laid out in Directive 2004/35/CE of 21 April 2004 on Environmental Liability with regard to the Prevention and Remedying of Environmental Damage. Finally, a new act has been passed, Act 26/2007, of 23 October, on Environmental Responsibility, which implements a new system of Responsibility for Damage to the Environment in Spain that will be commented on in the following paragraph.

§5. The Act 26/2007, of 23 October, as an Additional Source of Environmental Liability

377. The current Spanish legal regime regarding liability for environmental damages also has to take into account another special piece of legislation which became law because of the necessary transposition of European Parliament and Council Directive 2004/35/EC of 21 April 2004 on environmental liability with regard to the prevention and rectification of environmental damage and its subsequent amending acts. The main piece of Spanish legislation in this area is currently Act 26/2007, of 23 October, on Environmental Responsibility. As with the EU Directive, this Act follows the 'polluter pays' principle and establishes a liability regime with the aim of preventing and remedying damage to animals, plants, natural habitats, water resources and the land. The Spanish act is expanded to cover coastal waters and the coast itself. It should be noted that this liability scheme applies both to environmental damage which has already occurred and also to imminent threat of damage to the environment.

The liability scheme applies directly to certain specified occupational activities specifically mentioned in a list (Annex III) and to other activities in cases where the operator is at fault or negligent. In every situation it becomes necessary to establish a causal link between the damage and the activity in question. For those activities which are expressly listed by the act, the operator may be held responsible even if he is not at fault. The liability scheme applies to other activities besides those listed, and it applies not only when there is effective damage, but also when there is imminent threat of damage to species or natural habitats protected by Autonomous Community legislation. In these cases the operator will be held liable only if he is at fault or negligent. If several operators are jointly responsible for damage, they will have to bear the costs of repair jointly, severally or on a proportional basis.

As with the EU Directive, public authorities are also responsible for ensuring that operators take or finance the necessary preventive or remedial measures themselves. If the competent authority has carried out preventive and remedial actions itself, it can recover the costs from the operator responsible for the damage or the imminent threat of damage.

378. It will be useful to summarize the procedure to be followed in case of environmental damage to protected animals, plants, natural habitats, water resources and land. Natural or legal persons that have been adversely affected and environmental protection organizations may, subject to certain conditions, ask the competent authorities to act when faced with damage. Legal actions should be brought before a court or administrative body so they can review the lawfulness of the decisions and actions of the competent authority, or their failure to act. Remedies to be obtained could be, for example, preventive measures to be taken when there is an imminent threat of environmental damage. However, where environmental damage has occurred, it may be remedied in different ways. For example, when damage affects land, this must be remedied by decontaminating the land; when damage affects water or protected species and natural habitats, this must be remedied by restoring the environment to how it was before it was damaged.

Some of the articles contained in Act 26/2007 have been implemented by another regulation enacted by the State government through Royal Decree 2090/2008, of 22 December, which approves the regulations for partially implementing Act 26/2007, of 23 October, on Environmental Responsibility. The Regulation establishes a methodological frame for determining when environmental damage exists and outlines the general system to be followed when environmental damage has occurred. It also specifies the content of the articles in Chapter IV of the Act regarding the financial guarantees to be given, the different risk scenarios to be evaluated and the cost associated with repairing each one of these.

§6. Compatibility of the Different Environmental Liability Regimes

379. In the previous sections we have explained the basic lines of the different environmental liability regimes (civil, criminal and administrative). Since some of them could simultaneously apply to a specific case, they can overlap. It is necessary to draft the rules regarding the compatibility of the regimes.

I. *Civil Liability versus Criminal Liability*

380. Both types of liability can simultaneously arise in a specific case. Criminal infringements can lead to civil liability if they have caused damages or loss. Articles 109 and 116 of the Criminal Code establish the obligation of the guilty party to repair the damages caused by the criminal infringement. In this sense, civil liability questions are usually included in the action brought before the criminal court, which will decide upon both types of liability. Courts should reason and justify the valuation of damages and compensations. It is also possible to opt for deciding civil liability questions coming from criminal infringements in a subsequent civil proceeding. This is the common practice for criminal proceedings that do not reach the trial phase.

II. *Civil Liability versus Administrative Liability*

381. Two different cases must be distinguished. First, if the public administration caused the damage, the citizen cannot use the regular civil liability regime to recover loss. The procedure to be followed is the one explained above. Therefore, the applicant should first go to the public administration to ask for a remedy. The final administrative decision following the administrative proceeding will determine every type of liability involved. This single administrative decision is obviously subject to judicial review. Natural or legal persons who have suffered damage cannot thus bring any action other than the one described above to complain against the action (or lack of it) of any public administration.

Second, the exercise of the administrative punishing power. The public administration imposes the administrative sanction following the administrative proceeding established for this precise purpose (in the terms explained above). There will not be any separate civil procedure. The obligation to repair the damage is compatible with the administrative sanction. The administrative decision shall thus include the obligation of the person who caused the damage to restore the environment and impose compensation for damages caused. This administrative decision can be subsequently subject to judicial review.

III. *Administrative Liability versus Criminal Liability*

382. Given the peculiar concept of environmental crime (which requires the breach of administrative legislation), the classical principle *ne bis in idem* appears to be especially relevant in this context. This means that the same act cannot be punished twice, both criminally and administratively. If the public administration considers at any moment that some facts could constitute a criminal infringement, it must stop the ongoing administrative proceeding and inform the Public Prosecutor. The administrative proceeding will remain suspended until a judicial decision is finally rendered. If the Public Prosecutor, even though the administration has not informed it, takes knowledge of facts that could constitute a criminal infringement and starts criminal proceedings, the administrative proceeding is also suspended. The judicial decision binds the administration with regard to the proven facts. This means: first, if the judicial decision contains a guilty verdict – and a criminal penalty has been imposed – the administration cannot impose any administrative sanction; and second, if the judicial decision contains a verdict of not guilty, the public administration can impose an administrative sanction, but the factual background of the administrative decision is determined by the facts proven in the criminal proceeding. Finally, there is an interesting legal debate on this matter. If certain facts have been punished as administrative infringements, does the principle *ne bis in idem* impede a criminal proceeding in cases of serious violations? The Constitutional Court Decision 177/1999 of 11 October opted for the impossibility of subjecting these facts to a criminal proceeding. Later, the same Constitutional Court modified the initial criteria. This can be seen, for example, in Constitutional Court Decision 2/2003, of 16 January. After being sanctioned at the administrative level for an environmental infringement, it is possible to open a new criminal procedure to examine the same facts (without violation of the constitutional principle of *non bis in idem*) if the decision at the criminal level is proportional and 'discounts' the punishment imposed in the previous administrative procedure.

IV. Liability under Act 26/2007, of 23 October, on Environmental Responsibility and Other Liabilities (Administrative and Criminal)

383. As we have already said in §5, Act 26/2007, of 23 October, on Environmental Liability transposes into Spanish law European Directive 2004/35/CE of 21 April 2004 on Environmental Liability with regard to the Prevention and Remedying of Environmental Damage. In doing so, the Act has widened the circumstances under which environmental liability can be attributed in Spain. Article 6 of the Act specifies how the new liability regime will be compatible with the traditional regime in Criminal and Administrative law. To summarize, in general the responsibility established in the Act will be compatible with the criminal sanctions and with the administrative penalties that should be imposed for the same infringements under other laws (criminal or administrative)

384. When environmental responsibility under Act 26/2007 coincides with the liability under other criminal or administrative punitive procedures, the following rules should apply:

– Act 26/2007 will always be applied completely independently from all other procedures for repairing environmental damage caused by the operators of the economic or professional activities listed in Annex III of the Act.
– Act 26/2007 will always be applied completely independently from all other procedures when some or all of the operators of economic or professional activities adopt measures of prevention and avoidance of new damages.
– Measures for repairing environmental damage caused by economic or professional activities other than those listed in Annex III will only be mandatory when the specific administrative or penal procedure has determined the existence of willingness, culpability or negligence.
– Some compensatory measures should always be adopted in order to prevent costs from being recovered twice.
– If the entity or person responsible for the damage has been required by other laws to pay to prevent, avoid or repair environmental damage then the liability regime of Act 26/2007 does not need to be applied.

Part V. Juridical Actions of Individuals

385. In the previous chapters our analysis has focused on substantive environmental law. This part deals with the position of individuals and groups from a legal point of view. The question is to analyse how individuals and groups can:

- participate in the adoption of public decisions regarding the environment;
- challenge public decisions in this field;
- have access to the judicial process to achieve environmental objectives.

In short, this section aims to determine the role that individuals and groups are currently playing in this domain, as well as to anticipate as far as possible the role that both could play in the future. The concept of 'interested party' constitutes a crucial notion at this stage. The legislative bodies' understanding of 'public participation' will determine the definition of 'interested party' to a great extent. Both concepts thus shape the scope of the role of individuals and groups in environmental matters (as for instance, possibilities of active participation in decision-making bodies, the access to information, the participation in the elaboration of environmental regulations, the identification of people who can challenge administrative decisions, etc.). It should be noted that both Spanish legislation and the practice of the courts currently tend to enlarge the right of complaint and the legal standing to individuals and groups that did not enjoyed such rights previously. This is also relevant in environmental cases, where not only directly affected individuals are concerned. There are also certain provisions in sectorial legislation that include citizens' suit provisions. In any case, a widespread public participation is far from being achieved, since some traditional concepts regarding legal standing still remain valid.

The above remarks could also be applicable to environmental groups and NGOs. From a traditional point of view, they would be considered interested parties insofar as their rights or legal interests were directly affected. In these cases, they would always have sufficient legal interest to enjoy the right of complaint and right of action. But in environmental matters, there is currently less need for a direct relation between the complainant and the decision complained against.

Before going on it is worth mentioning the fact that Spain did ratify the Aarhus Convention on Access to Information, Public Participation in Decision-making and Access to Justice in Environmental Matters the 16 February 2005. This ratification has had a significant effect on day to day operations in Spain. As is well-known, in some points, and more precisely, when the possibility of participation must be ensured, the Convention is more generous than traditional ordinary national law, which we will look at shortly. The implementation of the mandates of the Convention in Spain has been particularly facilitated by the transposition of the so-called 'Aarhus Directives', in other words, the two directives introducing the Aarhus Convention to European Member States (Directive 2003/04/EC on public access to environmental information and Directive 2003/35/EC regarding public participation in environmental procedures). Both have been transposed into Spanish law by Act 27/2006, of 18 July, which regulates the rights to access information, to public participation and to justice regarding environmental matters.

Chapter 1. Administrative Remedies

386. This chapter deals with the possibilities of individuals and groups to input on environmental administrative decision-making. It is understood that participation does not mean decision, but to influence the final decision. The different ways for the citizens participating in environmental protection will be analysed – including the specific procedures that interested parties can use to challenge administrative decisions and regulations affecting the environment. It is worth noting that many of the available instruments have not been largely used yet. Even though this situation is progressively changing, mere legal provisions cannot immediately change a deeply rooted tradition of low citizens' participation in public matters.

§1. Constitutional Aspects of the Citizens' Participation

387. Spanish environmental law foresees several ways for the implication of individuals and groups in decision-making processes. Prior to analysing these specific instruments it is necessary to summarize the constitutional provisions on this matter.

The need to providing for public participation may be read from Article 45 of the Constitution, since it would constitute an adequate mechanism to give sense to the 'collective solidarity' referred to thereby. Article 45 contains no express reference to citizens' participation in environmental matters (unlike with users and consumers). We thus have to turn to other constitutional provisions.

Article 9(2) of the Constitution establishes, among the basic structural principles of the social and democratic State, that the public authorities must facilitate participation of all citizens in the political, economic, cultural, and social life. In addition, Article 23(1) recognizes the fundamental right of the citizens to participate in public affairs, directly or through representatives.

388. Apart from the Parliament, representative institutions and political parties, the Constitution foresees the popular initiative for presenting Bills (Article 87(3)). The Organic Act 3/1984 of 26 March regulates this instrument in a more precise way. It should be noted that no fewer than 500,000 valid signatures are required.

Article 125 states that citizens may participate in the administration of justice through jury trials, in the manner that the law may determine for certain criminal cases.

389. The citizens' participation in the public administration can be characterized by three basic ideas. First, the Constitution foresees the hearing of citizens (directly or through organizations and associations) in both administrative rule and decision-making procedures (Article 105(a) and (c)). Second, it also establishes the right to access to the administrative files and registers, except when these affect the security and defence of the State, the investigation of crimes, and the right to privacy (Article 105(b)). The Supreme Court Decision of 23 June 1999 already stated that in accordance with the Spanish constitutional system, Greenpeace Spain was entitled to require the public administration to provide information related to the organization's objectives. This decision also establishes that Greenpeace Spain enjoys legal standing before administrative tribunals to challenge administrative refusals to provide the requested information. And third, Article 129(1) foresees ways of citizens' participation in the activities of the public bodies whose function directly affects the quality of life or general welfare.

Finally, it must be noted that other constitutional provisions may have impact on this matter, for instance, the right of association – which facilitates the creation of environmental protection associations – and the right to access to justice and due process of law.

§2. Grounds for Participation

390. Education and information constitute main basic grounds for achieving an effective, successful and fruitful public participation. This section especially deals with questions regarding information.

391. Public participation consists of a reciprocal relationship between citizens and the public administration, as far as an exchange of ideas and information between them takes place. Sufficient, understandable, and up-to-date information could result in public participation constituting an effective instrument for controlling the arbitrariness of the public authorities. The Constitution establishes the right to access to the administrative files and registers, but the possibilities to obtain environmental information have been certainly enlarged by EU law.

The Spanish Act 38/1995 of 12 December on the Right of Access to Information on the Environment (amended by Act 55/1999 of 29 December), transposed European Directive 90/313/EEC on Freedom of Access to Information on the Environment into Spanish law. The latest Directives on this matter (Directive 2003/04/EC on public access to environmental information and Directive 2003/35/EC regarding public participation in environmental procedures) have been transposed into Spanish law by the new Act 27/2006, of 18 July, which regulates the rights to access information, to public participation and to justice regarding environmental matters This constitutes the State's basic legislation on this matter and is therefore mandatory for any public Entity in Spain The Act establishes the right of any person to access information on the environment held by public authorities at a reasonable cost, and without having to prove any particular interest. The current law guarantees this right to any person regardless of their nationality or place of residence. The privacy of the person who requests information should be ensured in any case. The public administration shall respond formally to a person's request for information as soon as possible, the standard time limit being one month. A reasoned explanation must be given for any refusal to provide the requested information. The administrative refusal to provide information will always be subject to administrative remedies and subsequently to judicial review. A request for such information may be refused if it affects commercial and industrial confidentiality, criminal investigation proceedings, national defence, public security, international relations, the confidentiality of the proceedings of public authorities, intellectual property, the confidentiality of personal data and/or files, material, the disclosure of which would make it more likely that the environment to which such material related would be damaged. A request for information may also be refused where it would involve the supply of unfinished documents or data or internal communications, or where the request is manifestly unreasonable or formulated in too general a manner, although even in these cases, partial and useful information should be provided.

The Spanish Act guarantees that public has the right to:

- Access environmental information held by the government or other public administrations, or by other entities working on behalf of the government or other public administrations.
- Receive information regarding the rights guaranteed by the current Act and to receive proper advice on how to exercise these rights.
- Receive assistance when seeking information.
- Receive information within the time limits established in Article 10 (normally, one month; exceptionally, two months depending on the volume and complexity of the request).
- Receive environmental information in the form or format chosen (under the terms specified in Article 11).
- Be told why the authorities will not give them all or part the information requested, and why the authorities will not give them the information in the form or format that was requested.
- See the list of taxes and prices that, depending on the case, are mandatory for obtaining the information requested, as well as the circumstances in which there is no payment required.

§3. Ways of Participation

I. Organic Participation

392. Organic participation refers to the possibility of citizens or groups being part of administrative bodies, intervening in certain stages of the decision-making process. In environmental matters this kind of participation is usually related to the public authorities' will to legitimate their actions. The main characteristics of this kind of participation can be summarized as follows:

- In most cases, citizens and groups can participate in consultative bodies rather than in decision-making bodies.
- The real weight of citizens and groups within these bodies should be analysed.

In some cases they are in a quite a weak position with respect to the other members.
– The way in which these representatives are chosen is also important, given that the public administration sometimes seems to be inclined to choose representatives from particular groups.

393. Citizens' participation can take place either in bodies representing their interests or in bodies of experts. The former usually include environmental organizations, enterprises and consumers' associations, which will be affected by the environmental administrative decision or regulation. Scientists, technicians, professors, etc., usually participate in experts' bodies. Administrative bodies where participation in environmental matters takes place have proliferated during the last fifteen years, at State, Autonomous Communities and local levels. Among them are the Environmental Advisory Board, the National Council of Water, etc.

II. Functional Participation

394. This concept refers to the different ways through which citizens and interest groups can participate in public affairs from an external position (i.e., without being part of any administrative body). It should be analysed how citizens can participate in both rule and decision-making administrative procedures, as well as the possibilities for reacting once the decision or regulation has been adopted. The laws providing functional participation on environmental matters should be read today in a more generous way, because of the Spanish ratification of the Aarhus Convention.

395. Another aspect that should be addressed has to do with the hearing of the citizens inside the administrative rule-making procedure. As we have already said, spanish public administrations have regulatory power. Article 105 of the Spanish Constitution establishes that the law shall regulate the hearing of citizens (directly or through organizations and associations) in the procedure of elaborating the administrative regulations which affect them. This provision has not, however, been extensively developed. Act 30/1992 does not deal with this matter in an extensive way, but Article 86 of such Act states something that is relevant to our purposes. It says that the competent administrative body can establish a citizens' hearing stage during the administrative rule-making procedure (if the specific nature of the particular procedure so requires). It is thus possible to establish a citizens' hearing stage in the administrative procedure for elaborating administrative regulations regarding the environment. This article also states that public administrations can establish other ways and instruments for facilitating the participation of the citizens (directly or through organizations and associations) in the procedure of elaborating administrative decisions and regulations which affect them.

Moreover, Article 24 of Act 50/1997 of 27 November on the Government sets up an administrative procedure for elaborating administrative regulations, which applies to the State administration. Once a regulation has been elaborated, citizens must be compulsorily heard – within a minimum period of fifteen days – if the regulation affects either their rights or their legal interests. Citizens can be heard directly or through organizations and associations directly related to the subject of the regulation. The public administration must justify the option. In addition, the competent administrative body must establish a citizens' hearing stage – fifteen days – if the specific nature of the particular regulation so requires. In any case, the citizens' hearing stage can only be avoided on the basis of serious reasons of public interest. Finally, it must be noted that these provisions do not apply to cases where these associations or organizations have already participated through reports or consultations in previous stages.

However, as has been mentioned, the current rights regarding public participation in the administrative rule-making procedure have been increased by Act 27/2006, of 18 July, which regulates the right to information, public participation and justice in environmental matters. This Act includes the right to:

- Participate in an effective and real way in the preparation, modification and review of plans, programmes and general regulations for the environment as specified in the Act.
- Access at an early date the most relevant information regarding those plans, programmes and general regulations.
- Formulate allegations and observations when all the options are still open and before any decision is adopted regarding plans, programmes and general regulations and to receive the guarantee that these allegations and observations will be taken into account by the corresponding Public Administration.
- Be publicly informed of the result of the procedure in which they have participated and to be informed of the reasons and considerations on which a decision has been adopted, particularly if any information relating to the public participation process was used to take this decision.

396. Participation in the administrative decision-making procedure: Article 105 of the Spanish Constitution foresees the participation of the citizens (directly or through organizations and associations) in the elaboration of administrative decisions. The law shall regulate the administrative procedure, guaranteeing when appropriate the hearing of interested persons. Article 31 of Act 30/1992 defines the concept of 'interested party'. Courts have interpreted this article in accordance with wide criteria in environmental matters, in such a way that the concept of interested party has been enlarged from the traditional notion relying on a 'direct interest'. Together with the more traditional interested parties, Article 31 of Act 30/1992 includes in this concept those persons whose individual or collective legal interests could be affected by the administrative decision, as well as the associations and organizations representing economic or social interests in the terms established by the law. Being an interested party implies enjoying certain rights within the administrative procedure. Among them are:

- to be informed about the status of the proceeding and to obtain copies of the documents included in the administrative file (Article 35(a));
- to bring allegations and documents at any stage of the proceeding, before the hearing stage takes place (Articles 35(e) and 79);
- to obtain information regarding the legal or technical requirements with which the actor should comply (Article 35(g));
- to use any pertinent lawful means to produce evidence (Article 80);
- to enjoy a hearing stage before the administrative decision is finally adopted (Article 84); – to obtain an express and reasoned administrative decision, as well as to be properly notified of the adoption of this decision (Articles 54, 58, 89);
- to use the pertinent administrative remedies (Article 107).

However, as has been mentioned, the right to public participation in important administrative decision-making procedures affecting the environment has been expanded by Act 27/2006, of 18 July, which regulates the right to information, public participation and justice in environmental matters. More precisely, as the Act specifies the additional rights given to citizens and entities which enable them to participate in an effective and real way, in specific administrative procedures such as the awarding of permits which are regulated in the legislation on the prevention and integrated control of pollution; the awarding of permits which are regulated in the legislation regarding genetically modified organisms; those procedures which include an EIA; the planning procedures foreseen in the legislation regulating water; and in the legislation regulating the assessment of the effects of certain plans and programmes on the environment.

397. Citizens' suit provisions: In spite of the wide understanding of the notion of interested party, there are cases where the link between the subject of the proceeding and the interest of citizens and associations appears to be very weak. This is not the case where the law expressly includes a citizens' suit provision. If the law expressly establishes such a provision, there will be no need to prove any specific interest, since any citizen or group has the status of interested party *ex lege.* Citizens' suit provisions enable any person or group to intervene in the administrative proceeding, as well as confer on them the right to access to justice asking for judicial review. Some examples of citizens' suit provisions in environmental law and connected legislation can be found in Act 22/1988 of 28 July on Coasts; D 833/1975 of 6 February on the Protection of the Atmosphere; Article 48 of RLD 2/2008, of 20 June, which approves the Redrafted Land Act, etc. Sectorial legislation coming from the Autonomous Communities has also established citizens' suit provisions in many cases.

Nowadays it is also necessary to take into account the special provisions included in Act 27/2006, of 18 July, which regulates the right to information, public participation and justice in environmental matters. Consequently, the Act gives standing and guarantees an administrative or judicial review of those actions and omissions by public authorities that contravene the rights to information and public participation recognized by the Act. It also includes a citizen's suit provision to prosecute actions and imputable omissions by the public authorities that contravene environmental legislation under the terms specified by the Act.

398. Public hearing: As explained above, the Spanish legislation foresees a public hearing stage in the elaboration of administrative regulations. This stage, which must be previously published in an official journal and enables any individual or group concerned with the proceeding to bring allegations or data, is also expressly established by multiple sectorial environmental norms. Besides the need to submit both land-use and environmental planning instruments to a public hearing, it must be noted that several environmental administrative procedures include such a stage (as for instance, EIA, authorizations for discharging wastes, etc.). That is why it is necessary to take into account the specific norm in question in order to determine the specific legal regime applying to the public hearing stage. During this period the administrative file can be consulted for the purpose of bringing allegations. Copies of documents can also be requested. All the allegations should be taken into account by the administrative body when adopting the final decision. This implies to adequately justify why certain allegations have been disregarded.

399. Consultative referendum: Article 92 of the Spanish Constitution contains a means of direct participation of the citizens in decision-making processes, subject to the discretionary and facultative use by the public administration. It establishes that political decisions of special importance may be submitted to a consultative referendum of all the citizens. It could constitute a relevant instrument for environmental purposes if certain conditions regarding previous information, alternative solutions, etc., are met. Local administrative decisions are the procedures where this instrument could likely be used most often. However, consultative referenda have rarely been undertaken, probably because of the high costs, political risks, etc. The decision to urbanize the Castell Beach in Palamós (Catalonia) provides an example of a consultative referendum where most of the population refused such a possibility.

400. Right of complaint: Article 29 of the Constitution states that all Spaniards shall have the right to individual and collective complaint, in written form, in the way and with the effects that the law shall define. This right also applies in environmental matters and is regulated, more precisely, by Organic Law 4/2001, of 12 November, which regulates the Right to Complaint. There are no strict formal requirements for exercising the right of complaint (just the identification and the signature of the citizen who exercises it). The administration is merely obliged to acknowledge the reception of the complaining paper. The right of complaint cannot result in any prejudice for the person who exerts it, except if it constitutes a criminal infringement. Individuals and legal persons can also address complaints to the State, Autonomous Communities (and even local) Ombudsmen. Since the latter can monitor the public administration's activity, they can make recommendations, suggestions, warnings, and even litigate in court.

401. Reporting administrative and criminal infringements: These constitute widely used instruments of public participation in environmental matters, likely because of their low cost – they do not require legal counsel. Any person who takes knowledge of facts that are likely to constitute an administrative infringement must report them to the public administration. The identification of the person reporting these facts, the facts themselves, the date when these occurred and the identification of the presumed liable persons – if possible – have to be brought to the public administration's knowledge. The public administration must inform this person whether the administrative proceeding for the exercise of the administrative punishing power has initiated, but only if this person requests the public administration to initiate such a proceeding. Reporting facts that are likely to constitute an administrative infringement does not imply that the citizen giving notice of these facts automatically becomes party to the administrative proceeding. On the other hand, it should be remembered that the Spanish Criminal Code devotes sixteen articles to environmental crimes. Any person who becomes aware of any criminal infringement of these articles must report it to the judge or the Public Prosecutor. This does not imply that the citizen giving notice of these facts becomes party to the criminal proceeding. We will deal with this matter in the chapter related to judicial remedies.

402. The right to administrative remedies: Generally speaking, every administrative decision – whether express or presumptive – can be challenged through administrative remedies in front of the public administration. Obviously this also applies to administrative decisions dealing with environmental matters. Administrative remedies are generally conceived for questioning the legality of a previous administrative decision. Administrative regulations are not subject to administrative remedies but directly to judicial review. Act 30/1992 establishes the legal regime applying to this matter. Some specific provisions can, however, be found both in sectorial legislation and in administrative procedural legislation related to the Autonomous Communities. Administrative remedies are available for interested persons. They must submit a plea, which should include the personal details of the interested person, as well as the identification of the challenged administrative decision and the reasons upon which the challenge is based. The anti-formalism principle applies to administrative remedies. It must be noted that administrative remedies do not require legal counsel – however, subsequent applications for judicial review do require legal counsel. Administrative remedies do not necessarily impede the execution of the challenged administrative decision. Such a suspending measure can however be granted by the administrative body dealing with the administrative remedy if certain circumstances are present (if damages difficult or impossible to repair could be caused by the execution of the administrative decision, or if the remedy is based on full nullity causes). If granted, the administrative body can adopt the necessary measures to both protect the public interest and ensure the effectiveness of the challenged decision. If new facts not included in the original administrative file have to be considered by the public administration, the interested persons will enjoy the right to bring allegations against them. The final decision will determine whether the remedy fails or is totally or partially accepted. In any case it should solve every disputed question. This administrative decision cannot worsen the situation existing before the remedy was brought.

403. Generally speaking, there are three kinds of administrative remedies: *alzada, reposición* and 'revision'.

As for the *alzada*, the remedy is addressed to a superior administrative body to review the decision of an inferior one. This remedy must be requested within a one month period (if an express administrative decision is challenged) or a three-month period (if a presumptive administrative decision is challenged). Once these terms have passed, the administrative decision cannot be appealed. The administrative body should decide on the remedy within three months. The decision on the remedy can be subject to judicial review.

The *reposición* is a facultative administrative remedy that can be used to appeal an administrative decision which exhausted the administrative procedure (therefore, when no *alzada* is provided by the law). This is brought before the administrative body which made the appealed decision. The statute of limitation coincides with that for the *alzada*. The administrative body should decide the remedy within a one month period.

The *revisión* is an extraordinary administrative remedy that can be used in a strictly limited number of cases, namely: (a) in cases where the administrative decision relied on factual error; (b) if new documents of essential value showing the wrongfulness of the decision later appeared; (c) if documents or witness testimony later declared to be false by a judicial decision influenced the administrative decision; (d) if the administrative decision resulted from any criminal infringement.

Chapter 2. Judicial Remedies

404. The present chapter focuses on the use of court proceedings for achieving environmental objectives. On the basis of the different types of judicial proceedings, the rules applying to the access to justice – legal standing – and the subject of lawsuits will be analysed. Aspects regarding the content of court decisions and court costs will also be considered. Given that environmental disputes could be decided by civil, criminal and administrative courts, this section deals with these proceedings separately in order to show their specific aspects. A brief explanation of the role of the Constitutional Court in environmental matters is also included.

§1. The Constitutional Court

405. The Constitutional Court has jurisdiction all over the national territory. It can decide upon environmental matters in a limited number of cases, which are always related to the constitutional provisions on environment. Constitutional Court decisions obviously have a relevant impact when deciding whether a specific environmental norm is compatible with the distribution of powers criteria laid down by the Constitution between the State and the Autonomous Communities. In the same sense, the Constitutional Court plays a major role in those cases where the compliance of an environmental Act with the constitutional provisions is in dispute. However, it must be noted that neither individuals nor associations have direct access to the Constitutional Court to contest the constitutionality of laws. They only have indirect legal standing – usually through political channels. Nevertheless, both individuals and associations can gain access to the Constitutional Court through the way foreseen in Article 163 of the Constitution. That is to say that if during any judicial proceeding the court considers that an applicable law upon which the validity of which the judgment depends may be contrary to the Constitution, it may bring the matter before the Constitutional Court.

406. On the other hand, the Constitutional Court decides appeals against violation of the rights and liberties referred to in Article 53(2) of the Constitution (i.e., the liberties and rights recognized in Articles 14 and 30 and the First Section of the Second Chapter of Title I – Fundamental Rights and Public Liberties). The right to enjoy an environment suitable for the development of the person as well as the duty to preserve it (Article 45) is not included among these fundamental rights. As explained in previous sections, Article 45 is included in Chapter III (Guiding Principles of Economic and Social Policy) of Title I of the Constitution. This means that any violation of this right cannot constitute the subject of the specific proceeding in front of the Constitutional Court foreseen in Article 53(2) of the Constitution. However, it is worth noting that the decision of the European Court of Human Rights of 9 December 1994 (*López Ostra v. Spain*) and subsequent similar decisions have had an important impact on this subject. In this sense, such a constitutional remedy for environmental purposes can now be used insofar as violations of other fundamental rights – life, domicile, health – are concerned.

§2. ADMINISTRATIVE COURTS

407. Considering the environment from a legal point of view and setting up a legal system dealing with environmental matter structured in multiple norms, requires an intensive and outstanding intervention of the public administration. Administrative action is usually undertaken through administrative decisions and regulations. Spanish administrative law gives the citizens the opportunity to apply to the courts for judicial review of either an environmental regulation or a administrative decision (in the terms that will be analysed below).

Given the major role played by the public administration in environmental matters, it can be said that judicial remedies for the protection of the environment must usually be brought to the administrative tribunals. Act 29/1998 of 13 July on the Administrative Judicial Review Procedure establishes the legal regime applying to this matter.

I. Court Structure

408. The Organic Act 6/1985 of 1 July on the Judicial Power and Act 29/1998 of 13 July on the Administrative Judicial Review Procedure determines the court structure with regard to administrative tribunals. These courts decide disputes between individuals and administrative bodies, or between administrative bodies, whose subject is normally related to an administrative decision or regulation. So, an administrative proceeding has been previously carried out. These administrative proceedings include granting administrative concessions and authorizations for the purpose of using public goods, torts claimed in front of the administration, checking the individuals' compliance with the conditions of any concession or authorization, monitoring of the individuals' compliance with the general legal provisions concerning environmental law, etc. Administrative decisions in proceedings for the exercise of the administrative punishing power are also subject to judicial review.

409. The jurisdiction of each judicial body is basically determined on the basis of the administrative body which made the challenged decision or regulation and on the specific matter dealt with in the administrative decision. Generally speaking, judicial review of local and Autonomous Communities' regulations is performed by the Superior Courts of Justice of the Autonomous Communities. With regard to administrative decisions of local bodies and Autonomous Communities, the Superior Courts of Justice of the Autonomous Communities are also the competent courts, except where Act 6/1998 has expressly attributed jurisdiction to the administrative tribunals (*Juzgados de lo Contencioso-Administrativo*). The administrative tribunals (single-judge courts with provincial jurisdiction) are competent to render judgments regarding certain administrative decisions dealing with environmentally related matters (e.g., licenses to use the soil and subsoil granted by the local authorities, administrative sanctions imposed by the local authorities, administrative sanctions imposed by the Autonomous Communities – limited to a certain height – on hunting, river fishing, unpleasant, unhealthy and noxious activities, etc.). Finally, it should be noted that, although these courts are competent in certain cases to review decisions of State administrative bodies whose jurisdiction does not extend all over the national territory, they cannot hear cases involving decisions from such bodies dealing with the State's public domain, special properties or expropriations.

The judicial review of decisions of the State administration is performed by:

- the Supreme Court (decisions of the highest bodies);
- the National Court (decisions of ministries and Secretaries of State);
- the Central Administrative Tribunals (for instance, in case of administrative sanctions imposed by State administrations with competence all over the national territory);
- the Superior Courts of Justice of the Autonomous Communities (which decide cases regarding decisions of the State administration without competence all over the national territory;
- except those attributed to the administrative tribunals –, and decisions of State administrations with competence all over the national territory in certain matters – personnel, special properties and expropriation);
- the administrative tribunals in the terms expressed in the preceding paragraph.

Finally, it must be noted that the judgments of the administrative tribunals and Central Administrative Tribunals can be respectively appealed to the Superior Courts of Justice of the Autonomous Communities or the National Court. There is no appeal from the judgment rendered other cases, but certain extraordinary remedies, as cassation, when so allowed.

II. Access to Justice

410. Article 19 of Act 29/1998 establishes the rules applying to the legal standing in judicial review proceedings. The following persons can gain access to the courts:

- individuals or legal persons having a right or legal interest in the matter;
- corporations, associations, groups and entities either affected or legally entitled to protect collective rights and interests;
- public administrations for challenging decisions or regulations of a different public administration;
- the Public Prosecutor;
- any citizen exercising a citizens' suit provision when expressly established by law.

A wide understanding of the second point would result in citizens and environmental interest groups having access to the courts to enforce the law for protection of the environment. This cannot be justified in all cases. The existence of a specific citizens' suit provision certainly facilitates the access to justice of the aforementioned persons. Citizens' suit provisions – when established – have not, however, been widely used, probably because of the absence of any rule which foresees the recovery of the court costs if the applicant succeeds. In general terms, the rules regarding legal standing in Spanish procedural law mainly rely on individual criteria, in such a way that the access to justice is commonly given to those entitled by individual rights or interests. The protection of collective and diffuse interests is slowly but steadily gaining access to the courts. In this sense, Article 7 of the Organic Act 6/1985 on the Judicial Power cannot be ignored, since it states that judicial bodies should protect both individual and collective rights and interests. As for collective rights and interests, this article expressly recognizes legal standing to corporations, associations and groups either affected or legally entitled to protect and promote these rights and interests. This provision has a relevant impact in environmental disputes. In current practice, courts rarely repeal any application on the basis that legal standing is absent. To conclude, we should remember the specificities regarding legal standing and citizen's suit provisions found in Act 27/2006 and that have been emphasized in the previous Chapter (in the paragraph on Functional Participation).

III. Defendants

411. A public administration which has carried out a challenged decision or approved a controversial regulation will always be the defendant party in judicial review proceedings. Together with the public administration, individuals or legal persons whose rights or interests could be affected by the judgment can also be defendant parties in these proceedings. Legal counsel is required in any case. Parties must also be assisted by a solicitor if a collegiate court (not a single-judge court) decides the case.

IV. Object of the Court Proceedings

412. Applicants can apply to the courts for judicial review of an environmental regulation, an administrative decision or a lack of action. The administrative decision (e.g., not granting a pollution license, not approving a land-use plan, imposing a sanction, adopting an environmental impact statement) can be either an express or a presumptive decision, and the administrative remedies, when provided, must have been exhausted before going to Court.

Since 1998 both applications for requiring the public administration to perform its duties and applications for judicial review of administrative actions which have not followed any administrative proceeding are accepted in Spanish law. These constitute quite important aspects with regard to environmental law. Applicants can require the court to quash an administrative decision or to strike down an administrative regulation insofar as it is unlawful. They can also ask for the adoption of measures to restore an altered situation (including compensation for damages caused). Finally, the applicant can demand that the public administration stops acting unlawfully, or require the administration to perform its duties.

V. Procedure

413. The applicant for judicial review brings a brief paper to the court identifying the challenged decision or disposition. Applications are limited to a two month period from the publication of the regulation or the notification of the challenged administrative decision), or to a six-month period (in case of a presumptive administrative decision). The court will require the public administration to send the administrative file and to notify the interested parties. Once the administrative file is received, the applicant will elaborate and bring to the court an affidavit (pleading paper) which sets out the basis of the applicant's case – containing the factual and legal background, the remedy he seeks, and the evidence. The respondent must reply to the applicant's affidavit with its own affidavit. Evidence in environmental disputes usually deals with modern technical means. There will be an oral hearing in certain cases, a conclusion stage, and finally the judgment. One of the most important challenges of administrative justice in Spain has traditionally consisted in achieving a quick and correct execution of the courts' judgments.

VI. Injunctions

414. Parties at any stage of the proceeding can ask the court for an injunction. For this purpose, the court will balance the interests and circumstances at hand. Injunctive relief, if given, may play a significant role in environmental disputes and will remain in force until the final judgment is rendered – insofar as the reasons that justified its granting do not disappear.

VII. Court Costs

415. The judgment will decide on court costs. They can be totally or partially imposed on a party, or up to a maximum amount. The general rule is that the party who has recklessly and maliciously litigated will bear the court costs in first instance proceedings. Appellant will bear the costs of the appeal if it fails.

§3. Civil Courts

I. Court Structure

416. Act 6/1985 of 1 July and Act 1/2000 of 7 January on Civil Procedure, establish the legal regime applying to this matter.

In environmental matters, civil courts hear cases on civil liability and '*acción negatoria*' (legal actions to refrain from doing a particular thing that disturbs the free enjoyment of possession).

In general terms, the Supreme Court, the Superior Courts of Justice of the Autonomous Communities, the provincial courts, the courts of first instance and the Justice of the Peace make-up the civil court structure in the Spanish Law. The courts of first instance will hear most cases and are set up as the general judicial bodies for deciding civil cases. The other courts (with the obvious exception of the Justice of the Peace) usually hear appeals from judgments. The territorial jurisdiction of the courts of first instance is organized by district. For determining the specific Court of First Instance holding jurisdiction with respect to a specific case, the Civil Procedure Act lays down a set of provisions which primarily focuses on the will of the parties. Secondary rules applying in the absence of either express or implied will of the parties are also established (as for instance, the domicile of the defendant, the place in which an individual carries out its professional or commercial activities, etc.). There are two main types of civil declarative proceedings: the common civil procedure and the oral proceeding. The proceeding to be followed in a concrete case primarily depends on the matter at hand. The value of the action (higher or lower than EUR 6,000) shall secondarily apply for these purposes.

II. Civil Liability Actions

417. As explained in the chapter devoted to liability questions, civil courts can decide environmental disputes related to contractual and non-contractual liability. Non-contractual liability constitutes the most usual type of civil liability related to environmental matters. Article 1.902 of the Civil Code contains a form of classical civil liability according to which, if a person causes damage to another with some degree of fault – usually negligence –, that damage should be compensated. The judgment of the civil court deciding the existence of civil liability will impose the obligation to restore the damage to the environment. Personal and economic loss should be also complementary compensated.

Civil liability actions are rarely brought to the courts in cases dealing with minor and diffuse environmental damages suffered by many individuals. Actions will neither succeed if the existence of damages effectively and certainly caused to persons and goods cannot be proved. That is to say that individuals and groups cannot successfully bring an action to claim for non-personally suffered damages.

The person directly injured or having suffered property loss will bring the action. Individuals or associations that have not been directly damaged cannot thus bring such actions to claim for injuries caused to third parties (irrespective of the seriousness of the damage). It cannot, however, be ignored that Article 7(3) of the Organic Act 6/1985 on the Judicial Power, expressly recognizes the legal standing of corporations, associations and groups either affected or legally entitled to protect and promote collective rights and interests. The association or the interested group bringing such an action will not, obviously, receive any compensation for damages that the court judgment may establish, such compensation being limited to the injured person or the public administration (if the damages are related to the State's public domain). Accepting the possibility of these associations receiving such compensations would imply creating an unpredicted source of income, as well as result in the person who caused the damage being exposed to an unlimited number of court cases. The possibility that these associations receive the restoration costs cannot be accepted in general terms either, even though a criminal court decision solving questions on civil liability arising from a criminal infringement had accepted this eventuality (Supreme Court Decision of 1 February 1997).

418. The plaintiff must bring the legal action against the person/entity that caused the damage. That is to say the person/entity that will pay to remedy the damage caused. Certain sectorial legislation (e.g., legislation on dangerous waste) foresees some alleviation of the plaintiff's burden of proof concerning the imputation of the damage. A causation link needs to be established between the damage and the action that caused it. As a matter of fact, the proof of causation raises the most significant obstacles in environmental liability cases, since these issues are frequently complex and high levels of technical and expert evidence are required. The judgment of the civil court deciding the existence of civil liability will impose the obligation to restore the damaged environment. Personal and economic loss should be also complementarily compensated, and appropriate corrective measures addressed to the prevention of new damages may be imposed.

419. As regards the procedure, the plaintiff submits a statement of claim (plea) to the court, containing the factual and legal background as well as evidence. The defendant must reply to the plaintiff's statement of claim. The court fixes an evidentiary period, a hearing stage and finally renders its judgment, which should be executed. The court can also grant injunctions. The judgment may decide upon court costs. Article 394 of the Civil Procedure Act establishes the general rules applying to this matter. In short, court costs in first instance proceedings will be borne by the party who has not succeeded at all – except in cases where the court reasonably appreciates the existence of severe legal or factual doubts. In cases of partially successful litigation, each party will bear the court costs that it has caused – except in cases of reckless or malicious litigation.

420. In the absence of specific sectorial legislation, Article 1.968(2) of the Civil Code will apply (statute of limitation). It establishes a one-year period for the plaintiff to bring actions against the person who caused the damage. This term counts from the moment at which the plaintiff took knowledge of the environmental damage (not from the moment when this damage was caused). There is, however, consensus on the need of enlarging such a term in case of environmental damages. The draft on civil liability concerning activities affecting the environment also inclines to this approach, since it establishes a three-year term from the moment at which the plaintiff took knowledge of the environmental damage. It also establishes that in case of repeated acts causing damages, the fixed three-year term will start counting from the moment at which the plaintiff took knowledge both of the last environmental damage and of the person or entity that caused it.

III. *Acción negatoria*

421. Together with liability actions, which are certainly the most widely used civil remedies in environmental matters, Spanish law foresees the possibility of bringing the so-called *acción negatoria.* This is a legal action aimed to force a person to refrain from doing a particular thing that disturbs the free exercise of possession. *Acción negatoria* could thus constitute a useful remedy in cases where disturbances are caused by noise, smoke, or any other kind of emissions from neighbouring properties. Article 590 of the Civil Code requires the plaintiff to be the owner or tenant of the land in question. In addition, the disturbing activity must cause damages to particular goods – otherwise this action cannot be brought before the court. Even though this is the general rule, it has been suggested that is would be possible to use the *acción negatoria* to prevent future damages.

The *acción negatoria* is a declaratory action. The plaintiff must prove its title, as well as the non-existence of the charge on the property that the other party intends to exert (encumbrance). It is necessary to prove that the activity in question causes damage, disturbs the free exercise of possession, and consists of an unlawful exercise of a right that the disturbing person does not properly hold. A causation link needs to be established between the disturbance and the action that caused it. The *acción negatoria* may play a relevant role in environmental matters, since both the objectives of stopping the disturbing action and obtaining compensation for damages can be reached in case of success.

There is a statute of limitation. In the absence of specific provisions, this action is limited to a thirty-year term (Article 1.963 of the Civil Code). An action can be brought before the court from the moment at which the free exercise of possession is disturbed.

Civil lawyers are certainly promoting the use of this action for environmental purposes, though it is not being exercised to a great extent at present. This situation, however, varies where an express legal provision clearly establishes the scope and limits of the action (as for instance, Article 544 of the Fifth Book of the Civil Code of the Autonomous Community of Catalonia).

§4. Criminal Courts

I. Court Structure

422. Pursuant to Article 9(3) of the Organic Act 6/1985 on the Judicial Power, the jurisdiction of the criminal courts includes all cases in which the laws defining criminal acts and providing for the punishment of the offenders are applicable, except for those expressly attributed to the military jurisdiction. There are several judicial bodies dealing with criminal matters in Spain, whose jurisdiction depends on the specific crime to be judged, the specific stage of the criminal procedure (pre-trial or trial) and the territorial jurisdiction of the judicial body. In short:

- the Criminal Chamber of the National Court (*Audiencia Nacional*) (which exercises jurisdiction all over the national territory) shall hear cases dealing with particular types of crimes expressly mentioned in Act 6/1985 (terrorism, acts against the Crown, etc.);
- provincial courts (*Audiencias Provinciales*) and criminal courts (*Juzgados de lo penal*, single-judge courts) both exercise jurisdiction within the province.

Their respective jurisdiction depends on the seriousness of the crime tried (i.e., on the seriousness of the punishment provided by the criminal laws). Provincial courts hear the most serious crimes, while criminal courts try the less serious ones. The pre-trial phase of criminal cases that will be heard either by provincial courts or criminal courts, are carried out by the Examining Magistrates:

- Examining Magistrates (*Juzgados de Instrucción*, single-judge courts) have district jurisdiction and hear cases regarding misdemeanours not attributed to Justices of the Peace.
- Justice of the Peace (*Juzgados de Paz*, single-judge courts) sit in municipalities where there is no Examining Magistrate. It is worth noting that it is not necessary to have any legal background to be appointed as Justice of the Peace. They hear cases regarding certain types of misdemeanours. Regarding territorial jurisdiction, the rule locus delicti comissi primarily applies. There are also secondary criteria to be used if it is impossible to determine the territorial jurisdiction following the primary rule.

There are basically three types of criminal procedures in Spanish law: the common criminal procedure for serious crimes, the abbreviate criminal procedure, and the criminal procedure for misdemeanours. The type of punishment foreseen for the specific infringement determines the concrete procedure to be followed.

Finally, it should be noted that quite complicated rules apply to the appeals of court decisions. In short (just limited to judgments and not exhaustively), judgments of Justices of the Peace and Examining Magistrates in misdemeanour procedures can be respectively appealed to Examining Magistrates and provincial courts. Judgments of criminal courts can be appealed to provincial courts. The Second Chamber of the Supreme Court hears cassation recourses when so allowed by the applicable legislation.

II. Actions and Remedies

423. As explained in previous chapters, the Spanish Criminal Code devotes sixteen articles to environmental crimes. Individuals breaching criminal norms, whether with criminal intent or negligence, may be prosecuted and convicted for criminal offences. As damages to individuals or goods can be caused by criminal infringements, criminal liability can also been accompanied by civil liability. Thus, the criminal court's decision usually will deal with civil liability questions. The judgment will refer to the obligation to repair the damage (i.e., restoration of the environment and compensation for damages). This makes criminal actions especially interesting for environmental purposes.

In Spanish law all citizens can: (a) report facts that are likely to constitute a criminal infringement to the Public Prosecutor or the judges, and (b) bring a criminal action before the court without the need of proving any direct legal interest. Criminal actions in Spanish law are thus generally conceived as citizen's suit provisions. This aspect, together with the possibility of the criminal court's judgment deciding on civil liability and the peculiar concept of the environmental crime, results in environmental associations using criminal remedies more often than administrative ones.

The first-mentioned possibility (reporting facts that are likely to constitute a criminal infringement) does not imply that the citizen giving notice of these facts becomes a party to the criminal proceeding; however (as explained below), he is entitled to be a party if he so desires. The notice can be written or orally given to the judge or at the police stations.

The second possibility (bringing an action) requires legal counsel and the assistance of a solicitor. In these cases the citizen becomes a party to the criminal proceeding (one of the prosecution parties together with the Public Prosecutor). This enables him to propose and produce evidence, bring allegations or pleas before the court, etc. Persons injured by the criminal action simply have to appear in court during the criminal proceeding. This is a path that is progressively being more used by environmental associations and interest groups, since that courts are inclining to consider them as injured persons in environmental crimes.

These factors are encouraging the use of criminal remedies by environmental associations and groups. Furthermore, some court decisions have accepted the possibility that these associations manage the amount of civil liability (in order to ensure that this amount is used for environmental restoration purposes – for example, *Grup per a la Defensa del Ter-*).

Selected Bibliography

Books

Alenza Garcia, J.F. *El sistema de la gestión de residuos sólidos urbanos en el derecho español.* Madrid: Ministerio de Administraciones Públicas, 1997.
Alenza García, J.F. *Manual de Derecho Ambiental.* Pamplona: Editorial Universidad Pública de Navarra, 2001.
Alenza García, J. & Sarasibar Iriarte, M. *Cambio climático y energías renovables.* Ed. Aranzadi. Cizur Menor, 2007.
Alonso García, M.C. *El régimen jurídico de la contaminación atmosférica y acústica.* Madrid: Marcial Pons, 1995.
Audivert Arau, R. *El régimen jurídico de la etiqueta ecológica.* Barcelona: Cedecs, 1996.
Barragán Muñoz, J.M. *Medio ambiente y desarrollo en las áreas litorales: guía práctica para la planificación y gestión integradas.* Cádiz: Universidad de Cádiz, 2003.
Baucells Lladós, J. & Vernet Llobet, J. (Coord.). *La prevención y el control integrados de la contaminación.* Madrid: Marcial Pons, 2004.
Betancor Rodríguez, A. *Instituciones de Derecho Ambiental.* Madrid: La Ley, 2001.
Blanco Lozano, C. *El delito ecológico. Manual operativo.* Madrid: Montecorvo, 1997.
Blanco Lozano, C. *La protección del medio ambiente en el Derecho penal español y comparado.* Granada: Comares, 1997.
Blanco Lozano, C. *La tutela del agua a través del Derecho penal.* Editorial J.M. Bosch. Barcelona, 2000.
Campins Eritja, M. & Pont Castejón, I. (co-ord.). *Perspectivas de derecho comunitario ambiental.* Bellaterra: Institut Universitari d'Estudis Europeus, 1997.
Canosa Usera, R. *Constitución y medio ambiente.* Madrid: Dykinson, 2000.
Caro-Patón Carmona, I. *El derecho a regar. Entre la planificación hidrológica y el mercado del agua.* Madrid: Marcial Pons, 1997.
Casado Casado, L. *Los vertidos en aguas continentales. Las técnicas de intervención administrativa.* Ed. Comares. Granada, 2004.
Casado Casado, L, et al. *La externalización de las funciones de control e inspección en materia de protección del medio ambiente.* Barcelona: Atelier, 2010.
CIMA Medio Ambiente, I. *Congreso Nacional de Derecho Ambiental: Ponencias.* Madrid: Imprenta Nacional del Boletín Oficial del Estado, 1995.
CIMA Medio Ambiente, I. *Congreso Nacional de Derecho Ambiental: Comunicaciones.* Valencia: CIMA Medio Ambiente, 1996.

De la Cuesta Aguado, P.M. *La prueba en el delito ecológico.* Madrid: Tecnos, 1995.

De la Mata Barranco, N.J. *Protección penal del ambiente y accesoriedad administrativa.* Barcelona: Cedecs, 1996.

De Miguel Perales, C. *La responsabilidad civil por daños al medio ambiente.* Madrid: Civitas, 1997.

De Miguel Perales, C. *Derecho español del medio ambiente, Civitas/Thomson-Reuters.* 3ª ed. Pamplona, 2009.

De Vicente Martínez, R. *Responsabilidad penal del funcionario por delito contra el medio ambiente.* Madrid: Universidad Complutense de Madrid-Ministerio de Justicia-Centro de Estudios Judiciales, 1993.

Domingo López, E. *Régimen Jurídico de las Energías Renovables y la Cogeneración Eléctrica.* Madrid: INAP, 2000.

Domper Ferrando, J. '*El medio ambiente y la intervención administrativa de las actividades clasificadas*'. Planteamientos constitucionales, vol. I. Madrid: Civitas, 1992.

Domper Ferrando, J. 'El medio ambiente y la intervención administrativa de las actividades clasificadas'. *La normativa del Estado y de las Comunidades Autónomas,* vol. II. Madrid: Civitas, 1992.

Embid Irujo, A. *Gestión del agua y medio ambiente.* Madrid: Civitas, 1997.

Embid Irujo, A. *Agua y territorio.* Cizur Menor: Thomson-Civitas, 2007.

Embid Irujo, A. (Dir.). *El derecho a un medio ambiente adecuado.* Madrid: Iustel, 2008.

Escobar Roca, G. *La ordenación constitucional del medio ambiente.* Madrid: Dykinson, 1995.

Esteve Pardo, J. (co-ord.). *Derecho del medio ambiente y administración local.* Madrid: Civitas, 1996.

Fanlo Loras, A. & Garrorena Morales, A. *La constitucionalidad de los nuevos Estatutos en materia de aguas. A propósito de la propuesta de Estatuto de Aunomía de Castilla-La Mancha.* Fundación Instituto Euromediterráneo del Agua, 2008.

Fernández de Casadevante Romaní, C. *La protección del medio ambiente en derecho internacional público, derecho comunitario europeo y Derecho español.* Vitoria-Gasteiz: Servicio de Publicaciones del Gobierno Vasco, 1991.

Garcia Delgado, J.L. & Jiménez, J.C. *Energía y Regulación.* Ed. Thomson-Civitas. Cizur Menor, 2007.

García Delgado, J.L. (Dir.). *Lecciones de Economía Española.* 4a ed. Madrid: Civitas, 1999.

García Rivas, N. *Delito ecológico. Estructura y aplicación judicial.* Barcelona: Praxis, 1998.

García Ureta, A. *Transposición y control de la normativa ambiental comunitaria.* Oñati: Instituto Vasco de Administración Pública, 1998.

Gómez Orfanel, G. (co-ord.). *Derecho del medio ambiente.* Madrid: Ministerio de Justicia e Interior, 1995.

Hava García E. *La tutela penal de los animales.* Ed. Tirant lo Blanch. Valencia, 2008.

Huerta Huerta, R. & Huerta Izar de la Fuente, C. *Tratado de Derecho Ambiental, Tomos I y II.* Barcelona: J.M. Bosch, 2000.

Jaria Manzano, J. *El sistema constitucional de protecció del medi ambient, Institut d'Estudis Autonòmics, Departament de Relacions Institucionals i Participació.* Barcelona: Generalitat de Catalunya, 2005.

Jordano Fraga, J. *La protección del derecho a un medio ambiente adecuado.* Barcelona: J.M. Bosch, 1995.

Junceda, J. *Cuestiones medioambientales.* Madrid: Colex, 1999.

Juste Ruiz, J. *Derecho internacional del medio ambiente.* Madrid: McGraw-Hill, 1999.

Lasagabaster Herrarte, I. (Dir.) – Lazcano Brotóns, I. – García Ureta, A. – Pérez García, C. *Derecho Ambiental. Parte Especial I. Espacios Naturales, Flora y Fauna, Montes, Paisaje.* Lete, Editorial, Pamplona-Bilbao, 2007.

Lasagabaster Herrarte, Iñaki (Dir.) – Urrutia Libarona, I. – Santamaria Arinas, R.J. *Derecho Ambiental. Parte Especial II.Productos Químicos, Transgénicos, Residuos*; Lete, Editorial, Pamplona-Bilbao, 2007.

Lasagabaster Herrarte, Iñaki (Dir.) – Arzoz Santisteban, X. – Uriarte Ricote, M. *Derecho Ambiental. Parte Especial III. Agua, Atmósfera, Contaminación Acústica.* Lete Editorial, Pamplona-Bilbao, 2007.

López Ramón, F. *Política ecológica y pluralismo territorial: ensayo sobre los problemas de articulación de los poderes públicos para la conservación de la biodiversidad. Madrid: Marcial Pons, 2009.*

Loperena Rota, D.I. *El derecho al medio ambiente adecuado.* Madrid: Civitas, 1996.

López Bustos, F.L. *La organización administrativa del medio ambiente.* Madrid: Facultad de Derecho Universidad de Granada-Civitas, 1992.

López Sako, M.J. *Regulación y autorización de los parques* eólicos. Cizur Menor: Thomson-Civitas, 2008.

Lozano Cutanda, B. *Derecho Ambiental Administrativo, Dykinson.* 10a ed. Madrid, 2009.

Lozano Cutanda, B. (Dir.). *Comentarios a la Ley de responsabilidad medioambiental. Ley 26/2007, de 23 de octubre.* Cizur Menor: Thomson-Civitas, 2008.

Lozano Cutanda B. – Gutierrez-Alviz Conradi, F. (Dir.). *Examen de la nueva Ley de acceso a la información, participación pública y acceso a la justicia en materia de medio ambiente.* Madrid: Consejo General del Poder Judicial, 2008.

Lozano Cutanda, B.-Alonso García, E. *Diccionario de Derecho Ambiental.* Ed. Iustel. Madrid, 2005.

Matellanes R., N. *Derecho penal del medio ambiente.* Ed. Iustel. Madrid, 2008.

Martín Mateo, R. *Manual de Derecho ambiental.* Pamplona: Thomson Aranzadi, 2003.

Martín Mateo, R. *Nuevos instrumentos para la tutela ambiental.* Madrid: Trivium, 1994.

Martín Mateo, R. Rosa Moreno. *Nuevo ordenamiento de la basura.* Madrid: Trivium, 1998.

Ministerio de Medio Ambiente. *Medio Rural y Marino, Anuario de Estadistica Ministerio de Medio Ambiente y Medio Rural y Marino 2009.* Madrid: Centro de Publicaciones, 2010.

Ministerio de Medio Ambiente. *Medio Rural y Marino, El medio ambiente y el medio rural y marino en España 2009.* Madrid: Secretaría General Técnica, Centro de Publicaciones, 2010.

Moreno Molina, J.A. *La protección ambiental de los bosques.* Madrid: Marcial Pons, 1998.

Moreno Trujillo, E. *La protección jurídico-privada del medio ambiente y la responsabilidad por su deterioro.* Barcelona: J.M. Bosch Editor, 1991.

Nieto Moreno, J.E. *Elementos estructurales de la la evaluación ambiental de planes y programas.* Aranzadi, 2011.

Nogueira López A. (Dir.). *Evaluación de impacto ambiental. Evolución normativo-jurisprudencial cuestiones procedimentales y aplicación sectorial.* Ed. Atelier. Barcelona, 2009.

Observatorio de la Sostenibilidad en España (OSE). *Cambios de ocupación del suelo en España: Implicaciones para la sostenibilidad.* Madrid: Mundi Prensa, 2006.

OCDE. *Análisis de los resultados medioambientales.* España, 2004.

Ortega Álvarez, L. (Dir.). *Lecciones de Derecho del Medio Ambiente.* Valladolid: Lex Nova, 2002.

Pallarés Serrano, A. *La planificación hidrológica de Cuenca como instrumento de ordenación ambiental sobre el territorio.* Valencia: Tirant lo Blanch, 2007.

Pérez Moreno, A. (Coor.). *El Derecho de la Energía.* Sevilla: IAAP, 2006.

Pigrau Solé, A. (Coord.). *Nuevas perspectivas de la responsabilidad por daños al medio ambiente.* Madrid: Ministerio de Medio Ambiente, 2006.

Pigrau Solé, A. (Dir.). *Acceso a la información, participación pública y acceso a la justicia en materia de medio ambiente: diez años del Convenio de Aarhus.* Barcelona: Atelier, 2008.

Piñar Díaz, M. *El derecho a disfrutar del medio ambiente en la jurisprudencia.* Granada: Comares, 1996.

Póveda Gómez, P. *Envases y residuos de envases: Nueva legislación.* Madrid: Exlibris Ediciones, 1997.

Prats Canut, J.M., M. Marquès Banqué & C. Morán Mora *Derecho penal ambiental y derecho comunitario. La Directiva IPPC.* Monografia de la Revista de Derecho y Proceso Penal. Pamplona: Ed. Aranzadi, 2002.

Quintero Olivares, G. & F. Morales Prats (Coords.). *Estudios de Derecho Ambiental. Libro Homenaje al Profesor Josep Miquel Prats Canut.* Valencia: Tirant lo Blanch, 2008.

Reyes López, M.J. (co-ord.). *Derecho Ambiental Español. Valencia, 2000.* Rocha García, E. de la. Práctica jurídica y administrativa respecto a la protección del medio ambiente Granada: Comares, 1997.

Rosa Moreno, J. *Régimen jurídico de la evaluación de impacto ambiental.* Madrid: Trivium, 1993.

Ruiz-Rico Ruiz, G. (co-ord.). *La protección del medio ambiente en el ordenamiento jurídico español.* Jaén: Universidad de Jaén, 1995.

Ruiz-Rico Ruiz, G. *El derecho constitucional al medio ambiente adecuado.* Valencia: Tirant lo Blanch, 2000.

Santamaría Arinas, R.J. *Administración pública y prevención ambiental: El régimen jurídico de la producción de residuos peligrosos.* Bilbao: Instituto Vasco de Administración Pública, 1996.
Sanz Larruga, F.J. (Dir.). *Estudios sobre la ordenación, planificación y gestión del litoral. Hacia un modelo integrado y sostenible, Fundación Pedro Barrié de la Maza.* Instituto de Estudios Económicos de Galicia, 2009.
Sanz Rubiales, I. *Los vertidos en aguas subterráneas. Su régimen jurídico.* Madrid: Marcial Pons, 1997.
Serrano Moreno, J.L. *Ecología y Derecho: Principios de Derecho Ambiental y Ecología Jurídica.* Granada: Comares, 1992.
Soler Manuel, M.A. (co-ord.). *Manual de gestión del medio ambiente.* Barcelona: Ariel, 1997.
Sosa Wagner, F. *Las actividades molestas: en especial el ruido.* Madrid: Tecnos, 1991.
Terradillos Basoco, J. *El delito ecológico.* Madrid: Trotta, 1997.
Valerio Martínez de Munian, E. *La legislación europea del medio ambiente: Su aplicación en España.* Madrid: Colex, 1991.
Valle Muñiz, J.M. (co-ord.). *La protección jurídica del medio ambiente.* Pamplona: Aranzadi, 1997.
Vera Jurado, D.J. *La disciplina ambiental de las actividades industriales.* Madrid: Tecnos, 1994.
Vera Jurado, D.J. *Legislación sobre actividades clasificadas e impacto ambiental. Normativa general y autonómica.* Madrid: Tecnos, 2000.
Vicedo Cañada, L. *Legislación aplicable a la planificación y gestión de recursos naturales.* Ed. UPV. Valencia, 2009.
Vilalta, E. *Acción de responsabilidad extracontractual por daños al medio ambiente.* Barcelona: J.M. Bosch Editores, 2002.

Articles

Alonso García, E. 'La participación de individuos en la toma de decisiones sobre el medio ambiente en España. Aspectos constitucionales'. *Revista Española de Derecho Administrativo,* no. 61 (1989): 49–65.
Arenas Cabello F.J. 'Marco normativo de la eficiencia energética y las energías renovables'. *en Revista Aranzadi de Derecho Ambiental,* nú. 13/2008.
Beltrán Aguirre, J.L. 'El medio ambiente en la reciente jurisprudencia del Tribunal Supremo'. *Revista de Administración Pública,* no. 134 (1994): 281–298.
Blanco Lozano, C. 'Acerca de algunas cuestiones básicas del Derecho penal ambiental en el nuevo Código penal'. *Cuadernos de Política Criminal,* no. 60 (1996): 705–730.
Blanco Lozano, C. 'Bases para la determinación del perjuicio ecológico en el Derecho penal español'. *en Revista de Derecho urbanístico y medio ambiente,* no. 163 (1998): 1019–1033.
Baucells Lladós, J. 'Comentarios al Título XVI del Código Penal de los delitos relativos a la ordenación del territorio y la protección del patrimonio histórico y del medio ambiente' (Arts 319 a 340) en Córdoba Roda, J., García Arán, M. (Dirs.)

Comentarios al Código Penal. Parte Especial, Tomo I, Marcial Pons, Madrid, 2004, 1.347–1477.

Calvo Charro, M. 'Contaminación de suelos y desertizatión en España'. *Revista de Derecho Urbanístico, Enero/Febrero* (1999): 143–177.

Canosa Usera, R. 'Aspectos constitucionales del Derecho ambiental'. Revista de *Estudios Políticos,* no. 94 (1996): 73–110.

Campins Eritja, M. 'La aplicación del derecho comunitario ambiental en España'. *Noticias de la Unión Europea*, no. 205 (2002): 9–27.

Casado Casado, L. 'Las competencias estatales y autonómicas sobre los parques nacionales a la luz de la reciente jurisprudencia constitucional. Nuevas perspectivas para las Comunidades Autónomas'. *Revista de la Administración Pública,* no. 172 (2007): 255–292.

Casado Casado, L. 'La contaminación por olores: un reto normativo pendiente'. *Revista Aranzadi de Derecho Ambiental,* no. 11 (2007): 279–303.

Casado Casado, L. 'Las administraciones públicas ante la contaminación lumínica. Análisis del modelo de prevención y control instaurado en Cataluña'. *Revista Española de Derecho Administrativo*, no. 134 (2007): 321–358.

Casado Casado, L. 'El papel de los municipios en la prevención, ordenación y control de la contaminación lumínica'. *Revista de Estudios de la Administración Local y Autonómica*, no. 304 (2007): 137–177.

Casado Casado, L. 'La potestad normativa local en materia de contaminación odorífera: la ampliación de las posibilidades de actuación municipal a partir de la Sentencia del Tribunal Supremo de 26 de julio de 2006'. *Revista Aranzadi de Derecho Ambiental*, no. 12 (2007): 151–167.

Casado Casado L. 'El derecho de acceso a la información ambiental a través de la jurisprudencia'. *Revista de Administración Pública*, no. 178 (2009): 281–322.

Castella García, A. & J.L. Giménez Mandado. 'La actividad gasista contemplada a través del Reglamento de actividades molestas, insalubres, nocivas y peligrosas'. *DDAA Primeras jornadas: Energía y Derecho*, t. II, E.V.E. (1988).

Cubel Sánchez, P. 'La caracterización de los residuos peligrosos en el ordenamiento jurídico español tras la Ley 10/1998 de 21 de abril de residuos'. *Revista Española de Derecho Urbanístico y Medio Ambiente*, no. 166 (1998): 163–187.

De La Varga Pastor, A. 'La consideración del suelo contaminado como residuo a partir de la STJCE de 7 de septiembre de 2004. Sus repercusiones en el Derecho alemán y en el Derecho comunitario'. *Revista Aranzadi de Derecho Ambiental,* no. 11 (2007): 115–131.

De La Varga Pastor, A. 'La coordinación entre la Ley 10/1008 de residuos y la Ley 26/2007 de responsabilidad medioambiental en materia de suelos contaminados'. *Revista Vasca de Administración Pública*, no. 84 mayo agosto (2009): 233–258.

Delgado Piqueras, F. 'Régimen jurídico del derecho constitucional al medio ambiente'. *Revista Española de Derecho Constitucional*, no. 38 (1993): 49–80.

De Rojas Martinez-Parets, F. 'La Ley 42/2007: el Estatuto de protección del patrimonio cultural y la biodiversidad'. *Revista Aranzadi de Derecho Ambiental*, no. 14 (2008): 207–226.

De Rojas Martinez-Parets, F. 'Una visión general sobre la nueva Ley de la red de parques nacionales'. *Revista Aranzadi de Derecho Ambiental*, no. 12 (2007): 221–233.

Embid Irujo, A. 'Usos del agua e impacto ambiental: evaluación de impacto ambiental y caudal ecológico'. *Revista de Administración Pública*, no. 134 (1994): 109–154.

Embid Irujo A. 'La política de aguas y su marco jurídico'. *Revista Aranzadi de derecho ambiental, ISSN 1695–2588*, no. 14 (2008): 13–27.

Garcia Ureta, A. & Arrospide Erkoreka, I. 'Sobre la transposición de tres normas ambientales comunitarias en derecho estatal'. *Revista Vasca de Administración Publica* 46 (1996): 39–43.

Gómez Rivero, M.C. 'Algunos aspectos de la responsabilidad de los funcionarios en materia ambiental'. *La Ley*, vol 4 (1996): 1239–1244.

Jaria Manzano, J. 'La participación del público en la evaluación ambiental estratégica'. *Revista Aranzadi de Derecho Ambiental*, no. 11 (2007): 213–222.

Jaria Manzano, J. 'Política ambiental y modelo territorial'. *Revista de Estudios Políticos*, no. 137 (julio -septiembre 2007): 217–245.

López –Medel Bascones J. 'El derecho a la información medioambiental'. *Revista española de Derecho Administrativo*, no. 144 (2009): 667–678.

López Menudo, F. 'El derecho a la protección del medio ambiente'. *Revista del Centro de Estudios Constitucionales*, no. 10 (1991).

López Ramón, F. 'Derechos fundamentales, subjetivos y colectivos al medio ambiente'. *Civitas – Revista Española de Derecho Administrativo*, no. 95 (1997).

Lozano Cutanda, B. 'La actividad sancionadora de la Administración en defensa del medio ambiente litoral'. *Revista de Derecho Ambiental*, no. 4 (1989).

Lozano Cutanda, B. 'La ecologización de los derechos fundamentales: la doctrina López Ostra c. España; Guerra y otros c. Italia; y Hatton y otros c. Reino Unido del TEDH y su recepción por nuestro Tribunal Constitucional'. *Revista Española de Derecho Europeo*, no. 1 (2002).

Lozano Cutanda, B. 'La responsabilidad por daños ambientales: la situación actual y el nuevo sistema de "responsabilidad de Derecho público" que introduce la Directiva 2004/35/CE'. *Justicia Administrativa*, no. 26, Enero (2005): 5–33.

Marqués Banqué, M. 'La aplicación del Derecho comunitario en la interpretación de los tipos penales. Especial referencia al delito ecológico'. *Revista de Ciencias Penales* 1, no. 2 (1998): 360–385.

Mora Ruiz, M. 'La ordenación jurídico-administrativa de las energías renovables: revisión en el marco de la Directiva 2009/28/CE, de Parlamento y del Consejo, de 23 de abril, de fomento de las Energías Renovables'. *en Revista de Derecho Urbanístico y MedioAmbiente*, no. 257 (2010).

Ortega Bernardo, J. 'Jurisprudencia en materia de residuos: Localización de instalaciones, producción y gestion'. *Revista de Derecho Urbanístico Noviembre* (2000): 41–81.

Pallarès Serrano, A. 'La organización administrativa del nuevo modelo de intervención ambiental de la Ley del Parlamento de Catalunya 3/1998, de 24 de febrero, sobre la Intervención Integral de la Administración Ambiental'. *Revista Vasca de Administración Pública*, no. 65 (I), enero (abril 2003): 103–147.

Pallarès Serrano, A. 'La participacion publica en el proceso de elaboracion de planes y programas en materia de medio ambiente. Especial referencia a los planes hidrologicos de cuenca'. *Revista de Administración Pública*, no. 176 (2008): 331–361.

Selected Bibliography

Paredes Castañón, J.M. 'Responsabilidad penal y "nuevos riesgos": El caso de los delitos contra el medio ambiente'. *Actualidad Penal*, vol. 1 (1997): 217–227.

Perdigó Solà, J. 'Organización administrativa del medio ambiente en los grandes municipios y áreas de conurbación'. *Derecho del Medio Ambiente y Administración local, Diputación de Barcelona.* Madrid: Editorial Civitas, 1996, 371–394.

Pérez Martos, J. 'La configuración jurídica del medio ambiente en el Derecho español'. *Revista de Derecho Urbanístico y Medio Ambiente*, no. 159 (1998): 169–200.

Prats Canut, J.M. 'Responsabilidad penal de las autoridades y funcionarios municipales en materia ambiental'. *Cuadernos Jurídicos*, no. 27 (1995): 32–49.

Prats Canut, J.M. & Marquès Banqué, M. 'De los delitos contra los recursos naturales y el medio ambiente'. In *Comentarios al Nuevo Código Penal*, edited by Quintero Olivares G. (dir.). 3a edn. Navarra: Thomson-Aranzadi, Cizur Menor, 2004, 1.655–1750.

Prats Canut, J.M. & Marquès Banqué, M. 'De los delitos relativos a la protección de la flora, fauna y animales domésticos'. In *Comentarios al Nuevo Código Penal*, edited by Quintero Olivares, G. (Dir.). 3a edn. Navarra: ThomsonAranzadi, Cizur Menor, 2004, 1750–1773.

Rodríguez-Chaves Mimbrero, B. 'Ordenación urbanística y medio ambiente. En especial espacios naturales protegidos'. *Revista de Derecho Urbanístico* (Septiembre–Octobre, 1998): 125–157.

Santamaría Arinas, R.J. 'Los residuos y la planificación urbanística'. *Revista de Derecho Urbanístico*, no. 147 (1996): 133–172.

Soler Matutes, P. 'La ley de intervención integral de la administración ambiental de Cataluña. Un nuevo marco administrativo para la protección del medio ambiente en el Derecho autonómico y un ejemplo de adaptación de la directiva IPPC en el Derecho Español'. *Revista de Derecho Ambiental*, no. 21 (1998): 37–46.

Soler Matutes, P. 'Derecho ambiental: Los programas de descontaminación gradual'. *Revista de Derecho Urbanístico* (Abril–Mayo, 1999): 93–103.

Index

The numbers here refer to paragraph numbers.

Index